The Ethics of Vulnerability

As concerns about violence, war, terrorism, sexuality, and embodiment have garnered attention in philosophy, the concept of vulnerability has become a shared reference point in these discussions. As a fundamental part of the human condition, vulnerability has significant ethical import: how one responds to vulnerability matters, whom one conceives as vulnerable and which criteria are used to make such demarcations matters, how one deals with one's own vulnerability matters, and how one understands the meaning of vulnerability matters. Yet, the meaning of vulnerability is commonly taken for granted and it is assumed that vulnerability is almost exclusively negative, equated with weakness, dependency, powerlessness, deficiency, and passivity. This reductively negative view leads to problematic implications, imperiling ethical responsiveness to vulnerability, and so prevents the concept from possessing the normative value many theorists wish it to have. When vulnerability is regarded as weakness and, concomitantly, invulnerability is prized, attentiveness to one's own vulnerability and ethical response to vulnerable others remain out of reach goals. Thus, this book critiques the ideal of invulnerability, analyzes the problems that arise from a negative view of vulnerability, and articulates in its stead a nondualistic concept of vulnerability that can remedy these problems.

Erinn C. Gilson is Assistant Professor of Philosophy at the University of North Florida, USA. Her research focuses on ethics and social thought from a feminist perspective and informed by contemporary European philosophy. She is currently exploring issues surrounding food ethics and the question of the significance of ethical failure.

Routledge Studies in Ethics and Moral Theory

1. **The Contradictions of Modern Moral Philosophy**
   Ethics after Wittgenstein
   Paul Johnston

2. **Kant, Duty and Moral Worth**
   Philip Stratton-Lake

3. **Justifying Emotions**
   Pride and Jealousy
   Kristján Kristjánsson

4. **Classical Utilitarianism from Hume to Mill**
   Frederick Rosen

5. **The Self, the Soul and the Psychology of Good and Evil**
   Ilham Dilman

6. **Moral Responsibility**
   The Ways of Scepticism
   Carlos J. Moya

7. **The Ethics of Confucius and Aristotle**
   Mirrors of Virtue
   Jiyuan Yu

8. **Caste Wars**
   A Philosophy of Discrimination
   David Edmonds

9. **Deprivation and Freedom**
   A Philosophical Enquiry
   Richard J. Hull

10. **Needs and Moral Necessity**
    Soran Reader

11. **Reasons, Patterns, and Cooperation**
    Christopher Woodard

12. **Challenging Moral Particularism**
    Edited by Mark Norris Lance, Matjaž Potrč, and Vojko Strahovnik

13. **Rationality and Moral Theory**
    How Intimacy Generates Reasons
    Diane Jeske

14. **The Ethics of Forgiveness**
    A Collection of Essays
    Christel Fricke

15. **Moral Exemplars in the Analects**
    The Good Person is *That*
    Amy Olberding

16. **The Phenomenology of Moral Normativity**
    William H. Smith

17. **The Second-Person Perspective in Aquinas's Ethics**
    Virtues and Gifts
    Andrew Pinsent

18. **Social Humanism**
    A New Metaphysics
    Brian Ellis

19. **Ethics without Morals**
    In Defence of Amorality
    Joel Marks

20 **Evil and Moral Psychology**
Peter Brian Barry

21 **Aristotelian Ethics in Contemporary Perspective**
Julia Peters

22 **Modern Honor**
A Philosophical Defense
Anthony Cunningham

23 **Art and Ethics in a Material World**
Kant's Pragmatist Legacy
Jennifer A. McMahon

24 **Defending Associative Duties**
Jonathan Seglow

25 **Consequentialism and Environmental Ethics**
Edited by Avram Hiller, Ramona Ilea, and Leonard Kahn

26 **The Ethics of Vulnerability**
A Feminist Analysis of Social Life and Practice
Erinn C. Gilson

The Ethics of Vulnerability
A Feminist Analysis of Social Life and Practice

By Erinn C. Gilson

NEW YORK AND LONDON

First published 2014
by Routledge
711 Third Avenue, New York, NY 10017

and by Routledge
2 Park Square, Milton Park, Abingdon, Oxon OX14 4RN

Routledge is an imprint of the Taylor & Francis Group, an informa business

© 2014 Taylor & Francis

The right of Erinn C. Gilson to be identified as author of this work has been asserted by him/her in accordance with sections 77 and 78 of the Copyright, Designs and Patents Act 1988.

All rights reserved. No part of this book may be reprinted or reproduced or utilized in any form or by any electronic, mechanical, or other means, now known or hereafter invented, including photocopying and recording, or in any information storage or retrieval system, without permission in writing from the publishers.

Trademark notice: Product or corporate names may be trademarks or registered trademarks, and are used only for identification and explanation without intent to infringe.

Library of Congress Cataloging-in-Publication Data

A catalog record has been requested for this book.

ISBN: 978-0-415-65613-9 (hbk)
ISBN: 978-0-203-07813-6 (ebk)

Typeset in Sabon
by Apex CoVantage, LLC

Contents

Acknowledgments ix

Introduction 1

PART I
The Normative Significance of Vulnerability

1 Responsibility for the Vulnerable 15
   Acknowledging Vulnerability and Dependence 17
   Alleviating Vulnerability 25
   The Implications of a Reductively Negative
   View of Vulnerability 31

2 Thinking Vulnerability with Judith Butler 40
   Vulnerability, Precariousness, and Precarity 42
   Violence, Vulnerability, and Norms 48
   The Normativity of Vulnerability 51
   Critical Comments 60

PART II
Analyzing Avoidance and Disavowal

3 The Ideal of Invulnerability 73
   The Pursuit of Invulnerability 75
   Invulnerability and Oppression 85
   Epistemic Vulnerability 93

4 Risk and Control:
The Formation of Entrepreneurial Subjectivity — 98
- Danger and Risk through a Foucaultian Lens — 99
- Shaping the Self through the Management of Risk — 108
- Risk, Privatization, and Responsibility — 111
- An Exemplary Case of the Perils of Privatization: Vulnerability and Food — 116

PART III
Rethinking Vulnerability

5 Vulnerability Beyond Opposition — 127
- Openness to the World: Rethinking Passivity with Merleau-Ponty — 130
- Vulnerability as an Ontological Concept: Resources from Deleuze's Philosophy of Difference — 134
- "force in their fragility": The Experience of Vulnerability in Cixous — 140

6 Vulnerability in Social Life:
Sexuality and Pornography — 148
- Sexuality, Embodiment, and Ambiguity — 149
- Vulnerability, Invulnerability, and Pornography — 154
- Responding to Pornography — 171

Conclusion — 177

Bibliography — 181
Index — 189

Acknowledgments

Books are the result of thinking and writing, but the thinking and writing that go into a book spring from so many other sources: the ideas, words, and feelings of others, and the conversations, relationships, and histories that one shares with them or observes. I feel fortunate to have parents who encouraged intellectual engagement, strove to offer me the best education possible, and, most of all, inspired a love of reading that has allowed me to peer into other worlds and investigate the depths of the one we inhabit. The curiosity and optimism possessed by my mother, Nancy Gilson, prompts me to see the world in new ways, and her unremitting concern for others stands as an example of how and why to care. The aesthetic appreciation and ability manifest by my father, Richard Gilson, makes the spaces in which we live more colorful and his skeptical disposition taught me the value of a healthy criticism. Caitlin Gilson, my sister, inspires me with her ability to transform patches of earth into budding, blooming, flourishing gardens, and to remain always energized in doing so. Above all, thanks go to Bryan Bannon, who read, digested, corrected, and commented on the book in its entirety as well as in its many previous incarnations. He put up with my undue proclivity for the semi-colon and em dash long enough to offer continual encouragement and support, and also did the dishes far more often than was fair (which I promise I'll make up to him). I am most grateful for the space we have made in which to be vulnerable together, and for discovering again and again the challenge in letting myself be so.

Writing, especially academic writing, can be an isolating endeavor and at times I've doubted that it was worth the energy when there is clearly so much else of value that needs to be done. Supportive colleagues, some more and some less well known to me, have affirmed the importance of the topic about which I am thinking and writing in this project. For that affirmation and for the confirmation that these words will find readers, which has inspired me to pull together the threads that comprise this book, I thank them. Mentors Len Lawlor, Mary Beth Mader, and Sarah Clark Miller were exceptionally supportive during graduate school and have been so continually. I have been especially grateful for Len's continued support as I veered somewhat off the Continental philosophy path. Members of a junior faculty writing group at the University of North Florida—Aaron Creller, Sarah Mattice, and Jon Matheson—gave helpful feedback on an earlier draft of Chapter Four. An early draft of Chapter Two benefited from the questions and comments of Linda Martín Alcoff, Devonya Havis, Robin James, and Kris Sealey during a Mentoring Workshop for women in philosophy in 2011. An earlier version of Chapter Three was published in *Hypatia* as "Vulnerability, Ignorance, and Oppression," v. 26, issue 2, 2011, pp.308–332, and the questions and comments of anonymous *Hypatia* reviewers prompted me to reflect on my underlying assumptions more thoroughly. Portions of this work were presented at various conferences over past years, so thanks are due to the audiences at those meetings whose queries and comments helped me to think through the ideas contained therein. Finally, a Faculty Development Research Grant by the Office of Academic of Affairs at the University of North Florida also facilitated the completion of this project.

Introduction

A journalist visits the only remaining clinic in the United States devoted to treating patients with Hansen's disease, more commonly known as leprosy. Ninety-five percent of people are naturally immune to what is a now curable bacterial disease whose harm stems from the way it causes degeneration of the peripheral nerves, resulting in numbness and often preventing those affected from feeling pain. The main focus of treatment, she notices, is managing stigma and teaching patients to care for themselves. They learn attentiveness to their own bodies to avert "the dangers of insensibility": to be mindful when cooking so as not to burn themselves, to tend to their wounds, and to check their bodies for even the most minor injury. For both patients and clinicians, the clinic is the site of lessons in empathy, an empathy born of the capacity to imagine pain that one does not experience oneself. Empathy emerges from "an act of imagination, of extending yourself beyond yourself," thus "[c]omfort is dangerous" because it dulls these imaginative capacities. A capacity for experiencing pain, imagined or real, and thus for empathy lies at the core of what it means to be human, the journalist concludes.[1]

Months after September 11th, 2001, a young Syrian American woman and her family are awakened and pulled from their beds in the middle of the night in Brooklyn. Officially, they are detained on immigration grounds—their visas are pending—but they are taken into custody as part of a drastic surge in arrests and detentions of Arab Americans because of inflated anxiety concerning terrorism in the wake of September 11th. A neighbor likely reported them as suspicious. The mother and her two daughters, the father and older son, and the juvenile son are taken to three separate facilities. No charges are filed, they are not deported, but they are imprisoned for nearly three months. The mother is allowed to make daily phone calls to her younger son who is being held by himself at a juvenile detention center in Pennsylvania, but she must plead daily with the prison counselor to place the calls. The counselor is often unsympathetic, impatient, and on at least one occasion reduces the mother to tears. Overwhelmed and frustrated by their powerlessness, the young woman challenges him in order to get the phone call to which her mother has a right. He responds by claiming that they must have done something wrong, they deserve to be there, and they "should have expected to be arrested." During the months after their release, she happens to see the counselor at a restaurant while she is dining with friends. She reminds herself of the injustice and his callousness, and summons courage before striding over to confront the man.[2]

In a small mountain town, an aging Chinese American widow reaches out to her neighbors, a Cambodian family with a troubled history that has recently relocated next door. As remnants of her past return, compelling her to reckon again with choices made, possibilities passed over, and loves lost, she faces the quiet loneliness of her present. Welcoming new immigrant neighbors—offering cookies, giving English and Chinese lessons, chauffeuring them to and fro, and making herself available as a confidante—is, at first, an act of kindness; she sees need and cannot but extend a hand. Yet eventually she is undone by the accusation that what she most fears is that the truth of her life has been that she needs others more than they need her. Need defines her as well, a need for companionship, affection, meaning, and community that entails that the wary outsider posture she has spent her life inhabiting must slowly be surrendered.[3]

All of these stories are scenes of vulnerability. What joins them—crossing the different situations, persons, and ways of being vulnerable—is the fact that vulnerability is pervasive, fundamental, shared, and something we cannot ever entirely avoid. Each story also reveals the complexity, diversity, and ambiguity of what it is to be vulnerable, the way it is both extraordinary and mundane, conducive to both empathy and outrage, a product of injustice and a virtue one develops to contest injustice. Across the diverse instances of vulnerability, a common sense of vulnerability is underscored: vulnerability is defined by openness and, more specifically, to be vulnerable is to be open to being affected and affecting in ways that one cannot control. Each story indicates further that, as an ethical disposition, intersubjective vulnerability is a matter of practice. It is far from given and indeed is often quite rare. Its presence can only be cultivated just as we so often cultivate its absence: distance and detachment, the security and comfort of the familiar, imperviousness and composure, in a word, invulnerability. Counterposed to the attitude of invulnerability so clearly displayed by the prison counselor, is the idea embodied by the patients and clinicians at the Hansen's disease clinic that vulnerability is the basis for learning and for empathy, connection, and community, and that only by being vulnerable can one extend oneself beyond oneself. The practices by which one extends oneself, relinquishes barriers, or summons the wherewithal to expose oneself are myriad.

In the case of the clinic, the school of empathy, patients are physically vulnerable to the effects of the disease. Their simple physical vulnerability inheres in the likelihood of harm that stems from the absence of pain. Thus, they must develop an attunement to what they do not feel, which leads to a different kind of vulnerability. Less tangible but equally important is this vulnerability found in cultivating attentiveness and imaginative capacities.

It mitigates the social vulnerability of a leprosy diagnosis that comes from a history of exclusion, widespread social stigma, and internalized fear despite the relative incommunicability of the disease. Through attunement to their bodies in daily practices, patients learn to care for themselves as they would care for someone they love. Yet it is patients and clinicians both who learn vulnerability as a mode of awareness and openness that emerges from imagining what it is to feel otherwise. It is like working in a utopia, one doctor says, where they can "care without measure." In this context, vulnerability is a capacity for imagining, feeling, and seeing that does not exclude, close off, or make recourse to exculpatory truisms in order to avoid empathy and identification. Whether they are surveying their bodies for blisters and cuts or caring for others "without measure," they are practicing how to experience their own vulnerability in conjunction with that of others.

Arab American families detained as part of post-September 11th witch-hunts were vulnerable in many senses: physically, legally, and psychologically. Yet, what also stands out in the abovementioned story is the young woman's bravery, which is far from unconditional but rather is shot through with uncertainty, fear, and sadness. It is a kind of bravery that grew out of powerlessness and was rooted in vulnerability. Her ability to position herself in front of someone who disempowered and demeaned her and to challenge the firmness of his worldview comes from a place of vulnerability; by doing so, she opens herself up. Moreover, her desire to fight back, to contest his position of comfort and security, involves a recognition that injustice is paired with an invulnerable disposition; the wrong done to her and her family is a result of imperviousness, an unwillingness to hear and see others who challenge one's preconceived notions or basic worldview. In a very different context, Gish Jen's protagonist, Hattie Kong, learns that she must work to allow barriers to dissipate, and open herself to her own vulnerability and need. She is aware of the complexity of vision—of how some ways of seeing prevent us from seeing otherwise, of how one's vision can be so strong as to be blinding—and grows aware that although she sees others' shortsightedness, she may need to look again at her own. In this story, vulnerability is a process of letting go of that to which one has always held on—ways of understanding one's self, interpretations of other's actions, established beliefs—so that one may see better.

From the abovementioned narratives, we can see better why vulnerability is of ethical importance and also why it poses ethical problems. Vulnerability is unsettling. The experience of vulnerability presents us with the reality of fallibility, mutability, unpredictability and uncontrollability. We are affected by forces outside our control, the effects of which we can neither fully know nor fully control. Thus, experiences of vulnerability can also prompt fear, defensiveness, avoidance, and disavowal. Where the ability to predict and control is valued, the inability to do so is perceived as a failing and thus to be avoided at all costs. Hence, we are often ill at ease with vulnerability because it is a form of exposure to that with which we are unfamiliar or uncomfortable. Moreover, where our vulnerability is felt as exposure to others who seek to do us harm, it becomes a condition that precipitates violence (see Murphy 2012). For this reason, among others, vulnerability is of ethical concern: if being vulnerable leads to defensive violence, is there not good reason to seek to lessen our vulnerability? If in some cases, being vulnerable also means being susceptible to pain, stigma, and injustice, then do we not have an ethical obligation to diminish vulnerability? Wherein lies the precise ethical significance of vulnerability? I began this work by recounting these three narratives in order to introduce complexity into these basic questions, but also in order to gesture towards the answers they will receive: first, that vulnerability names a complex set of experiences and conditions for which no unequivocal ethical prescription will be adequate; second, that we must consider in more depth what we mean by vulnerability and what it is like to experience it in order to begin to venture ethical responses to vulnerability, both as one experiences it oneself and as one witnesses others experiencing it; and, third, that perhaps what matters most is how we deal with vulnerability in the mundane, common practices of everyday life. It is in these practices—those of listening or failing to hear, asserting control or abandoning pretenses, changing course or steadfastly adhering to the tried and true—that our attitudes toward vulnerability, ethical or not, both develop and manifest.

In virtue of the complexity and significance of vulnerability, thinking about vulnerability has surged in recent years, spanning diverse fields with various aims and motivations.[4] In particular, as concerns about violence, war, terrorism, and the definition of life, humanity, and animality have garnered attention, the concept of vulnerability has become a shared reference point in these discussions within philosophy and theory. Vulnerability is regarded as definitive of life, a condition that links humans to nonhuman animals, and an experience that roots us in the corporeality of our existence. It is also a state that is intimately tied to violence, acts of which render us more vulnerable while also laying bare a preexisting vulnerability of which we have been ignorant. Thus, vulnerability is a topic of concern, on the one hand, because it is a fundamental part of the human condition, and, on the other hand, because it is regarded as having significant ethical import: how one responds to vulnerability—by tending to vulnerable others or by neglecting or abusing them—matters, whom one conceives as vulnerable and which criteria are used to make such demarcations matters, how one deals with one's own vulnerability matters, and how one understands the meaning of vulnerability matters. Although all of these issues make vulnerability a concept of enormous ethical salience, it is this last one that is one of the overarching concerns of this work. Though much attention has been paid to vulnerability as a feature of life that merits ethical concern, less attention has been paid to how we think, talk, and feel about vulnerability and little theoretical effort has been devoted to elaborating fully what is meant when we talk of vulnerability. Indeed, the meaning of vulnerability is usually taken for granted and the term is thought to require no additional explanation. Thus, it is frequently assumed that to be vulnerable is to be susceptible to harm. One of the major claims I develop is that there are specific, very problematic "non-logical implications" of this view of vulnerability. Cheshire Calhoun's notion of "non-logical implications" refers to the "'explanatory beliefs' whose general acceptance would have to be supposed in order to explain the rationality of the particular patterns of philosophical conversation and silence which characterize moral theory" (1988, 462). Non-logical implications are often the result of unwitting exclusions and contractions in emphasis, and, when politically salient, can become ideologies. They are the implicit background assumptions of a community that have not been made explicit and upon which the coherence of the community's theory or worldview rests. The non-logical implication of the intuitively accepted idea that vulnerability is susceptibility to harm is a reductively negative understanding of vulnerability. Common presumptions about vulnerability are reductively negative in two ways: first, they constitute an implicit understanding of vulnerability that equates it with liability to injury, weakness, dependency, powerlessness, incapacity, deficiency, and passivity; second, these assumptions also often devalue vulnerability, deeming it a condition or quality that is bad. Vulnerability is understood in a reductively negative way both by definition and in terms of its value. These implications are non-logical since few expressly aver that vulnerability itself is pernicious but predominant patterns of thought and behavior rely upon such a value judgment. Throughout this work, I question this view of what it means to be vulnerable. I contend that this understanding of vulnerability prevents the concept from possessing the normative value many theorists wish it to have and does so because it imperils ethical responsiveness to vulnerability, both our own and that of others.

Accordingly, the trajectory of the book follows two central questions concerning the role of vulnerability in ethics: First, how does vulnerability operate as an ethical resource, both as a fact about the human condition that forms the basis for ethical obligations and as an experience we undergo that can compel ethical responses to others? Second, what picture of vulnerability is drawn in our theoretical conceptions of it and in the accumulated social meanings that surround it? The argument of the book joins these two questions to reflect on how our views and ideas—both implicit and explicit, theoretical and everyday—about vulnerability affect how we treat vulnerable others and how we deal with our own vulnerability. I argue that how we think about vulnerability influences the extent to which it can be an ethical resource. Our tacitly accepted understanding of vulnerability relies on the conceptual linkages between vulnerability and the other aforementioned concepts, and is grounded in problematic assumptions that devalue being vulnerable. These negative connotations overdetermine the meaning of vulnerability in a way that makes it difficult to think about, experience, and respond to vulnerability in an ethical fashion. When vulnerability is regarded as weakness and invulnerability is prized, attentiveness to one's own vulnerability and ethical response to vulnerable others remain out of reach goals. I maintain that to enable genuine recognition of vulnerability it is necessary to challenge the normative construal of invulnerability as desirable and vulnerability as undesirable.

The first part of the book explores the normative significance of vulnerability. In the context of a general inattentiveness to this dimension of human life throughout the history of ethical and social theory, a variety of thinkers have sought to foreground the idea of vulnerability. Chapter One focuses on the role of vulnerability in ethical theory, articulating how it serves as a ground for ethical responsibility. I focus primarily on the accounts offered by Alasdair MacIntyre and Robert Goodin for two reasons: both theorists expressly focus on vulnerability, making it a core concept that is continually thematized throughout their work, and both develop ethical theories—virtue-based and utilitarian, respectively—according to which responsibility derives clearly from vulnerability.[5] The chapter then interrogates the conceptual linkages between vulnerability and other notions such as dependency, suffering, and harm in order to highlight the limitations of these approaches, the most significant of which is an implicit reliance on the reductively negative view of vulnerability. Chapter Two turns to the ideas of vulnerability and precariousness articulated by Judith Butler, finding in her recent work a much more substantial and nuanced account of the nature of vulnerability, which can allay some of the concerns about an ethics of vulnerability. Specifically, I contend that Butler's account augments our understanding of the ethical and political salience of vulnerability in four ways. First, it offers a more complicated picture of the relationship between vulnerability and normativity by conceiving norms as 'doubled,' both ideals to which we aspire and often constraining standards. Second, this view of norms makes possible critique of problematic social norms, including those that attend vulnerability, and positions critique itself as ethical practice rather than as a departure from ethical norms. Third, her account begins to distinguish different levels of vulnerability or precariousness and distinct modes of vulnerability rather than invoking vulnerability as a uniform phenomenon. Fourth, Butler avowedly does not equate vulnerability with susceptibility to harm. I conclude the chapter by suggesting that vulnerability and violence remain too closely tied in Butler's work, and that, in order for vulnerability to serve as an ethical resource rather than the source of ethical problems, we must move beyond an account of vulnerability that binds it to acts of violence. Furthermore, we need to consider how predominant social practices, norms, conditions, and structures enshrine a reductively negative understanding of vulnerability and so obstruct critical, ethical responsiveness to vulnerability.

Thus, the second part of the book engages in a critical assessment of the links between the socioculturally pervasive overvaluation of invulnerability, repudiation of vulnerability, and the negative understanding of vulnerability. In Chapter Three, I propose that avoidance of vulnerability takes the form of pursuing a sense of invulnerability through concrete everyday practices and patterns of thought. The ideal of an invulnerable self is defined by complete self-sufficiency, self-sovereignty and autonomy, independence from others, and an imperviousness to being affected, even if these are impossible aims. Drawing on conceptualizations of ignorance as an ethically and politically inflected condition, I contend that the pursuit of invulnerability amounts to ignorance of vulnerability. This pervasive ideal of invulnerability exists only when vulnerability is negatively construed and perceived as something to fear. The ideal of invulnerability is an oppressive one because it ties vulnerability to those people, social positions, and qualities that are deemed inferior, devaluing those positioned as 'lower' or less capable. In Chapter Four, I consider how individuals comport themselves in relation to risk in order to constitute themselves as invulnerable. Risk and vulnerability are often understood in conjunction with one another or even as synonymous—to be at risk is to be vulnerable—yet risk, like vulnerability, is a complex socially mediated phenomenon, not simply a 'natural' occurrence. The main theme of the chapter is the interplay of risk and control in contemporary political-social-economic relations, which I explore through Michel Foucault's work. Contrary to the simple equation of risk and vulnerability, which entails viewing the management and control of risk as a way of reducing undesirable vulnerability, I propose that it is in relation to risk that we seek to shape ourselves as invulnerable subjects. Managing risk while appearing to embrace it, I argue, is central to developing the entrepreneurial form of subjectivity that is the paradigm for invulnerability in capitalist Western societies. The chapter concludes that the ideal of invulnerability demands not just the rejection of vulnerability but also the devaluation of, and dissociation from, those individuals and groups that are culturally positioned as vulnerable (who are at risk or regarded as failing to take requisite risks), hampering the impetus to assume responsibility for shared vulnerability. Such refusal of responsibility is a product of the intensification of habitual mundane practices that preclude individuals from understanding themselves as constituted in and through relations with others, that is, as sharing in vulnerability with them.

The third part shifts from diagnosis to construction, developing the more complex concept of vulnerability that is needed if vulnerability is to function as an ethical resource. Chapter Five summarizes the problems that arise as a result of the negative understanding of vulnerability—problems of hierarchical and inequitable distribution, fixity, negative overdetermination, and homogeneity—and articulates in its stead a nondualistic concept of vulnerability that can remedy these problems. Drawing on the work of twentieth century French philosophers Maurice Merleau-Ponty, Gilles Deleuze, and Hélène Cixous, I develop an alternative concept of vulnerability that has four central features: first, vulnerability is 'univocal,' which means that in its most basic sense it is said of all beings in the same way, second, vulnerability is a condition of potential rather than an already determined condition of harm, third, vulnerability is both ambivalent and ambiguous in how it is experienced and in its value, and, fourth, vulnerability has a diversity of manifestations.[6] Chapter Six applies this account to one particular type of vulnerability, that of sexuality and, more specifically, the kinds of vulnerability at stake in pornography. Rather than condemn or defend pornography, I examine how responsiveness to vulnerability can operate as criterion for ethical evaluation of the content of sexually explicit material and consumer interaction with it. In particular, I draw upon the analyses of the third and fourth chapters to investigate whether and how common pornographic representations of sexuality and habits of consumption contribute to the pursuit of invulnerability.

CONTEXT AND ORIENTATION

By way of introduction, some remarks on the orientation, background, and methodological choices made throughout the book are necessary. One may wonder why I have chosen to take vulnerability as the focal point of this work. Why not a term less beset with conceptual confusion and multiple meanings?[7] Why not a clearer and more precise term, such as fragility? Or frailty? Perhaps because of its ambiguity, the elasticity of its meaning, vulnerability is a concept with much weight and intuitive significance. It traverses disciplines, spanning bioethics, social work, international relations, feminist theory, law, sociology, and philosophy, among others. Although each field invokes the notion with its own particular aims and motivations, there is continuity among them. Talk of vulnerability indicates concern about the susceptibility of others to violation and injury, evinces awareness and anxiety on the part of the relatively privileged about their own exposure to forces outside their control, and points to an incontrovertible fact about the human condition. All of which is to say that vulnerability has widespread salience and application. Its breadth, complexity, and variability make it important and interesting. For these reasons I also reject the self-evidence of the dictionary definition of vulnerability as susceptible to injury and the simple interpretation of its etymology as the ability to be wounded. As indicated by the brief stories with which I began, to be vulnerable is not always or simply to be susceptible to injury. Rather, vulnerability can have positive manifestations and value, enabling the development of empathy, compassion, and community. To comprehend the multiplicity of ways we experience being vulnerable, we cannot endorse a narrow definition of the term.

Thus, the analyses developed herein are part of a lineage of feminist thought that aims both to revalue devalued notions, such as vulnerability, and rethink conventional dualist understandings of key concepts. As Val Plumwood argues in *Feminism and the Mastery of Nature* (1993), feminist thought must move beyond positions that endorse uncritical equality and uncritical reversal in order to disrupt the dualisms upon which they both rely. The aim of uncritical equality is for women to achieve a status equal to that of men, which requires women's participation in "exclusionary ideals of humanity and culture" and fails to contest inequity and domination in general (27). The aim of uncritical reversal is to put an end to masculine domination by revaluing what have typically been considered feminine traits and values; it fails to challenge the dualisms that have been instrumental to the domination of women because it simply switches which side of dualism is esteemed. Although some work in the field of care ethics might be perceived as feminism of uncritical reversal, many care ethicists follow the shift Plumwood urges and seek to redefine and transform conventionally dualistic categories. In her much anthologized essay "Feminist Reconceptualizations in Ethics," Virginia Held advocates a transformation of central concepts in ethical and political theory, such as public/private, reason/emotion, and the self, given the way gender bias has been systemically built into normative theory (1998). Likewise, in another classic essay, Cheshire Calhoun argues that in light of the non-logical implications of our ideologies surrounding them, we need to rethink core ideas of what constitutes moral knowledge, moral obligation, moral motivation, and the moral self (1988). Joan Tronto maintains that it is necessary to reconceive autonomy as an achievement rather than a given and in so doing give serious thought to how it is achieved, to the relations of care that are the precondition of autonomy (1995).[8] Eva Feder Kittay's important work on dependency critiques both the norm of independence as a fiction, one belied by the inevitability of dependency, and equation of autonomy with independence (Kittay 2011). The valorization of independence and self-sufficiency both reduces care to a means to an end (that of independence) rather than a value in itself and renders dependence incompatible with dignity. If the reality of human life is that we are always dependent to varying degrees, then our conception of autonomy ought to reflect such facts of dependence, interdependence, and the significance of care-giving and receiving rather than relegating them to the status of exceptional and abnormal. This tradition of feminist work is the background for the reflections on vulnerability I undertake, and, in particular, for the challenge to the reductively negative view of vulnerability I develop. Another trajectory in recent feminist thought has focused more overtly on vulnerability, seeking to think about ethical response as embodied, relationally constituted, sociohistorically situated, and as a kind of experience that might enable "a nonappropriative or nonviolent relation with the other" (Murphy 2012, 23).[9] Accordingly, one of the central aims of this project is to reconceptualize vulnerability as more than mere weakness, passivity, incapacity, and absence of autonomy and thus set the stage for revaluing vulnerability as an ethical disposition, a complex and ambiguous experience, and a multifaceted condition.

One implication of this feminist orientation is that although the main focus is the ethical significance of vulnerability—its role in ethical theories, its ability to prompt ethical response or occasion ethical failure, its viability as a virtue of sorts—the intertwining of ethics and politics is also of utmost concern. From a feminist perspective, or at least from the feminist perspective I adopt here, one cannot divorce ethics from politics. The sense of the 'political' that I employ is broad, following Iris Marion Young's understanding of it, and refers to relationships of power and social connection, dynamics of oppression, and structural injustice rather than more narrowly to political processes and decisions (Young 2004, 376–377). The consequence is that ethics cannot be regarded as free of power dynamics, including those pertaining to gender, but rather must be perceived as a space of political contestation. Thus, as I understand it, ethics is not purely a matter of private or individual decisions; it involves the actions of individuals, to be sure, but those choices and actions are only conceived and received as ethical or not because of a broader political, socioeconomic, and historical context. This context and how it frames standard perceptions of ethical action requires interrogation. Thus, as will be explored in Chapter Two, we must remain attentive to the ways social arrangements and norms and economic exchange and activity inflect normative judgment. Another element of a feminist perspective is paying attention not only to sex/gender as an axis of experiential and analytic concern but to other axes of salient social difference, including race, socioeconomic class, nationality, ethnicity, and disability/ability. I strive throughout for such attentiveness to axes of difference in order to take into account how they shape self-identity, how situation and social structure affect the experience of these categories of identity, and how vulnerability varies in relation to social identity.

The other significant influence is twentieth century European philosophy, in particular the existential-phenomenological, deconstructive, and post-structuralist traditions. Throughout the book I draw directly on the work of figures such as de Beauvoir, Sartre, Foucault, Deleuze, Merleau-Ponty, and Cixous, and implicitly on the ideas of many others. My orientation toward vulnerability is guided by the existential-phenomenological focus on the primacy of experience and the concern of transcendental philosophy for the conditions that make possible experience. Indeed, I consider vulnerability to function as a transcendental condition of sorts to the extent that the concept points to an openness and plasticity that makes possible transformation, a claim that I develop further in the fifth chapter. Yet, from an ethico-political perspective, what matters most is how we experience vulnerability and what we make of that experience. Post-structuralist and deconstructive analyses of power and social relations provide nuance to how we understand experience, calling attention to both the value-laden quality of what appears to be neutral (knowledge, categories of thought, description of experience), and the sociohistorical contingency and situatedness of normative prescriptions. In light of this orientation, therefore, what is meant by 'ethics' calls for some clarification. From a post-Nietzschean perspective, the foundation for prescription or normative judgment is called into question. The tenuous nature of normative claims is highlighted by Nietzsche's claim that the search for foundations, origins, and ultimate justifications reveals more about the character of those seeking such grounds than the truth of the claims. The belief in a transcendent foundation for ethics—whether it is God, reason, or scientific truth—is always a belief, always a choice made from within life by a living being. It thus entails positing, from a perspective internal to life itself, an external perspective from which complete justification would be possible. There can be no such outside perspective, one that might be called 'objective' or 'impartial,' hence the prevailing critique that any pretense to such a perspective merely masks the partiality and particularity of those who purport to inhabit it (see Benhabib 1987). As Margaret Urban Walker summarizes, "I do not recognize something that sets morality's terms and standards anterior or exterior to human life and human beings' awareness and judgment" (2007, 5–6). From an existential perspective, one that I take to be consistent with Walker's expressive-collaborative model for ethical theory, any basis we have for making ethical claims is immanent, internal to human life and experience. All choice of standards, criteria, principles, and grounds for evaluation is a choice. The consistency of such ethical benchmarks is likewise internal. On de Beauvoir and Sartre's account, for example, the coherence of standards for ethical action is determined by whether they are consistent with the freedom that makes choice-making possible, that is, whether or not they are standards the realization of which constitutes a pursuit of freedom as a value. Post-structuralist perspectives on ethics are similarly oriented toward immanent criteria for ethical evaluation rather than, as is sometimes erroneously thought, characterized by the total absence of such criteria.[10]

Thus, the ethical sensibility of a feminist analysis of vulnerability strongly contests the focus on decontextualized principles, detached reasoning, and "*disembedded and disembodied*" selves that has characterized much of the history of ethical thought (Benhabib 1987, 158). To focus on vulnerability is to focus on a pervasive immanent condition rather than to postulate transcendent bases for claims about what we ought to do here and now. Consequently, an ethic of vulnerability roots ethics in experience and the conditions for the possibility of experience, that is, both in specific instances of vulnerability—such as grief, loss, bodily dissolution, and the violence occasioning them—and in vulnerability as a common condition. Accordingly, the prescriptions involved in this project are minimalist, comprising preludes to future work and suggestions for how vulnerability might figure positively into our critical reflections of ethics. If vulnerability is "an ontological condition of our humanity" it means that vulnerability forms the basis for any ethics whatsoever (Rogers, Mackenzie, and Dodds 2012, 12). If we are not vulnerable, we have no need for ethics, and it is precisely because we are vulnerable—can be affected and made to feel sorrow, concern, or empathy—that we feel any compulsion to respond ethically. Ethical action thus entails preserving vulnerability as such a condition and crafting ethical values that both condemn the myriad ways it is exploited and encourage the cultivation of forms of vulnerability that enhance shared social life. The aim would be not to deny, via our actions, the very basis of our action and existence. In calling our attention to the irrevocably immanent terrain of ethics and politics, and in rooting ethics and politics on this terrain, the discourse of vulnerability enables us to consider ethics as a practice of problematizing actual ethical failure and success. My aim in so doing so is neither to judge nor to praise but rather to gesture toward how we might better understand how to respond to vulnerability.

NOTES

1. Drawn from Solnit 2013.
2. Drawn from "Rasha" in Bayoumi 2008.
3. Drawn from Jen 2010.
4. Beyond philosophy, vulnerability is a theme in sociology (Turner 2006), international relations (Schick and Beattie 2012), feminist legal studies (Satz 2009, Fineman 2008), as well as in popular psychology (Brown 2010).
5. Vulnerability is clearly a major theme in many accounts of feminist ethics and care ethics in particular. It might appear inauspicious to focus on two male theorists when so many women have written and published on similar themes; their contributions have not been overlooked and will be central to the critique I offer of Goodin and MacIntyre. I offer this narrower reconstruction of ethical theories centering on vulnerability because these two accounts expressly thematize vulnerability whereas in feminist ethics notions like dependency, attachment, connection, and relationality are the main focus.
6. Readers familiar with the traditions of European Continental thought will likely note the absence of Emmanuel Levinas from this list of figures. Although vulnerability is an important theme in Levinas' philosophy, he will not appear as a substantial interlocutor in this work for a variety of reasons that I can only briefly delineate here. First, Butler's thinking on vulnerability is significantly influenced by Levinas and, I believe, she refines the insights present in his work in valuable ways. Second, much of what I find to be of value in Levinas' work on vulnerability also appears in that of the philosophers discussed herein and without some of the politically problematic baggage that plagues his work; especially suspect from the perspective of an ethics of vulnerability that is concerned with the differential distribution of vulnerability are his statements concerning Palestine. Third, since my aim in this chapter in particular as well as throughout the book is to challenge an understanding of vulnerability that reduces it to susceptibility to harm, Levinas' thematization of vulnerability—as an almost always violent, traumatic, and certainly forceful encounter with the Other—runs counter to my aims.
7. See Rogers, Mackenzie, and Dodds 2012 for articulation of some of the confusion surrounding the term and the need to integrate different understandings of it.
8. MacIntyre follows this line of thought as well. Also see Mackenzie and Stoljar 2000 for feminist views of relational autonomy.
9. See Butler 2004a, 2004b, and 2009, Cavarero 2009, Bergoffen 2011, Diprose 2002, Guenther 2006, Murphy 2012, and Oliver 2008.
10. I discuss this point with respect to Deleuze's ethics in Gilson 2011.

Part I
The Normative Significance of Vulnerability

1 Responsibility for the Vulnerable

Some notion of vulnerability is generally assumed in our everyday discussions of ethical dilemmas as well as by theoretical and philosophical treatment of questions of ethical and political relevance. Vulnerability is presumed to be a common feature of the human condition, a basic susceptibility that all possess. As such, an idea of vulnerability underlies our notions of harm and well-being, interests and rights, equality and inequality, and duties and obligations. The central concepts of ethical, political, and social theories rest upon the simple fact that we can be affected by those others with whom we share our world, that is, that we are vulnerable to one another and to the hazards of our environment. To put the point simply, it is only because one is vulnerable that one can be harmed or benefited. The institution of rights, for instance, protects one's interests insofar as one is a vulnerable party and the deprivation of these rights heightens one's vulnerability. Correspondingly, the pursuit of an ideal like equality can remedy injustice, which can be understood as the unjust distribution of vulnerability. Likewise, positive and negative ethical obligations, which demand that we refrain from harming others and act so as to aid them, derive from the basic fact that we are vulnerable creatures. Even Kant's justification for the duty of beneficence makes reference to the simple truth that we need one another and our mode of existence is such that we cannot but call upon others to offer support. It is apparent, therefore, that normative projects typically involve minimizing vulnerability and protecting those who are vulnerable through the establishment of legal rights and political institutions, the performance of ethical obligations, and the pursuit of social and ethical ideals.

These simple points about the normative significance of vulnerability lead to three conclusions. First, vulnerability is something fundamental; it is an unavoidable feature of human existence that is present from the start and never goes away. The creation of ethical and political principles and ideals as a way to cope with our vulnerability indicates that although we can modify our vulnerable state, we cannot do away with it entirely. Vulnerability is inherent both in our physical being, our corporeality, and in our social being. Second, the centrality of vulnerability to ethics demonstrates that vulnerability carries with it some normative force; it calls for response and, moreover, for particular kinds of response. Our vulnerability prompts us to try to prevent vulnerability from being turned into harm or from being unequally distributed or addressed. More specifically, it is vulnerability that compels or motivates ethical action; if an individual is invulnerable, unaffected, there is no compulsion to care for, aid, or meet obligations to this person. It is her vulnerability that is the basis for such compulsion; if our care, aid, or dutiful action had no effect on her or on us, then we would not feel obliged to provide it. Third, in ethical, political, and social philosophy vulnerability is most commonly considered a precondition to hazard and harm. It is regarded as a state that is to be avoided, minimized, and prevented, and, if it cannot be avoided, that warrants protection and assistance. Although vulnerability is not typically understood to be the same as harm, it is thought of as the condition that leads to it; it is seen as tantamount to harm.

There are important connections between these three points. We might conclude that vulnerability's normative force derives from the way it is a condition of particular liability to harm and that it merits response because without appropriate response, injury, harm, or violation is more likely to occur. Yet, there is also a peculiar tension between the first and third points: if vulnerability is a fundamental, unavoidable condition, then we can never fully or adequately protect ourselves from the harm that might result from it. If we conceive our basic vulnerability as always a precondition to injury and suffering, we find ourselves constantly pursuing an unachievable security and safety, that is, the total alleviation of vulnerability.

Denial is one oft noted consequence of the fundamental, unavoidable quality of vulnerability and the view that vulnerability leads to harm. This dimension of our experience is one in which we find ourselves affected by and at the mercy of others, and, if the foregoing description is accurate, liable to be injured at their hands. On this understanding, as vulnerable we are weak and passive, and defenselessly undergo the actions of others. Such a view of ourselves is one that is likely to be eschewed and repudiated since it is inconsistent with idealized conceptions of active and autonomous agency. One strategy for minimizing the import of vulnerability has been to regard vulnerability as an exceptional state, a kind of extreme incapacity and frailty that leads to dependence on others as caretakers. Vulnerability, thus, is the condition of the very young and very old, and those who are physically or mentally disabled, and constitutes a distinct departure from our normal mode of functioning. Thus, it is consigned to the borders of human experience rather than the center, considered a marginal condition rather than a central one that must be taken into account for adequate theorizing. Consequently, although vulnerability is a vital concern for ethics, politics, and social life, it is a little addressed topic and an experience the value of which has been denied. In the late twentieth century, a number of thinkers from a variety of traditions have come not only to recognize the importance of vulnerability but also to attempt to place it at the center of their theories of ethics and politics. This chapter investigates their efforts and, in particular, the ways in which they attempt to take stock of the temptation to deny vulnerability.

ACKNOWLEDGING VULNERABILITY AND DEPENDENCE

Work in the field of feminist ethics over the past four decades or so have made admirable efforts to shift the rather myopic focus of ethical and social-political discourse from the independent, rational, and implicitly male agent to a subject of ethics and politics that is socially situated, interdependent, and not fully rational and transparent. The ethical agent in feminist discourse is one who is situated with respect to race, gender, socioeconomic class, and other salient differences. Theoretical work of this type has also involved the kind of analysis of dependency and vulnerability that is crucial if one is not to assume that autonomous actors simply emerge fully formed from nowhere and if one seeks to develop a more comprehensive understanding of self-identity, relationships, reasons for action, character, and the nature of responsibility. The notion that the care typically performed by women is a central feature of ethical life brings the conditions that necessitate such care to the fore. In this context, feminist thinkers and others have endeavored not only to revalue and call attention to previously neglected or devalued aspects of human existence, but also to examine the political and ethical implications of "dependency work," that is, the work of caring for those who because of "youth, severe illness, disability, or frail old age" are dependent upon others "in order to meet essential needs" (Kittay and Feder 2002, 2). Feminist ethics has also extended this consideration of dependency and vulnerability to analysis of how these conditions are not exceptional ones but rather integral parts of the human condition in general (Kittay 1999). Following in this tradition, theorists concerned with contemporary ethical, social, and political life have come to see the import of human vulnerability. For instance, by placing human dependency at the center of his theory of virtue Alasdair MacIntyre's *Dependent Rational Animals* poses a notable exception to the trend that ignores vulnerability. Since the concept of vulnerability receives deliberate and noteworthy treatment in MacIntyre's text, his account will be our starting point for exploring how vulnerability can operate as a focal point in theories of ethics.

MacIntyre's Argument

MacIntyre describes his project in *Dependent Rational Animals* as a corrective to his earlier landmark texts *After Virtue* and *Whose Justice? Which Rationality?* (1999, x). Specifically, his aim is to explain how particular ethical "forms of life" are possible for beings that possess a particular biological constitution, that is, to provide a developmental account of virtue. This project is situated against the backdrop of a philosophical landscape that has ignored and minimized both human vulnerability and disability, and the continuity between humans and nonhuman animals (ix). MacIntyre seeks to remedy this pervasive oversight by fully acknowledging animality, disability, and vulnerability and by assessing what transformations they effect in moral philosophy when given due consideration. Without an account of the centrality of these dimensions of human existence to life we construct an inadequate picture of human development and a skewed portrayal of what makes us the kind of beings that we are, for instance, one that draws a sharp distinction between human and nonhuman animals.

MacIntyre links a philosophical lacuna—the absence of consideration of vulnerability—with the tradition of privileging mind over body and, coupled with that dualism, human over animal. Our bodily existence links us to other animals, but human capacity, autonomy, rationality, and uniqueness have continually been conceived as stemming from the ways in which we are unlike, and superior to, these animals. Preserving our distinct abilities and status has consequently been contingent upon denying our continuity with nonhuman animals, underrating the significance of our bodily experience, and thus distancing ourselves from the facts of vulnerability that define our existence. The systematic disregard of vulnerability, disability, and dependence in philosophical inquiry is a product of "habits of mind that express an attitude of denial towards" these dimensions of life and "[t]his failure or refusal is perhaps rooted in, is certainly reinforced by the extent to which we conceive ourselves and imagine ourselves as other than animal, as exempt from the hazardous condition of 'mere' animality" (1999, 4).[1] This all too common rejection of vulnerability is also linked with a refusal to acknowledge its concomitant, dependency, and with conceptions of human virtue that rely on the standpoint of those who are "self-sufficiently superior" and aspire to complete autonomy, requiring repudiation of dependency (7). Given that "human identity is primarily . . . bodily and therefore animal identity[,]" this distaste for our animality and dependency leads to a rather woeful misconstrual of who we are and how we should live.

Consequently, MacIntyre rebuffs the idea that vulnerability is an exceptional state, one in which the majority of us only sporadically and unluckily dwell as children and elders, and when we are ailing, injured, or disabled in some way. It is, instead, a condition that we all share as "dependent rational animals." The first part of MacIntyre's argument is thus oriented toward establishing that humans are indeed "dependent rational animals," whose capacity for rationality manifests certain striking similarities to the capacities of nonhuman animals. He develops this claim by elaborating a notion of prelinguistic practical knowledge that serves as a precondition for the use of language and thus for more explicit, linguistically expressed forms of knowledge. Our more implicit ways of knowing are the developmental basis for what we have come to recognize as knowledge: propositional statements, logical arguments, and truth claims established through them. This implicit form of knowledge is characterized as interpretative since it is formed through social interaction, recognition of others and responsiveness to them, and perception of their behaviors (1999, 14–15). This prelinguistic mode of belief is not limited to the time before we learn language, but persists throughout our lives and "provide[s] matter for characterization by exercise of" our linguistic abilities (36–37). It is this kind of capacity for prelinguistic interpretative knowing that humans share with many species of nonhuman animals.

Thus, in MacIntyre's view, our capacities for rationality are rooted in our dependent nature, in our sociality, and in our embodied existence. Even as we strive to become "independent practical reasoners," those who are capable of assessing what is good and how to achieve it, we do not abandon the quality of dependence that defines our early lives; we rely on others throughout this process of development. The status of "independent practical reasoner" is defined by three critical development shifts: (1) from having reasons to evaluating those reasons as good or bad and, in response, altering both reasons for action and actions themselves, (2) from simply having desires to taking a reflective distance from one's own desires and evaluating them and their relationship to the good that one desires (Are they oriented toward that good? Or do they thwart one's ultimate aim?), (3) from being cognizant of just the present to being cognizant of the future as we imagine it for us as a set of possibilities and alternatives. The development of all of these capacities requires the participation of others and so reveals the continued dependency at the heart of our independence: although at first we learn from others what to value and consider good, we come to make our own choices but only are able to do so because of these others and through their instruction, guidance, and conflicts with them (1999, 84). As a consequence, "[a]cknowledgement of dependence is the key to independence" (85).

This picture of human development leads MacIntyre to a correspondingly transformed view of virtue. If dependence is a formative part of our nature, rather than a limited dimension of our experience or a deficient mode of functioning, then the virtues that we need to cultivate in order to live well include those that are premised upon acknowledging dependence (1999, 120). He elaborates these virtues by explaining how our fundamental dependency places us in a web of relations of giving and receiving in which we receive support and care from others as well as provide it to them. By being located in these relationships, we cannot isolate what we as individuals take to be good from what is good for others: for my own flourishing, I need care and sustenance from others and from the communities in which I am situated. The flourishing of those others and those communities are thus integral to my own flourishing. In this way, what is good for them is good for me. One consequence of this account is that there are genuinely shared, communal goods, ones that enable us to become independent practical reasoners. The virtues of acknowledged dependence are the set of virtues that guide us in our relationships of giving and receiving. Included among them are just generosity and misericordia, as well as gratitude and related virtues of receiving well. Misericordia, which is often translated as mercy, pity, or compassion, names the way in which one feels called to act because of the suffering of another and the capacity to extend this feeling to those outside of one's immediate community in a way that is proportionate to their need. As such, misericordia is part of a composite virtue that MacIntyre labels "just generosity," which is defined by uncalculating giving and "attentive and affectionate regard" (122). One gives what is justly due (because it is what is needed), and so in the exercise of this virtue both justice and generosity are found. Even as just generosity and misericordia expand the bounds of a community by extending generosity to those outside of it who are in need, they are the basis for a shared social and political life: "what each of us needs to know in our communal relationships is that the attention given to *our* urgent and extreme needs, the needs characteristic of disablement, will be proportional to the need and not to the relationship" (124). Such virtues of giving provide security not from vulnerability but from abandonment and social exclusion. The corresponding virtue of "graceful receiving" (121) includes the ability "to exhibit gratitude, without allowing that gratitude to be a burden," and graciousness to inept or inadequate givers (126). These virtues are only found to be valuable once we recognize our vulnerable and dependent condition, so developing them requires that we acknowledge dependence. When we are able to acknowledge that we possess "urgent and extreme needs," or might in the future, then the value of uncalculated giving proportionate to need rather than to felt connection becomes apparent. If acknowledgement of dependence is prerequisite to cultivating these virtues, then forgetfulness or denial of one's dependence prevents their cultivation and so prevents the flourishing of a shared social and political life.

MacIntyre often explains acknowledgement of dependence in terms of how those who are conventionally able-bodied relate to those who are disabled and understand themselves in relation to them. We acknowledge dependence when, with respect to those who are disabled, "we have to say: this could have been us. Their mischances could have been ours, our good fortune could have been theirs" (1999, 100–101). This acknowledgment leads us not only to the recognition that we are obliged to provide care to others who are disabled but also to see such care as a common good: " . . . our interest in how the needs of the disabled are adequately voiced and met is not a special interest, the interest of one particular group rather than of others, but rather the interest of the whole political society, an interest that is integral to their conception of their common good" (130). MacIntyre thus locates those who are dependent, disabled, and vulnerable at the center of a social and political community. Another significant feature of his account is the criticism he offers of ignorance of these dimensions of life. He charts the trajectory of this ignorance from disregard for the issues of vulnerability, dependence, and disability, which stems from repudiation of the embodied nature of human existence, which flows from a rejection of our animality. One related error is the link made between physical appearance and the value of individual human beings, which leads to a dismissal of the contributions of those who are physically disabled and disfigured. Dominant social norms esteem more highly those who meet the norms of physical attractiveness, underestimating and devaluing the intelligence and other positive qualities of those who do not, leading to the conclusion "that, in responding to those whose appearance has affronted us, we have assumed that from *them* at least we could have nothing to learn" (137). This assumption is, of course, a woeful, discriminatory error, one rooted in the aforementioned more fundamental misconceptions.

Thus, more adequate acknowledgment of vulnerability involves awareness both that things could have been and could be otherwise—"Their mischances could have been ours, our good fortune could have been theirs"—and that the development of one's mental and physical capacities is due to one's dependence on others. It also requires that this awareness figure into how we live: that those who are especially vulnerable and dependent be recipients of the just generosity of those who are able to give, be valued as members of a social and political community, and that others act as proxies for them if they are unable to participate fully in the social and political sphere, endeavoring to represent their concerns and speak for them. Accomplishing these aims, MacIntyre's account suggests, will require that we contest the social norms that prevent awareness of vulnerability and the accompanying restructuring of social relations, and transform the social environment so that the norms through which it operates are not based on erroneous conceptions of the human condition (137).

The Image of Vulnerability in MacIntyre's Account

MacIntyre's expanded version of a virtue ethic admirably gives a central place to human vulnerability and dependence, generating a theory of virtues and of social and political organization on the basis of full comprehension of these most basic facts. This perspective emphasizes the contingency of the present—that it could be otherwise—and the persistence of vulnerability, dependence, and disability in our lives. It thus attempts to destabilize the normalcy and inevitability of the status quo of ablebodiedness, for instance, by compelling recognition that it is not a given and is a bodily capacity that one may possess in virtue of reliance on others. Although MacIntyre's approach is a commendable departure from the philosophical norm because it emphasizes the cultivation of ways of thinking and feeling that grow out of dependency without outgrowing it and without demoting it to an inferior state, in this section I seek to raise some additional questions about the understanding of vulnerability that is involved in his account.

Throughout his analysis, MacIntyre consistently pairs vulnerability and affliction. The opening line of the first chapter states, "We human beings are vulnerable to many kinds of affliction[,]" and the main concerns of the book are "two related sets of facts, those concerning our vulnerabilities and afflictions and those concerning the extent of our dependence" (1999, 1). Throughout, vulnerability is referenced as vulnerability to affliction, suffering, harm, or injury. This point is made even more clearly by the characterization he offers of flourishing and the goods needed to flourish; our understanding of flourishing is intimately tied not only to our idea of goodness but also to our ideas of harm and vulnerability. MacIntyre states, "[w]hen we identify the harms and dangers to which dolphins [for instance] are exposed and the nature of their vulnerability to those harms and dangers, we presuppose a certain notion of dolphin flourishing" (63). We conceive that which interferes with our ability to achieve the goods necessary for flourishing as harms and dangers, so our idea of harm relies on an idea of what it means to live well. To be vulnerable in this case is to have one's capacity to achieve necessary goods and thus to flourish put at risk (63–64). In particular, the process through which we develop the capacities of independent practical reasoners is vulnerable to deformation (75). Thus, our dependence on others and on social institutions to facilitate our development enhances our vulnerability; failures on the part of parents, guardians, schools, etc. can hinder development. A more complex system of dependence leads to greater vulnerability.

What is curious about these formulations is that MacIntyre strives vigorously to recode dependence as positive, breaking with traditional idealizations of independence and self-sufficiency, but does not seek to detach vulnerability from its common connection with susceptibility to harm, suffering, and weakness. Vulnerability is thought primarily in a negative sense, but relations of dependence on others are construed as sustaining us and facilitating our development into more interdependent beings on whom others can depend. Conceived in this way, vulnerability is understood as the condition that results from dependence. If dependence is our default condition, then, following MacIntyre, vulnerability to harm or injury would be a condition that results from the failure to meet the needs of a dependent being adequately. Vulnerability remains a state in which one is susceptible to being harmed, to having one's capacities diminished, and thus to having one's well-being hindered.

So why question the depiction of vulnerability as a negative condition, and the amalgamation of vulnerability and affliction? What is the difference between these terms? According to MacIntyre, affliction often involves a loss of continuity and the deprivation that attends such loss; in particular, affliction can stem from loss of continuity in our relationships with others (1999, 8). So, the extent to which disability is dis-abling or an affliction depends on the extent to which others, the society, and the social structure fail to support the disabled individual; a disability is experienced as affliction when the disabled person loses specific forms of continuity with others and his social world (e.g., can no longer access particular spaces in that world because they are not physically accessible) (75). Affliction, therefore, entails loss. Vulnerability, however, does not. Despite its etymological origin in the Latin *vulnerāre*, "to wound," vulnerability is not equivalent to suffering, harm, loss, hardship, or pain. Rather, vulnerability is the condition that makes these things possible. Even when conceived negatively, vulnerability is understood as susceptibility to harm, not the harm; it is the ability to be wounded, not the wounding. It is a condition of potential rather than a state of actual injury. As such, it cannot be predetermined that the outcome of vulnerability is negative.

This distinction between vulnerability and affliction illuminates a different angle of the relationship between vulnerability and dependence. If vulnerability is a condition of potential rather than one equivalent to affliction, then rather than being the condition that results from dependence—a condition in which one's development is liable to be hindered, for instance—vulnerability is the condition that makes possible dependence. We are dependent and rely upon others, requiring their assistance and support, because we are vulnerable, open to being affected by our environment and by these others. This ability to be affected, however, leads not only to possible harm and loss but is also the basis for the positive forms of connection and transformation. This alternative understanding of vulnerability merits far more discussion and thus is the main topic of Chapter Five. Here my concern is simply to call attention to the way in which vulnerability is depicted even in an account as sensitive as MacIntyre's. To summarize this concern, it is helpful to turn once again to the type of reflection he believes enables awareness of our vulnerability and dependence:

> It matters also and correspondingly that those who are no longer children recognize in children what they once were, that those who are not yet disabled by age recognize in the old what they are moving towards becoming, and that those who are not yet ill or injured recognize in the ill and injured what they often have been and will be and always may be. It matters also that these recognitions are not a source of fear. (146)

Although it is important not to understate the power of such recognitions, what is of interest is how this description fits with the earlier one in which "we have to say: this could have been us. Their mischances could have been ours, our good fortune could have been theirs" (100–101). What MacIntyre prescribes here is in many ways a dose of humility and a recognition on the part capable, able-bodied adults of their good fortune: it is only by chance that we are not ill, injured, or disabled and only a matter of the vagaries of time that we are now capable adults. This prescription for awareness, however, leaves intact the sense that it is preferable, better, and superior not to be old, injured, ill, disabled, or infantile, and thus that these are inferior conditions that we ought to try to avoid even as we recognize their inevitability. Although MacIntyre wishes us to learn from those who are disabled or otherwise particularly vulnerable, it seems that what we ought to learn is that we should count ourselves lucky, and not that those who are physically disabled might possess capacities and perspectives that the able-bodied are not in a position to conceive, or that children might have unique ways of perceiving the world and capacities for curiosity that are lost in adults. The request for awareness that is made is that we aim not to fear being weak, not to fear mortality, not to fear bodily limitation and decline. Yet, if we continue to regard old age, disability, illness, and injury solely as conditions of weakness and limitation, conditions we are lucky to avoid, then we persist in perceiving them simply as negative states and fail to imagine how we might find different perspectives, experiences, and modes of strength and capacity in these conditions.

Although he devotes little space to an explication of this concern, at the core of MacIntyre's project lies the imperative to alter the social environment so that we might begin to recognize the centrality of vulnerability, dependence, and disability in our lives rather than regarding these experiences as conditions to fear and avoid. Working to transform social norms surrounding disability, dependence, and related issues such as physical appearance is crucial to creating this kind of change in the social environment. Dominant norms deem dependence a form of weakness and incapacity, esteeming total self-sufficiency and independence, and so suppose disability to be a prospect-hindering misfortune that relegates a person to utter dependence. The rhetorical nature of these norms paints all forms of dependence and disability with a broad brush, of course, failing to take into account the wide variety of ways in which a person can be dependent or disabled, and the variations in experiences of dependence and disability. Such social norms also presume that to be vulnerable is to be open to harm. In accord with such norms, dependence is necessarily a form of vulnerability because to rely upon others is to allow one's fate to leave one's own hands and rest in those of others, opening oneself to harm at their hands. Thus, dependence is eschewed because it increases vulnerability. This stance ignores that we cannot but depend on others—true and complete self-sufficiency is an impossibility—and that vulnerability is a unavoidable feature of life and, as such, is not simply an opening to harm but an opening to all experience, negative, positive, and ambiguous. Changing social norms such as these is vital to the aim of human flourishing via acknowledgment of dependence, but it is not solely our norms concerning dependence and independence, and disability and capacity that must change. At the center of these social norms is a particular image of vulnerability as susceptibility to harm; dependence is devalued not only because it is construed as weakness, an inability to do things for oneself, but because it is understood as a way of making oneself vulnerable to others and thus liable to be hurt. Although MacIntyre argues for foregrounding vulnerability, challenging its exclusion from the philosophical landscape and its repudiation in everyday life, he does not challenge how we conceive vulnerability. My main contention throughout this book is that the image of vulnerability that equates it with susceptibility to harm is central to the oversights and denials that define response to it. Vulnerability has been ignored and repudiated not only because we associate related experiences of dependence, disability, and affliction with our bodily nature and thus with our animality, but precisely because we regard the openness of vulnerability as an openness to injury and our bodily existence as the site of such potential injury.

ALLEVIATING VULNERABILITY

Whereas MacIntyre offers an account of ethics and social and political organization that emphasized virtue, Robert Goodin depicts a model of ethics and politics that draws our attention to the significance of vulnerability for duty and responsibility.[2] Like MacIntyre, Goodin's aim is to demonstrate how vulnerability generates responsibility. Goodin's work is of particular interest because he explores how responsibilities of various types share the same foundation in vulnerability. Although the model he develops is quite different from MacIntyre's, the two have common basic premises such as the importance of expanding the moral community beyond those to whom one initially believes one is obligated, e.g., family, friends, compatriots. In addition to explicating Goodin's "vulnerability model" to reveal another way of formulating the ethical relevance of vulnerability, this section also raises similar questions about the understanding of vulnerability employed in Goodin's account. In particular, since his theory calls our attention to the specific relationship between vulnerability and responsibility, my critical concern is directed toward the impact a negative understanding of vulnerability has on responsibility: the question I aim to unpack is whether conceiving vulnerability as susceptibility to harm, weakness, passivity, and incapacity limits or alters the way in which responsibility is taken for vulnerable parties or for one's own experience of vulnerability. Before turning to this question, it is necessary to lay out Goodin's framework of responsibility for the vulnerable.

The Vulnerability Model

On Goodin's "vulnerability model," our responsibilities to others are proportionate to their vulnerability to us. It is vulnerability that generates and explains responsibility; I am responsible for those others who are vulnerable in relation to me and am responsible because they are vulnerable to me. Thus, vulnerability is the basis for both special responsibilities to others with whom one is close and responsibilities to others in general; one may be more responsible for one's friends and family precisely because the close ties one has to them may render them more emotionally vulnerable, for instance. This model poses an alternative to the common contractual model of special responsibilities in which such responsibilities are voluntarily assumed and one is responsible because one made a commitment or promise to which one must adhere. The vulnerability model does not contradict the view that some special responsibilities are voluntarily assumed but rather seeks to explain the source of the obligation apart from this choice:

> It is their vulnerability, not our promises or any other voluntary act of will on our part, that imposes upon us special responsibilities with respect to them. . . . If I promised and others are depending on me in consequence, then I am obliged to do as I promised—not because I promised, but merely because they are depending on (i.e., are vulnerable to) me. (1985b, 777)

The source of such special obligations is not the fact that we take on these obligations but that in so doing we institute or maintain relationships of dependency and vulnerability. We have such responsibilities in view of this vulnerability regardless of whether or not we have chosen to assume them.

The basic premise of the vulnerability model is explained further through Goodin's definition of vulnerability, which is also of particular concern for the analysis that follows. First, vulnerability is defined as synonymous with dependency; Goodin states, "I use 'vulnerability' and 'dependency' interchangeably to refer to the following situation: A is vulnerable to B if and only if B's actions and choices have a great impact on A's interests" (1985b, 779). Here "vulnerability" indicates the significant effect we can have on one another's interests and needs, and the way this effect indicates dependency. If A is not dependent on B, then B's actions will not affect A's interests in a significant way. Second, vulnerability is also defined as "a matter of being under threat of harm" where that "harm is not predetermined" (1985a, 110, 112). Vulnerability generates a responsibility to protect the vulnerable party precisely because the harm that threatens is not predetermined and inevitable; that is, something can be done to avert the harm and thus there is a responsibility to do it. Therefore, dependency lies in needing the other person to perform the action or make the decision that will fulfill basic needs and prevent harm.

Consequently, both vulnerability and responsibility are relational concepts; one is vulnerable or responsible in virtue of the relationships one has to other individuals and groups. This feature of the vulnerability model, Goodin maintains, facilitates adjudication of moral claims and attribution of responsibility because we have stronger claims with respect to those to whom we are more vulnerable. To determine who is responsible, we must ask both " . . . *to what* the persons or things are vulnerable . . . [and] . . . *to whom* the persons or things are vulnerable" (1985a, 112). There are a couple of distinct advantages of the vulnerability model. First, rather than simply prescribing that the needs of the most vulnerable should be met, the vulnerability model indicates who should take responsibility and meet those needs, specifying that the person or group in relation to whom the needy are most vulnerable is responsible. The extent of responsibility is also weighed in terms of the extent of vulnerability, such that responsibility is proportionate to the control one has over another's situation and interests, and the extent to which another's interests are at stake (1985a, 118). Second, task responsibility—who is responsible for protecting the vulnerable—does not necessarily coincide with causal responsibility, which is attributed to whoever caused the vulnerable party to be in the situation in which she finds herself (1985b, 780). Since responsibility stems from vulnerability, the relevant factor in assigning responsibility is not who caused what but who is in a position to remedy or improve the situation.

Overall, Goodin's approach significantly expands our moral and social responsibilities, extending them to encompass all those who are vulnerable to us regardless of proximity, which perhaps includes the environment and animals. In particular, it offers a compelling foundation for the claims of global justice. Goodin's aim, however, is not just for the vulnerability model to justify remedies for existing injustices but for it to justify preventative strategies such as the welfare state, which "is the principal mechanism through which we discharge our collective responsibilities to protect our vulnerable compatriots" (1985a, 145). Goodin's reasoning for the claim that the state is the most appropriate party to discharge these collective responsibilities depends upon the stipulation that the primary responsibility in relation to vulnerability is to prevent exploitative vulnerability relationships. Ethically unacceptable vulnerabilities, those that we ought to seek to prevent, are ones where the likelihood of exploitation is strong. Goodin specifies that the potential for exploitation arises and the vulnerability relationship becomes "morally objectionable" when the following four conditions are found: (1) there is a power asymmetry in the relationship, (2) the vulnerable party needs what is provided by the dominant party, (3) the vulnerable party can only access those resources through the relationship to the dominant party, and (4) the dominant party controls, and can withhold, those resources (1985a, 195–196). The mechanism of the welfare state provides for the needs of the vulnerable, and so prevents them from having to enter into inequitable and potentially exploitative relationships in order to meet these basic needs. Additionally, the distribution of resources through the state is made a matter of law and right; "it is possible to vest that [vulnerable] person with a legal entitlement to assistance" and so prevent the fourth condition from arising (1985b, 785). Those who are tasked with distributing resources are not in control of whether or not recipients receive them; they receive them as a matter of right.

Goodin's reasoning concerning the welfare state stems from two related points. First, although we can distinguish between what we take to be 'natural' vulnerabilities and 'social' vulnerabilities, the 'natural' vulnerability inherent in our physical existence is always mediated by social arrangements (see Turner 2006). Given that many seemingly natural dependencies or vulnerabilities are in fact socially constituted and exacerbated by social arrangements, we have responsibilities not just to protect the vulnerable from exploitation but further to prevent and limit vulnerability itself. That is, if the forms taken by vulnerability are not wholly natural, then our aims are different ones: beyond protecting the vulnerable, we can seek to reduce vulnerability as much as possible by altering the social arrangements that contribute to it. Second, however, Goodin also acknowledges that in many ways vulnerability is an unavoidable feature of life and "absolute invulnerability is an impossible ideal" (1985a, 192). We live in a world in which interdependence is crucial to survival and wellbeing, and is a more suitable ideal to which to aspire than total independence and invulnerability. So, the overall aim of protecting the vulnerable is oriented toward preventing exploitation of those who are vulnerable to harm by instituting social and political arrangements (i.e., the provisions of a welfare state) that enable people to avoid asymmetrical vulnerability relationships.

Perceiving Vulnerability

Goodin's account offers valuable insight into the significance of vulnerability for ethics and politics. By demonstrating that the obligations that we intuitively accept are in fact based upon the vulnerability of those to whom we are obligated, he establishes a case for expanding ethical responsibility. If vulnerability is the ground for ethical responsibility—that which calls us to respond to, care for, and protect others—then we are obliged to respond to any others who are particularly vulnerable in relation to us. This response need not, and indeed should not, be solely individual but can in many cases be the response of a collective; in particular, the state as a collective agent is well-suited to protecting the vulnerable by meeting their basic needs and enabling them to avoid potentially exploitative vulnerability relationships.

There are, however, concerns to be raised about this account. Margaret Urban Walker's helpful criticism of Goodin's vulnerability model illuminates some of its limits. In Walker's view, the idea of vulnerability that Goodin invokes depends significantly on our implicit "*understandings* of the relationships, practices, and incidental situations" that comprise "his example cases," in particular, the cases of special obligation such as the parent-child relationship (2007, 86). Our conclusions regarding who is the responsible party, how extensive that responsibility is, and what are unacceptable and immoral vulnerabilities vary in different cases because we have differing understandings of the relationships, practices, and situations under consideration. Further, both these determinations about the extent of responsibility and vulnerability, and further implicit presumptions about needs, wellbeing, rights, and capacities, are culturally and socially specific. For instance, Walker wonders about Goodin's paradigmatic case, the parent-child relationship, asking, "Is it really 'obvious' who just 'is' responsible for a child's well-being? Is the bar of minimal well-being really set independently of practices which determine who will in fact or who must respond?" (2007, 89). Our conception of the wellbeing of a child is formed in the context of normative presumptions about who does and ought to care for children (their biological parents), and these presumptions are shaped by social conditions (labor practices, whether or not there are social structures to support working parents, living arrangements, and so on).

Thus, Goodin's vulnerability model insufficiently accounts for how obligations are socially formed through institutions, practices, expectations, and norms. Indeed, Goodin admits as much when he attempts to address one possible criticism of the vulnerability model. This criticism "would hold that some sort of circularity is involved in deriving responsibilities from vulnerabilities that arise only because some people have conventionally been assigned responsibilities in that regard" (1985a, 124). The response he offers to this circularity objection is simply to note that there are two different kinds of ethical issues at stake here, one concerning whether or not I should do 'x' and one concerning whether or not the rule that tells me I should do 'x,' or the "existing allocation of responsibility" that holds me to be responsible, is a just or desirable one (125). For Goodin, the first issue concerning the discharge of our ethical responsibilities is the more pressing one and so we must accept the "existing allocation of responsibility" as dictating ethical prescriptions until we have changed it. This stipulation, however, is not quite a response to either Walker's criticism—which suggests that we cannot separate the question of what to do from the question of how responsibility is allocated—or the concerns I raise below.

Goodin's account declines to address this concern both because it separates ethics from issues of social organization and norms, and because it correspondingly presumes a simple and linear relationship between vulnerability and responsibility. The vulnerability model offers up a rather direct logic of the relationship between vulnerability and responsibility: vulnerability exists and manifests in a dependency relationship, and so the responsible party is the person to whom another is vulnerable and upon whom the other is dependent. Thus, his account "retains a linear model" in which vulnerability leads to responsibility, but does not include the "feedback loop" between the assignment of responsibility and the constitution of new patterns of vulnerability and responsibility (Walker 2007, 89–90). The way in which the attribution of responsibility can engender vulnerabilities is thus overlooked. Walker's consideration of this phenomenon emphasizes that the assignment of responsibilities that one cannot perform can lead to a vulnerability to blame and shame. Moreover, if we sidestep a more complex understanding of the relationship between responsibility and vulnerability—including how they are not mutually exclusive and are part of a "feedback loop"—then we will fail to account for how peoples' vulnerabilities can be exacerbated by the very mechanisms designed to protect or aid them. As

Walker suggests, in the welfare state for which Goodin argues, people are particularly vulnerable to having to make their needs fit into social institutions so that they are "administrable."

The "linear model" in which Goodin places vulnerability leads to the conclusion that vulnerabilities are, even if modified by social circumstances, at least reasonably easy to identify and analyze, and that responsibility for them is fairly easy to attribute. Yet, as Walker's criticism reveals, although we might be justified in basing responsibility on vulnerability, the relationship between the two is not a direct linear one in which the nonvulnerable party simply assumes responsibility for the vulnerable party. Nor are vulnerability and responsibility autonomous phenomena, separate and independent from one another. Instead, the same individual may be both vulnerable and responsible, the assignment of responsibility may produce new vulnerabilities, the mechanisms through which we seek to protect the vulnerable may also render them vulnerable in different ways, and, additionally, these others forms of vulnerability may be less visible to us. Both vulnerability and responsibility are social phenomenon, and their ethical salience cannot be divorced from their social constitution since it is an understanding of this constitution that enables us to assess their ethical status. Walker's criticism thus helps us to see that what is at stake in dealing with vulnerability is not just how to prevent the exploitation of vulnerable parties but also how to recognize the complexity of the relationship between vulnerability and responsibility, and diverse different forms of vulnerability. Identifying vulnerability and attributing responsibility is also a question of perception, understanding, and social norms. It is not just a matter of discharging existing ethical responsibilities within the already given framework through which we understand and allocate vulnerability and responsibility.

Thus, our interrogation of Goodin's vulnerability model reveals an additional concern that must be added to the concerns raised previously about the negative understanding of vulnerability. Goodin, even more overtly than MacIntyre, reduces vulnerability to susceptibility to harm in addition to equating vulnerability and dependence. Yet, the consequence of this image of vulnerability now becomes apparent: this understanding of vulnerability, and the understanding of responsibility that accompanies it, narrows the field of our ethical perception. That is, the tacitly presumed ideas of vulnerability (that it is susceptibility to harm) and responsibility (that it is directly and clearly derived from vulnerability) constrain what we are able to perceive as vulnerability such that we see only the most obvious instances of vulnerability relations, those sanctioned by dominant social norms. Although both Goodin and MacIntyre are attuned to the way vulnerability is conditioned by social, economic, political, and legal arrangements and institutions, they fail to recognize how the norms of the social world—the very norms that are expressed through social arrangements and institutions—affect our perception of vulnerability. On their ethical models, the perception and recognition of vulnerability is taken for granted. Even though MacIntyre focuses on the way vulnerability is denied, these denials are simple rejections of vulnerability, not failures to perceive it. What vulnerability is, and who is vulnerable and why, is assumed, not questioned. Yet, if vulnerabilities are shaped by social conditions and only emerge as products of those conditions, then it is fair to say that our perception of vulnerabilities is equally socially shaped: where and whether we see it, whose vulnerability we perceive and respond to, how we regard the differing vulnerabilities of different parties, and so on are all socially mediated.

The absence of such an awareness of the social constitution of the perception of vulnerability has significance consequences for an ethics of vulnerability. Assuming responsibility for vulnerable others, or demanding that other parties take responsibility, requires that one first have perceived and recognized someone's condition as a vulnerable one. Responsibility for vulnerability hinges on perceiving vulnerability as such, as that which calls for response. The issues of perception, understandings, and social norms raised by Walker link the two concerns I have introduced: the negative conception of vulnerability, and the insufficient awareness of the social shaping of perceptions of vulnerability and responsibility. Without that awareness, the views we have considered thus far are unable to take into account how the dominant image of vulnerability (as negative) might impact and limit how we are able to take responsibility for vulnerability.

Following from these concerns, the suggestions I wish to make in the succeeding section are threefold. First, that the pervasiveness of the negative understanding of vulnerability, which deems it tantamount to harm, constrains our ability to take responsibility for vulnerability, both our own and that of others. Second, in light of the impact of our implicit understanding of vulnerability on ethical responsibility, a more critical account of the relationship between social norms and ethical prescriptions is needed, which is developed in Chapter Two. Third, a more nuanced picture of vulnerability needs to include a series of distinctions that can help us think through the meaning of vulnerability more completely.

THE IMPLICATIONS OF A REDUCTIVELY NEGATIVE VIEW OF VULNERABILITY

An ethics focused on vulnerability proposes a particular relationship between ethical obligation and vulnerability: that vulnerability demands ethical responsiveness via caring for and protecting the vulnerable, mitigating their vulnerability, and cultivating the virtues that enable one to do those things well. We have ethical obligations because others are vulnerable to us, as both MacIntyre and Goodin argue, and in light of the fundamental vulnerability that we all share and cannot avoid, as MacIntyre establishes. Vulnerability is thus a ground for ethical obligation; it gives us reasons to act ethically and, simply put, those reasons are either to avert harm or to facilitate flourishing. We are, however, not always or even often compelled by these reasons. In other words, rather significant failure attends our relationship to vulnerability. As MacIntyre indicates, we deny and are afraid of vulnerability both in ourselves and in others. This fear hinders not only our ability to develop the virtues of acknowledged dependence but also our ability to assume and call for responsibility in relation to those who are most vulnerable. It is clear from MacIntyre's account why denial and fear of vulnerability would hinder the cultivation of virtues. Why, however, would responsibility for vulnerable others be diminished as well?

Whilst it is frequently conceded that the meaning of vulnerability goes beyond the way it opens us to harm, this other aspect of vulnerability—as the basis of care and love—remains neglected and the concept retains a negative connotation.[3] In the space that remains, I outline the case, developed throughout subsequent chapters, that a predominantly negative view of vulnerability limits the power vulnerability has to motivate responsible action. In brief, the line of reasoning goes as follows: (1) vulnerability is equated with weakness and powerlessness, with negative traits, (2) the link between vulnerability and weakness makes us likely to repudiate our own vulnerability and dissociate with vulnerable others, and (3) repudiating our own vulnerability facilitates repudiation of responsibility for vulnerable others. Correspondingly, a significant part of what enables the exploitation of vulnerability and rejection of responsibility for vulnerable others is the persistence of the idea that vulnerability is to be avoided. This idea is possible because vulnerability is associated with being harmed, passive, and weak, and thus is incompatible with ideal notions of mastery, competence, and wellbeing. Even on MacIntyre's account flourishing is incompatible with those states that we consider the most vulnerable ones; to be vulnerable is to have one's ability to live well potentially compromised. This preconceived view of vulnerability as susceptibility to harm is aligned with other dualist patterns of association concerning power, gender, and autonomy, all of which render vulnerability something to be overcome rather than something to be experienced, avowed, or understood. Our implicit assumptions and most theoretical elaborations polarize vulnerability by conceptually opposing it to capability, strength, autonomy, activity, wellbeing, and other desirable conditions. The polarization of vulnerability contributes to a narrowed sense of responsibility; it can encourage the view that those who are vulnerable—in the sense of being weak, needy, and dependent—are inferior and undeserving of care. Overall, the negative view prevents both adequate responsibility for others and dealing with one's own vulnerability in an ethically aware manner.

In order to develop this claim, I turn to a perhaps unlikely source: the criticisms of the notion of vulnerability developed in a variety of applied fields—such as social work and development policy—in which vulnerability has a central role. These lines of criticism, which find fault with the notion of vulnerability, clearly explicate the problems with a reductively negative understanding of vulnerability and bring into focus the particular pitfalls of this understanding, as well as providing reasons not to jettison vulnerability as a valuable concept but rather to rearticulate it in a way that expresses its full significance. Concerns about the discourse of vulnerability are often rooted in the practical consequences of the concept. In fields like social work, bioethics, and international development politics, the concept of vulnerability is commonplace. Its use merits scrutiny from both a theoretical perspective (from which we might ask, does this concept operate within our theoretical framework in a valuable way?) and a practical perspective (from which we might ask, what effect does the use of this concept have on those to whom it is applied?). On many accounts, the concrete, practical consequences of vulnerability are thought to undermine the theoretical and practical aims that it is intended to achieve.

Kate Brown summarizes three distinct but interrelated concerns about the practical consequences of the concept: (1) vulnerability is a patronizing, paternalistic, and oppressive concept; (2) vulnerability becomes a premise for an instrument of social control; and (3) vulnerability has stigmatizing and exclusionary consequences (2011, 316). The first criticism stems from the way in which individuals' vulnerabilities are naturalized, negatively coded as hindrances, and both their situation and the harm that befalls them because of it are regarded as inevitable. Paternalistic treatment is the obvious consequence of this approach to vulnerability. Thus, the second criticism of vulnerability follows from this first: if the population in general or specific groups within it are intrinsically vulnerable, paternalism secures them against the harm that would be the purportedly necessary consequence of their vulnerability. Social control—either overt control in the name of protection or subtle control through the normalization of socially desirable behavior, attitudes, and self-conceptions—is the result; worries about vulnerability legitimate such control. Lastly, vulnerability has an isolating and stigmatizing effect insofar as it is linked with being different and 'other,' and insofar as there is a slippery slope between being exposed to dangers and risks, engaging in risky behavior, and being or posing a danger. Those who are especially vulnerable are those who fall into this latter category, but this classification excludes them from the group of those who deserve protection because, as Brown notes, "it would seem that we do not see vulnerability in those we fear" (2011, 317).

The view that vulnerability involves a patronizing and stigmatizing attitude is explored further in Gregory Bankoff's consideration of whether vulnerability forms part of "western discourse" on international development. Bankoff describes how vulnerability is part of a conceptual lineage in international relations that invokes and affirms oppositional categories, subscribing to 'us' versus 'them' thinking, the foreignness of the 'other,' and a corresponding spatialization of this foreignness via the construction of 'hazardous' and 'safe' zones. In this context, vulnerability is often understood as susceptibility to natural disasters in particular, and is often naturalized and regarded as a product of the intrinsic features of a region. This perspective "denies the wider historical and social dimensions of hazard and focuses attention largely on technocratic solutions" (Bankoff 2001, 24). Florencia Luna echoes the view that the concept of vulnerability is often used to shift attention, blame, and responsibility onto the individual and away from the social and historical conditions that generate risk and danger. Luna notes that in bioethics, use of the concept of vulnerability produces an emphasis on the characteristics of the vulnerable group rather than a consideration of the research protocol that might create and/or exacerbate vulnerability (2009, 127). Even when the impact of social conditions such as poverty are taken into account, the deployment of the discourse of vulnerability still stigmatizes and excludes. Even when those who are susceptible are not blamed for failing to take necessary precautions, the hazardous regions are still contrasted with those that are privileged and invulnerable; the expertise, technology, and aid that will save 'them' emanates from the Western 'us.' Ultimately, "the concept of vulnerability still encourages a sense of societies and people as weak, passive and pathetic" (Bankoff 2001, 29). Thus, it falls prey to all three of the critiques articulated by Brown; it is oppressive, controlling, and exclusionary not just nationally but globally.

Although Brown and Bankoff identify a number of clear problems with the concept of vulnerability, their analyses focus on the consequences of the deployment of the concept and do not attempt to investigate why the concept has these consequences. By identifying the core features of the understanding of vulnerability that is being deployed, a reductively negative one, we can shed light on precisely what makes vulnerability a problematic notion. In so doing, we will see how it is this particular formulation of the concept of vulnerability that has negative effects; the concept of vulnerability is resoundingly criticized because of how vulnerability is understood, because of the way the concept itself is formulated.

First, vulnerability is conceived as a negative state, a weakness, and a hindrance; moreover, it is defined in a simplistic and oppositional way that opposes 'vulnerable' people to 'normal' people. As Luna observes, in the bioethics context the 'vulnerable' person is usually defined in contrast to the default "paradigmatic research subject"—a mature, autonomous, capable, consenting adult—and so is typically conceived as being incapable of protecting her own interests and lacking power; the vulnerable person is by definition weak, incapable, and powerless (2009, 23, 25). Second, vulnerability is regarded as a relatively fixed state; the same people, groups, and regions are deemed vulnerable without variation over time, thus confining those labeled 'vulnerable' to that negative state. The fixity of vulnerability paired with its negative connotation generates many of the problems identified. Those identified as vulnerable are not regarded as capable of transforming their situation or exercising agency; indeed, agency is regarded as incompatible with vulnerability, which is just hindrance not a resource or site for the development of capacity.[4] If vulnerability is something entrenched, sometimes even naturalized, then the seemingly logical result is patronizing, paternalistic, and controlling interaction. When thought as a fixed state, the assistance of other, better, more invulnerable parties is needed to rise above conditions of vulnerability. The fixity of this concept of vulnerability both fixes people in vulnerability and fixes vulnerability as a negative state. Theoretical problems also arise from this picture of vulnerability. As Luna concludes, utilizing vulnerability as a fixed label (1) makes problems appear simple when they are usually complex, in particular by (2) failing to address the way different forms of vulnerability overlap and create complexity, and (3) makes it challenging to account for changes by fixing the situation of the vulnerable person; ultimately, "[t]here is a lack of flexibility in this way of considering vulnerability" (2009, 24). Lastly, because vulnerability is viewed as a simple and negative state, and as relatively fixed, it is conceived in a way that entrenches inequity and hierarchy rather than acknowledging commonality and seeking equity. As oppositional and fixed, those who are vulnerable must appeal to or comply with those who occupy the role of invulnerable savior, those who are not weak but strong, not passive but active, not pathetic but admirable.

The criticisms of the concept of vulnerability thus take for granted a rather common but simplistic and dualistic conception of vulnerability. They highlight the perilous consequences of this picture of vulnerability but do not problematize the picture itself; in so doing, these critical perspectives uncover the unmistakable pitfalls of a reductively negative view of vulnerability. They give voice to a specific and, in this case, technical—and highly problematic—usage of the idea of vulnerability, but not to the vulnerability that underlies life in general, the vulnerability inherent in corporeality and sociality. As Brown notes, the concept "now seems to be used less in its relational sense . . . and more as a stand-alone term (i.e. calling someone vulnerable)" (2011, 314). In these applied fields, it is used to categorize, isolate, and label those who are vulnerable, setting them apart from those who are not, and there is little to no practical manifestation of the recognition that vulnerability is a shared condition. Moreover, vulnerability is value-laden—enmeshed with neoliberal ideals like self-sufficiency, meritocracy, and individual responsibility and blame—while its use purports to be value-neutral (Brown 2011, 318). Vulnerability, though, is a problematic concept not because it simply is oppressive, controlling, and stigmatizing. Rather, when vulnerability is conceived as inherently negative, relatively fixed, and inequitably attributed, then it has oppressive, controlling, and stigmatizing effects.

This reductively negative image of vulnerability is a dualist construction of vulnerability. For instance, it involves a facile distinction between power and powerlessness, according to which power is thought of as the ability to defend oneself, and to control and perhaps do harm to others. Thus, vulnerability—being open and susceptible rather than defensive—cannot but be understood and experienced as powerlessness. With these understandings, we are more prone to adopt attitudes of arrogant self-sufficiency than to acknowledge shared vulnerability because doing so would be to admit weakness, defenselessness, and subject oneself to humiliation.[5] The self is then defined via a repudiation of vulnerability, which may be projected onto others against whom one defines oneself. Thus, when vulnerability is encountered in others it is likewise eschewed. Moreover, when vulnerable others for whom we might be responsible are viewed as weak, needy, and powerless, they become the object of arrogant attitudes. In seeking to preserve the sense of the self as competent, powerful, and strong, one may define oneself as a self-sufficient, capable individual in contrast with those whom one deems incapable and dependent. Such attitudes toward others and the self work against responsibility, and are anchored in a negative conception of vulnerability.

The impact of social norms and ideals concerning self-sufficiency, competency, and power on our understanding and experiences of, and responsibility for, vulnerability cannot be underestimated. These norms implicate fundamental and deep-rooted ideas concerning capacity and incapacity, disability, and gender. Thus, they are not myths or misconceptions that can be easily dispelled. Deliberate critical effort is required to identify and analyze the workings of such norms and ideals. The effect they have on our idea of vulnerability, and thus on whether and how responsibility is taken, indicates the need both for this work of critique and for a more thorough account of the relationship between social norms and ethical prescriptions. This kind of account begins in the next chapter.

In light of the detrimental effect an almost purely negative understanding of vulnerability has on our ability to respond ethically to vulnerability, a more nuanced picture of vulnerability is needed. Such a conception of vulnerability would not fall prey to simple and reductive intuitions about what it means to be vulnerable, nor reduce vulnerability itself to any of the particular consequences it may occasion, such as harm. The full account of a concept of vulnerability is developed in Chapter Five, but here I briefly introduce a few central distinctions that are crucial for comprehension of the various dimensions of vulnerability. These conceptual distinctions aid in distinguishing vulnerability from the other notions with which it is typically associated, unburdening it of the weight of these presumptions. As with any set of conceptual distinctions, they are intended to facilitate understanding and inclusion of nuance but are not meant to capture definitively some necessary truth about the way things universally are.

To begin, it is important to distinguish—at least conceptually—vulnerability as an experience of a person or group of people from vulnerability as a condition. There is, of course, much coincidence between experiences of vulnerability and the condition of being vulnerable; those who experience themselves as vulnerable find themselves in the condition of vulnerability. Yet, we may also feel ourselves to be vulnerable when the reality of our social condition renders us far less physically vulnerable than others. As a condition, vulnerability is attributed to people; however, they may or may not experience themselves as vulnerable. Throughout this chapter, the primary focus has been on vulnerability as a condition and, insofar as it is negatively construed, as a condition of being compromised in a way that might lead to harm. The rationale behind this distinction is to enable awareness of the difference between how we understand vulnerability in general—both as a universal condition that all share and as a condition of those in specific circumstances—and how vulnerability is felt and experienced by those who are in such conditions. We can outline certain features of vulnerability when we understand it as a condition, but we ought not imagine that this delineation entirely explains or encompasses the myriad experiences of vulnerability that we and others have. Second, we should distinguish between two different ways one can experience vulnerability and be in a vulnerable condition. A fundamental or primary vulnerability—vulnerability as a universal condition that all share—can be distinguished from particular constituted patterns of vulnerability. Since the former refers to an unavoidable feature of life and a basic structure of human experience, it makes sense to call it "ontological vulnerability" and term the latter "situational vulnerability."[6] Ontological vulnerability is an unavoidable receptivity, openness, and the ability to affect and be affected. Situational vulnerabilities are the specific forms that vulnerability takes in the social world, of which we have a differential experience because we are differently situated. These include, but are not limited to, psychological/emotional, corporeal, economic, political, and legal vulnerabilities, which can and do overlap, interacting with and reinforcing one another. Our situational vulnerabilities are significantly inflected by the most salient social differences like race, class, gender and sexuality, disability, nationality, and so on. Ontological and situational vulnerability are essentially two distinct levels at which we can be vulnerable and experience this vulnerability.

Distinguishing two levels of vulnerability, and vulnerability as both a condition and an experience helps to decouple vulnerability from the conditions like powerlessness and weakness with which it is conflated. Breaking these associations is integral to an ethics of vulnerability since binding vulnerability to ideas of weakness, incapacity, passivity, and powerlessness is both reductive and facilitates denials of vulnerability and rejections of responsibility. This twofold distinction requires that when speaking, writing, and making policy about vulnerability we (1) specify the patterns and characteristics that define any condition of situational vulnerability, both recognizing that these are not necessarily accompanied by the negative valence we have come to expect and locating them within particular sociohistorical contexts rather than naturalizing them, and (2) acknowledge a level of vulnerability that pertains to us all rather than jettisoning vulnerability from our self-conception. Specifying the conditions of different situational vulnerabilities obliges us not to speak of vulnerability in generic and indeterminate terms (as susceptibility to harm), but in terms of how it is manifested in concrete relationships and practices. Calling attention to the particularities of situations of vulnerability also facilitates a critical interrogation of those relationships and practices. Yet, without conceptualizing vulnerability as ontological as well as situational, we may be prone to think of it as the reified, fixed property of certain types of individuals. In this way, we may fail to see the economic, political, and social dynamics that contribute to particular forms of situational vulnerability. This slippage is encapsulated in common sentiments like "those living below the poverty line are vulnerable to disease" or "women are vulnerable to sexual assault," which can collapse into the beliefs that "the poor are dirty, lazy, and incapable of caring for themselves" and "women are vulnerable, weak creatures." When vulnerability loses its character as a condition that can take diverse forms in the social world, it is naturalized as a property (rather than condition or experience) that pertains only to women, people of color, or the economically disadvantaged, and, concomitantly, is viewed solely in a negative light as weakness, inability, and openness to harm. The distinction between ontological and situational vulnerability avoids this reification by establishing that it is the ontological vulnerability that is shared by all that is unavoidable, whereas the situational forms of vulnerability are not necessary; that is, it forces attention to the naturalizing error of reification and to the socially mediated quality of vulnerability. Moreover, identifying vulnerability as an ontological condition enables us to see it as an open-ended condition that makes possible love, affection, learning, and self-transformation just as much as it makes possible suffering and harm. This more comprehensive understanding challenges the prevailing view that vulnerability is just an inability or deficit. By keeping in mind the fact of ontological vulnerability—the fact that we are now and always vulnerable—we also may be able to check the tendency to elevate ourselves above those others who we deem vulnerable. An understanding of vulnerability that does not equate it with susceptibility to violation is both more accurate as well as able to acknowledge vulnerability as a shared condition because it does not participate in the polarization of incapacity and capacity, power and powerlessness, weakness and strength. Such a conception of vulnerability is needed for any ethics that places vulnerability at its center. In order to be able to be truly responsive to the specific ways we affect others, we must take responsibility for ourselves. Thus, taking responsibility for vulnerability demands that we avow our own vulnerability rather than deny it simply because it brings with it the specter of weakness. This avowal, as will be clear in the next chapter, is not necessarily made easier by a more nuanced understanding of vulnerability, but such an understanding is necessary nonetheless.

NOTES

1. We consider animal life to be both "mere" and "hazardous" because we view animals as just bodily creatures. What is "hazardous" about animality to the speciesist human is the animal's lack of "mind" and thus the animal's inability to think, to plan, to avoid dangers, etc.

2. More recently, others have expanded our understanding of the normative salience of vulnerability to suggest that vulnerability grounds human rights. See Bergoffen 2011 and Turner 2006.
3. Love is commonly invoked as a positive form of vulnerability and intimate relationships are arenas in which vulnerability is thought to be necessary. Intimacy demands vulnerability, and a life without intimacy is considered inhuman. The fact that few if any other desirable and positive forms of vulnerability can be referenced is telling. One point to be made is that invoking love is a safe way to acknowledge the unavoidability of vulnerability but it infrequently does much to expand what we mean by vulnerability or our sense of to whom we are responsible in light of vulnerability.
4. Bankoff's account also develops this line of reasoning. He contends that the view of progress, development, and change that follows from this view of vulnerability—a linear narrative of progress—fails to take account of cultural adaptability and the development of culturally specific coping practices in contexts of vulnerability, thus depriving people of autonomously developed forms of agency (Bankoff 2001, 30–31). See also Hutchings 2013.
5. See MacIntyre's criticism of the attitude of "self-sufficient superiority" in Aristotle (1999, 7, 127), O'Neill 2005 on neediness and humiliation, and Young 2002 on the difference between autonomy and the rhetoric of self-sufficiency that stigmatizes dependency.
6. This terminology follows Heidegger's distinction between the ontic and the ontological. As will become clear, I do not map the distinction between ontic (or situational) and ontological onto that between experience and condition (or structure), whereas for Heidegger the ontological is structural. For instance, we might wish to explore what it is like to *experience* ontological vulnerability rather than limit it to being a condition that makes possible our experiences of (situational or ontic) vulnerability.

2   Thinking Vulnerability with Judith Butler

In Jeanette Winterson's story of existential meditation, "A Green Square," the narrator ponders the significance of a recurring memory of sailing in a small boat on the gleaming Irish Sea and experiencing a happiness as clear, deep, and glimmering as the sea itself. Why does this image return again and again, the narrator wonders, and what could it signify?:

> The vulnerability of it. The insolence. Isn't that the winning human combination? Isn't that us, tumbling through the years? To suffer. To dare. Now, the sufferers don't dare and the darers don't suffer. Perhaps that's what's wrong with us all. Wrong with now, sharded people that we are. (2000, 201)

Although in this short passage Winterson's narrator pairs vulnerability with suffering and insolence with daring, and so at first glance seems to conceive vulnerability in the same reductively negative way as the accounts described in the previous chapter, there is more to this literary invocation of vulnerability. The error of the present—"what's wrong with us all" and "wrong with now"—is the separation of suffering and daring, of vulnerability and insolence. In the lines that follow—"The boat in the water. At every turn the waves threaten. At every turn I want to push a little further, to find the hidden cove, the little bay of delight, that fear would prevent" (ibid)—it is apparent that the joy and clarity that accompanies this image arise only from the unique combination of vulnerability and insolence. The vulnerability of being at sea surrounded by waves that might overcome one's small craft is what impels the narrator onward. It is only in being vulnerable that one can truly dare. Without the accompaniment of vulnerability, daring fails to be a way to risk oneself and becomes mere self-assertion or even domination. Without the accompaniment of a certain temerity, vulnerability can be mere suffering. The challenge, the joy comes from being vulnerable in one's daring.

The wrong, on the other hand, that leads us to be "sharded people" is the division of suffering and daring such that some only suffer and others only dare; some are vulnerable while others take advantage of their vulnerability.

We would be right to hear in this assessment a parallel to the position Goodin puts forth, but the musings of Winterson's narrator also raise different issues. We ought to think not just about the inequity of vulnerability relationships and the need to minimize undue vulnerability, but also about the importance of experiencing vulnerability. In Winterson's brief reference to vulnerability, we can see intimations of two important ideas: first, that vulnerability is not necessarily to be eschewed but rather is central to ethical existence and, second, that its eschewal produces only sharded persons and fragmentation, which is a problem not just because it is an injustice but also because of its implications for the human personality.

This chapter develops these two thoughts through an explication of the idea of vulnerability suggested in Judith Butler's recent work. I argue throughout the chapter that Butler's work provides a much more substantial and nuanced account of the nature of vulnerability than the accounts previously described. One methodological difference between Butler and those theorists that accounts for the superiority of her account is the view they take of the relationship between ontology and ethics, politics, and the social sphere. For Butler, ontology is necessarily political and social, and thus has ethical implications. The activity of making ontological distinctions—e.g., about what it means to live, to be human, to be vulnerable—is undertaken in a social, political context, and those distinctions and choices cannot be separated from this context or somehow purified of the power relations, biases, assumptions, and history that compose this context. The centrality of the political dimension of ontology and the ontological dimension of ethics and politics to Butler's approach marks it as distinctive in several respects.

Although I will conclude that there remain questions to raise about Butler's thinking on vulnerability, I contend that it adds significantly to an understanding of the nature of vulnerability in four specific ways. First, it offers a more complicated picture of the relationship between vulnerability and normativity by conceiving norms as "doubled." Norms are doubled insofar as they operate both as ideals to which we aspire and as often constraining standards. Butler's point is not that some norms are constraining and others are desirable benchmarks, or even that social norms are constraining whereas ethical or moral norms are desirable and justified. Rather, her insight is that norms can operate in both ways simultaneously. So, instead of considering just the way in which norms for ethical action require responsiveness to and responsibility for vulnerable others, we are able to see how we are also vulnerable to norms themselves and, moreover, wonder about the norms that delimit how we think about vulnerability. Second, this understanding of norms makes possible criticism of problematic social norms, including those norms that attend vulnerability, and (in marked contrast to Goodin's dismissal of the circularity objection) positions critique itself as ethical practice rather than as a departure from ethical norms. Third, rather than discussing vulnerability as if what is meant by the term is apparent and thus assuming that vulnerability is some general, uniform phenomenon, Butler's account begins to make the kind of distinctions I proposed were necessary in the last chapter, differentiating between a fundamental form of vulnerability that is shared and the various ways political-social context modifies (exacerbating or reducing) such basic, shared vulnerability. Accordingly, she treats vulnerability as having distinct modalities, such as linguistic and bodily vulnerability, that are experienced in distinct ways. Lastly, Butler avowedly rejects the equation of vulnerability with susceptibility to harm. Though I will raise questions about the extent to which her thinking about vulnerability breaks from the pattern of linking vulnerability with harm and violation, her direct consideration of this issue sets her approach apart. Butler only articulates some of these contributions to a theory of vulnerability overtly, thus my aims are twofold: to sketch a picture of the sense of vulnerability that we find in her work, extrapolating from the ideas of precariousness and precarity that she does expressly thematize, and to elaborate on the connection between normativity and vulnerability, fleshing out a more complex picture of an ethics of vulnerability.

In the section that immediately follows, I examine the two key concepts—precariousness and precarity—that form the core of much of her recent work. In the process of distinguishing these two concepts, I also explicate some of the other key concepts that will help us to understand the dual function of norms and the way in which ontology is a political endeavor. The second section of the chapter focuses on the issue of violence. Since the ethical position that Butler develops is one of nonviolence and the substance of that position entails a complex relationship to both aggression and violence, it is important to consider how aggression is distinct from violence and how violence relates to norms. In the third section, I turn to the question of the normativity of vulnerability, elaborating how vulnerability can generate certain ethical norms. The final section addresses what I see as the limitations of Butler's account, introducing two distinct sets of concerns that will be taken up in subsequent chapters.

VULNERABILITY, PRECARIOUSNESS, AND PRECARITY

The theme of vulnerability is implicit in all of Butler's work, yet it is only in her more recent work that she has begun to treat it directly. One of the focal points of *Precarious Life* is bodily vulnerability, especially as it pertains to undergoing suffering and being subject to violence but also in a more general sense: "[t]he body implies mortality, vulnerability, agency: the skin and the flesh expose us to the gaze of others, but also to touch, and to violence, and bodies put us at risk of becoming the agency and instrument of all these as well" (2004a, 26). Through the body, we are exposed, opened onto the world and to others even as for others we are the ones to whom they are exposed and vulnerable. In this sense, vulnerability is universal, an inevitable part of embodiment. In *Frames of War,* Butler's terminology shifts and becomes more precise. Here she takes up the idea that runs throughout *Precarious Life*—that life is precarious—and theorizes the concepts of precariousness and precarity more directly as conditions pertaining to life in general. Although vulnerability, precariousness, precarity, injurability, suffering, and interdependence are all part of a "new bodily ontology," precariousness becomes the central concept of this ontology (Butler 2009, 2).

Precariousness is meant to refer to the way in which lives "can be expunged at will or by accident" (2009, 25), to the way that "to live is always to live a life that is at risk from the outset and can be put at risk or expunged quite suddenly from the outside and for reasons that are not always under one's control" (2009, 30). Precariousness indicates tenuousness, fragility, and insecurity given the absence of control. More specifically, however, it is tied to the possibility of loss. The sense that a life is precarious—requires sustaining, is subject to death—requires the prior recognition that there is life, that there is something or someone of value, whose absence would be missed, whose loss would be grieved. In this sense, life is a normative concept not a purely descriptive one. Accordingly, precariousness exists in a particular relationship with grief and the possibility of grief (grievability): insofar as grief indicates that a loss has been felt, that a life has been valued and, indeed, has been valued *as* a life, "the apprehension of grievability precedes and makes possible the apprehension of precarious life" (2009, 15). By apprehending a life as grievable, and thus as precarious, one sees the very fragility of life and sees it as cause to sustain that life (rather than as an opportunity to annihilate, neglect, or abuse it).

The apprehension of lives as grievable and precarious requires the ability to perceive someone or something as part of the community of the living in the first place. The precariousness of lives can be acknowledged or ignored but must be apprehended prior to such an avowal or disavowal. Accordingly, Butler distinguishes apprehension, which is a more implicit form of grasping that grows out of one's very perceptual capacities, from a more overt, conscious form of recognition, which operates on a distinct plane. Whereas recognition demands a level of conscious cognition, apprehension "is less precise, since it can imply marking, registering, acknowledging without full cognition" (2009, 4–5). Recognition involves "conceptual forms of knowledge" (insofar as it is recognition of particular features of a person's identity and of rights) but apprehension can be more or less implicit, and is connected to what we are able literally to perceive (or not) and what meaning we then derive from what we perceive (ibid). So, apprehension underlies and makes possible the conferral of recognition. One must, for instance, be able to apprehend someone's life as precarious and the loss of that life as grievable in order to recognize the existence of a right to life. Conversely, the inability to apprehend someone's suffering as undue, grievous, or distressing precludes recognition of that person's humanity.

In sum, the precariousness of lives is not immediately perceived, understood, or recognized; it is not a given. Rather, our ways of perceiving life—of seeing its precariousness or failing to see it, for instance—are structured by conditions of intelligibility, which Butler describes as frames. This terminology is used quite deliberately because of its connotations: a frame gives us an image set within certain bounds. By placing the image within a frame, we ensure that it is regarded in a particular way and the frame itself supplements the image, influencing how it is viewed. A frame is not just a framework, some neutral way of making sense of things, but is a meaning and value-laden organizational structure. Frames, thus, are conditions of intelligibility that make possible or preclude the apprehension, in this instance, of lives as possessing a particular kind of significance. Frames "organize visual experience" (2009, 3). The terminology of framing and frames is an extension of the more Foucaultian notion of 'grids of intelligibility,' which is central to Butler's work. The idea of a grid of intelligibility refers to the way certain sociohistorical *a priori* conditions make possible—render intelligible—a phrase, a statement, a way of thinking, a discourse, etc., and are conditions without which that statement, way of thinking, etc. would be unintelligible. The idea of 'frames' that delimit our ways of perceiving and understanding implies, in addition, that something always exceeds the frame. What is not contained within the frame remains incomprehensible, unperceivable within its terms, but also, in its unintelligibility, defines as intelligible what is circumscribed by the frame. So, frames are not just limiting conditions that set the horizons of the meaningful, but are guidelines that are permeable, breakable precisely because they set boundaries. What is outside the frame is not inaccessible—thoroughly imperceptible and unintelligible—but shadows what is understood, operating as that which will shift, break, and remake the frame.

The idea that our ways of apprehending—our basic modes of perception—are framed, delimited by the social and cultural conditions in which we find ourselves and through which we have acquired an understanding of the world, is crucial to our understanding of precariousness in two ways. First, it demonstrates how the precariousness of life may or may not be apprehended and recognized. Second, it leads Butler to distinguish between precariousness in general and a narrower idea of precarity. Precarity is the "politically induced condition" in which precariousness is maximized for some populations and subjects, and minimized for others (2009, 26). Linking one and two, if the precariousness of some lives is not apprehended or recognized, and thus those lives are not sustained, then the consequence is likely increased precarity. So, precarity is a modification of a fundamental state of precariousness, exacerbating or diminishing it.[1] It is thus a product of the frames through which we apprehend life.

A central point Butler makes by distinguishing precariousness and precarity is that precariousness is not simply due to 'natural' events (such as natural disasters) or conditions (such as old age or ill health), nor is it even simply a matter of the material conditions of existence or social arrangements. Instead, precarity is politically induced: it emerges because lives are perceived through the lens of certain dominant frames. Life is particularly precarious if one happens to live in a locale where violence is common, or where access to clean and safe water is limited. But violence may be common and may go unchecked, and water may be scarce or go unsanitized because of how lives are differentially valued. Some lives are regarded as more valuable and significant than others, their precariousness apprehended immediately, and thus violence against them curtailed or prevented and safe(r) water supplied to them more readily. A frame that eclipses the lives of rural, poor, nonwhite people, for instance, intensifies the precariousness of their existence and often does so to the benefit of urban, wealthy, white or otherwise ethnically and racially privileged people.

Accordingly, frames both sustain and fail to sustain lives. The relationship between perception or apprehension, and "material reality," however, is a complex and somewhat circular one (2009, 25). How lives are perceived conditions the material support they find and yet this material reality also conditions whether and how lives will be perceived. The precariousness of some lives might remain unacknowledged, leading to a failure to condemn the exploitation or eradication of those lives, but conditions of exploitation and material impoverishment also circumscribe the way lives are understood. Framing, thus, is not just a matter of how people are regarded or overlooked, but of the practices that coincide with, support, and perpetuate that way of regarding them, linking material conditions to the differential ways of regarding lives.

Although precariousness and precarity are intertwined concepts—precarity is just precariousness exacerbated—there are significant differences in how Butler conceptualizes them and the role they play in the ethics she proposes. For instance, in contrast with precarity, which is politically conditioned, precariousness is "the condition of being conditioned"; it is definitive of life itself and reveals "life as a conditioned process" (2009, 23). Precariousness is importantly generalizable, a feature of *all* life. Accordingly, Butler's ontological understanding of precariousness is distinguished from an existential one by an emphasis on substitutability rather than individualization (2009, 14). Precariousness is akin to an existential sense of finitude in that it emphasizes the fragility of existence, but it serves a different purpose. Precariousness calls our attention not to the tenuousness of our own individual lives—our own mortality, the inevitability of our death, our isolated and unique being—but rather to the way this tenuousness is shared, the way any of us might be substituted for another and so are interchangeable when it comes to the precariousness of life. Understood in this way, precariousness is an ungrounded ground for "positive social obligations" (2009, 22).[2] To the extent that I am vulnerable and my life is precarious, it is also because I am bound to others. Yet, I can only live in terms of my ties to others, the ambivalence of which sustains me, allows me to survive, as well as exposing me to injury of various sorts. Social bonds condition my existence, rendering it precarious and, simultaneously, making it possible. Only recognition of this dynamic can ground—immanently rather than transcendently—responsibilities. On Butler's account, therefore, it is the fundamental nature of precariousness and its universalizable quality that makes it a normatively salient concept, a basis from which we might derive positive social and ethical commitments. The relationship between normative pursuits and precariousness, precarity, and vulnerability will be explored in greater detail in the following sections.

Thus far I have focused on the concepts of precariousness and precarity, emphasizing the difference between them. Differentiating between precariousness as a general condition of all life and precarity as "politically induced," enables Butler to bring the political and social nature of precariousness to the fore. Whether and how precariousness is apprehended, through what interpretive frames it is understood, has important implications both for normative aspirations and for how we understand norms themselves. Before turning to these issues, it is likewise necessary to assess the differences between precariousness and vulnerability.

One way to highlight the difference between the two states is to consider the consequences or outcomes of them. As has been described, precariousness refers to the tenuousness of existence, the instability of persistence; it is the precariousness of life itself. As such, the term implies the risk of loss: loss of life and loss of the features—both physical (e.g., food, bodily safety and integrity) and emotional or psychological (e.g., esteem, dignity)—that are vital to living beings. The outcome of increased precariousness (of precarity) is loss.[3] For these reasons, precariousness is a narrower concept than vulnerability. It is a particular form of being vulnerable, one consonant with MacIntyre's understanding of vulnerability: being vulnerable to loss(es) that affect one's ability to persist and/or thrive in life.

Thus, vulnerability is a more general notion than precariousness, with a broader scope and application, in a few ways. First, it involves a more pervasive uncertainty and instability; it is openness to destabilizing alterations in general, not to losses in particular. Second, although vulnerability pertains to life, it is not a condition that is limited to life as precariousness is. Life is precarious and vulnerable, but precariousness in this conceptualization pertains only to life whereas other things can be regarded as vulnerable. For instance, if we consider the vulnerability of ecosystems or the feeling of sensitivity that we call emotional vulnerability, then we see that neither necessarily involves loss in the aforementioned sense. What makes these examples both instances of vulnerability? The ecosystem is vulnerable to change, to shifts in the conditions and relations that compose it, and the sensitivity of emotional vulnerability might be understood as a greater attunement, an openness to feeling. Vulnerability, thus, concerns ways of being affected, what we can call affectivity. So, third, the outcome of increased vulnerability is not inevitably loss although it may be in some cases.

Whereas increased precariousness produces increased exposure to "injury, violence, and death[,]" the consequences of increased vulnerability are indeterminate (2009, 25).

Consequently, although the concepts seem quite similar, indistinct even, there are some significant differences between vulnerability and precariousness. Even though Butler does not distinguish the two terms, such a distinction is a logical consequence of her understanding of precariousness. For instance, she notes that the purpose of positive social and ethical "obligations is to minimize precariousness and its unequal distribution" (2009, 22). Since precariousness is a fundamental feature of life itself, eliminating it is an impossible goal but minimizing it and reducing the inequality of precarity are desirable goals. For this reason, vulnerability is not homologous with precariousness (or precarity, for that matter). As we will see in the subsequent sections, the purpose of social and ethical obligations is not one of minimizing vulnerability. Instead, the connection between vulnerability and responsibility is more complicated, and the imperative to reduce vulnerability can be understood as part of the source of ethical problems. In this way, Butler's account will lead us to a different understanding of the relationship between vulnerability and responsibility from the account Goodin offers.

This broader conception of vulnerability is also necessary to begin to understand the relationship between norms and vulnerability, and the complexity of our relationship to norms. So, for instance, we may say that we are vulnerable not only because we are living, embodied beings but also because of the way in which we occupy a social world ordered by given norms (for recognition, intelligibility, acceptability, and so on). We are not just vulnerable to the actions of others, or in terms of our need for them, but are vulnerable to norms themselves given how such norms define and structure sociality (as a sociality that preexists us and is the condition of our emergence as ourselves). As Butler writes in *Giving an Account of Oneself*, the self "has no story of its own that is not also the story of a relation—or set of relations—to a set of norms. . . . The 'I' is always to some extent dispossessed by the social conditions of its emergence" (2005, 8). Yet, it is only because we are vulnerable that norms can operate as they do. That is, the vulnerability of the self—its susceptibility to impression, its malleability and openness, its formation and mutation through relation—is the context in which norms are produced and reproduced both critically and conventionally. Thus, the relation between vulnerability and normativity is co-constitutive. Vulnerability enables the functioning of norms and norms can render us vulnerable. It is only given this co-constitutive relation that norms are also 'vulnerable' to destabilization and alteration through reiteration. So, it is clear that vulnerability and normativity are intimately intertwined, and are so bound up with one another because of the way in which ethics and social-political reality are entwined (2009, 35; 2005, 25). The normative social-political frames that are the conditions of our perceptions, feelings, and responses delimit who and what we regard as life worthy of ethical concern. This framing does not, however, entail that we must abandon norms; rather, it means that we must recognize that norms have a "doubled truth" insofar as they both are normalizing and constraining, and are values that orient transformative action (2004b, 206).

VIOLENCE, VULNERABILITY, AND NORMS

On Butler's account, norms and vulnerability are closely intertwined and both are linked to violence in a number of ways. Following from the doubled nature of norms, norms can themselves be violent but norms can also enjoin us not to act violently.[4] This tension is the ambivalent starting point for Butler's ethics of nonviolence, which is explored further in the next section of this chapter. Here I consider the nature of violence and its role in Butler's views about vulnerability and ethics. Because violence is a particular way of affecting others and being affected by others, it is a specific consequence of vulnerability. We are vulnerable to violence, among other things, but violence is premised on vulnerability. That is, if we were not vulnerable, violence would not be possible.

Thus, one of the points Butler makes most insistently is that acts of violence can make us more acutely aware of the precariousness of our lives and of vulnerability in general: "Violence is surely a touch of the worst order, a way a primary human vulnerability to other humans is exposed in its most terrifying way, a way in which we are given over, without control, to the will of another, a way in which life itself can be expunged by the willful action of another" (2004a, 28–29). Violence reveals the vulnerability that underlies it: the physical vulnerability of the body that is injured by a bombing, the legal vulnerability of the noncitizen displaced by war, and the emotional vulnerability that accompanies these events. Yet, violence calls our attention to more than just the capacity of the body to suffer. There is also the vulnerability of being subject to an unanticipated violation that can usurp one's ability to control one's self, one's circumstances, and one's conduct. Furthermore, violence makes manifest the vulnerability of simple human interdependence. As Butler notes, the "primary human vulnerability to other humans is exposed in its most terrifying way." We discover in acts of violence an extreme form of the most fundamental dynamic: the way in which we are always vulnerable in relation to one another.

The seemingly straightforward answer to the question of how norms, vulnerability, and violence are related is complicated as a consequence of this understanding of the revelations of violence. Rather than hold that in light of pervasive vulnerability we need ethical norms that condemn violence and promote nonviolence, Butler asks a different set of questions, ones about what to do about the inevitability of aggression in the context of such interdependence. One central concern, which animates *Precarious Life* in particular, is that of how to respond in the aftermath of violence. On this point, Butler's reflections are inspired by the atmosphere in the United States after the events of September 11th, 2001 and are addressed to that audience, those who have witnessed or experienced violence but are otherwise relatively privileged. Once one has been subject to violence and in some way made more aware of precariousness, the question of how to respond to and deal with violence ethically should be posed differently:

> Only once we have suffered that violence are we compelled, ethically, to ask how we will respond to violent injury. What role will we assume in the historical relay of violence, who will we become in the response, and will we be furthering or impeding violence by virtue of the response that we make? To respond to violence with violence may well seem 'justified,' but is it finally a responsible solution? (2004a, 16)

This shift in focus highlights how violence is born of prior violence or, at least, the perception of such violence. For this reason, meeting violence with further violence only perpetuates "the historical relay of violence" and thus may not be an ethical form of response. Moreover, as Fiona Jenkins emphasizes, violent responses to violence prevents violence from operating as "testimony to vulnerability or to the specificity of injury" (2007, 164).

The questions of who we are and who we become when we act violently lead Butler to an investigation of the roots of violence in psychic life, which is simultaneously an inquiry into how the self is formed. Although I will not delve too deeply into these questions, I will explicate briefly the distinction Butler draws between the violent formation of the self—the violence of sociality and the norms that compose it—and the physical violence that is the result of the actions of such selves. In particular, I will focus on what qualifies as violence, what difference there might be between violence and aggression, and what role aggression has in ethics.

In "The Claim of Non-Violence," Butler deals extensively with the issue of the meaning of violence. In particular, she responds to the critique Catherine Mills levies that there is a tension at the heart of Butler's nonviolent ethics. Mills contends that Butler's account of the "normative violence" that shapes the self is at odds with her demand for an ethics of nonviolence: "if the appearance of the ethical subject is itself productively constrained by social norms and is thus dependent on violence, then it is unclear in what sense an ethics could be nonviolent" (Mills 2007, 135). In reply, Butler suggests that there is no reason to think that "all normativity is founded in violence"; indeed, we can imagine various norms for which "violence" is not an apt descriptor and various occasions on which norms operate in ways that are not violent (2009, 169). She thus deliberately leaves room for norms that find their source or impetus elsewhere, outside of violence.[5]

Mills' criticism, moreover, presumes a rather unilateral sense of violence, one that paints all violence with the same brush and glosses over significant differences between different sorts of violence. Consequently, the main point of Butler's response is to distinguish "the violence through which the subject is formed"—the violence of social norms and frames—from "the violence with which, once formed, we conduct ourselves" (2009, 167). These types of violence operate in different ways, take different forms, have different roots and means of transmission, and serve different functions. Thus, we equivocate if we take them to mean the same thing and hold that because selves are formed through the violence of norms they cannot pursue a practice of nonviolence. As Butler notes, to advocate nonviolence when it comes to "the violence the subject wages" is not then to contend that we must deny or eradicate the violence through which the subject becomes an ethical subject (2007, 185). Indeed, to return to the point made above, she suggests that it might be "precisely because—or rather, when—someone is formed in violence, [that] the responsibility not to repeat the violence of one's formation is all the more pressing and important" (2007, 181). Rather than preclude an ethical practice of nonviolence, the violent formation of the self is what makes this kind of ethics a necessity. The idea here is a more complicated version of the claim that we only need ethics because we are not gods. It is only because we are complex creatures who are opaque to ourselves, shaped through processes and relations that are not of our deliberate choosing and exceed our control, and prone to (potentially violent) responses that reflect that formation that we can and must strive to practice nonviolence. If we understood ourselves fully, could control ourselves fully, had some pure and nonviolent history, we would have no tendency to engage violently and thus no need of an ethic of nonviolence.

Butler, however, also expresses some skepticism about the use of the term 'violence' and so proposes that aggression is perhaps the more accurate term when referring to the violence through which the self is formed. We can understand the difference between aggression and violence as the difference between a tendency toward destructiveness (aggression) and the expression of that tendency in acts that injure and harm (violence). Whereas violence is forceful action (physical or not) that produces harm, aggression is a drive that may be expressed in varied ways (2009, 48). The destructiveness of aggression is not always violent and, moreover, is undeniably part of positive social change, including critique. Indeed, the practice of nonviolence that Butler advances is one that "involves an *aggressive* vigilance over aggression's tendency to emerge as violence" (2009, 170; emphasis mine). Nonviolent practice is aggressive, and is so not just in its attempt to counter violence but also because it is always a struggle, a coming to terms with one's own aggression. One is aggressive when it comes to one's own potential to act violently. Thus, while violence is a violation of the bonds of interdependence that comprise our vulnerability, aggression is not always such a violation.[6]

THE NORMATIVITY OF VULNERABILITY

On Butler's account, these notions of violence, aggression, vulnerability, precariousness, and precarity present us with the opportunity for thinking and practicing ethics and politics in ways that depart from the standard paradigms, for example, outside of the liberalism-multiculturalism debate. In particular, these ideas animate a different conception of responsibility and shift the terrain of our political debates from, for instance, "identity politics" to "precarity and its differential distributions" in hopes of enabling new leftist political coalitions (2009, 32).[7] A focus on vulnerability, precariousness, violence, and aggression alters the normative landscape of ethics and politics. The particular concern of this section is to examine how these notions effect this change, and what precise normative significance vulnerability and precariousness hold. To provide context for this discussion, however, it will be valuable to specify the sense of norms and normativity at work in Butler's philosophy.

As more than a few commentators have noted, in her more recent work Butler's orientation has shifted from social and political critique to a concern for ethical life. Although some view this shift as almost an abandonment of the critical and political dimension of her earlier work, the understanding of ethical norms and normativity in general that Butler develops in texts like *Undoing Gender* (2004) and *Frames of War* (2009) constitutes a clear integration of the political into the ethical.[8] The sense of normativity with which she works is one that operates at the complex intersection of ethics and politics. In this way, Butler's view of normativity is a departure from conventional ideas about normativity in ethics and social and political philosophy. Rather than divide the ethical sphere from the social and political spheres, isolating norms proper to each, or distinguish sharply between social norms and moral norms, regarding the former as requiring critique and the latter as providing the basis for critique, Butler attempts to explore the way in which social conditions underlie and shape ethical norms. Her aim is to make sense of the way "our moral responses . . . are tacitly regulated by certain kinds of interpretive frameworks" (2009, 41). Thus, in Nietzschean fashion, critique takes as its target not just oppressive or constraining social norms but moral norms as well, which are just as likely to operate in ways that are exclusionary or undemocratic and yet are accorded greater weight. Therefore, Butler claims, "moral theory has to become social critique if it is to know its object and act upon it"; that is, if moral theory is to be ethically responsive—contextually relevant and temporally modulated—then it must involve critique of the interpretive frames that condition it and may limit its comprehension of ethico-political issues (2009, 35). In this way, Butler's account remedies one of the central problems with the accounts of an ethics of vulnerability offered by MacIntyre and Goodin.

The emphasis on the importance of critique is crucial when it comes to making sense of the doubled nature of norms. If the norms that govern social life are imbricated in the norms that guide ethical life, then norms are both constraining and normalizing ways of ordering the world and its inhabitants, and, at the same time, shared values and principles that guide our actions and aspirations (see 2004b, 206, 221). So, Butler links a Foucaultian understanding of the norm as a normalizing operation of power with the aspirational sense of norms.[9] In the former sense, a norm is "a principle of comparison, of comparability, a common measure" (2004b, 51). Norms are not necessarily restrictive or coercive (although they can be), but rather are measures that facilitate the hierarchical ranking of individuals and that operate as continuous corrective mechanisms.[10] Because the norm creates a continuum of normality, it "integrates anything which might attempt to go beyond it" in the sense that all behavior—proximate to or distant from the norm—is framed in relation to the norms that pertain to it (2004b, 51). Rather than being an external constraint, a norm circulates within social practices, which manifest the norm and are the medium of its reproduction.

On Butler's account, these features of norms pertain as much to moral norms as they do to social norms. It seems, though, that the normalizing and corrective operation of norms would preclude them from being ethical ideals for action. Simply put, if norms are merely social conventions, then the moral norms that demand the transformation of convention so that it accords with an ideal are also just conventions. There appears to be little way to differentiate ideals from mere convention and thus little way to justify our ideals as grounded in some way. For this reason, the practice of critique is as integral to moral theory as social theory. Without critique, moral norms do rely as much on convention, presumption, and given interpretive frames as social norms do. In this context, critique is far from a mere negative evaluation or judgment. Rather, critique can be defined as a practice of reflection that aims not to judge and evaluate but to "bring into relief the very framework of evaluation itself" (Butler 2004c, 307).[11] Critique brings to light the delimiting conditions of our knowledge, the epistemological constraints that are the product of ontological framing, by adopting "an interrogatory relation to the field of categorization itself" (ibid, 310). This "interrogatory relation" to our given categories for understanding places them in question rather than acceding to and assuming them, and so can reveal them both as a basis for evaluation that is contingent rather than given and as generating an evaluation that is not always just or adequate. In this way, critique reveals the "illegitimacy" of certain laws, power structures, institutions, and forms of authority (ibid, 308). Thus, critique always emerges in response to a particular way of being governed, a particular form of authority, a particular power dynamic, a particular set of restrictions, and is an ongoing practice rather than a onetime act of judgment (304).[12]

What, then, does a normative theory that puts critique at its core look like? One significant point of difference between such a theory and more traditional normative theories is the role accorded judgment and the view taken of its importance. For traditional normative theories such as utilitarianism and deontology for example, judgment is the means for ethical action and thus indispensable; one must judge prior to action in order to act rightly. In contrast, Butler adopts a purposeful skepticism about moral judgment. In "Non-Thinking in the Name of the Normative," she turns to the conception of normativity implicit in anthropologist Talal Asad's book *On Suicide Bombing*. Asad, Butler contends, develops a compelling normative account that focuses on understanding rather than on moral judgment:

> He is . . . standing to the side of the 'for and against' arguments [concerning suicide bombing] in order to change the framework in which we think about these kinds of events or, rather, to understand how such phenomena are seized upon by certain moral and cultural frameworks and instrumentalized for the purposes of strengthening the hold of those frameworks on our thinking. (2009, 152)

So, the concern expressed in the title of the chapter is that the normative—here exemplified in being "for and against"—is all too often utilized in order to preserve the status quo and render thought unnecessary. Moral condemnation, however appropriate it may seem and ultimately may be, is non-thinking, and this kind of non-thinking response to problematic and complex events only re-entrenches the normative framework from which it is derived. It neither leaves an opening for understanding nor provides any motivation to understand the events that have taken place or our own interpretations of those events.

A cautious resistance to judgment and justification, and an emphasis on critique becomes all the more important when we consider the purportedly clear but often blurry line drawn between the activities of description and prescription. As Butler observes, both definition and description can perform the work of judgment. The ways we define things and describe phenomena predetermine the kind of judgment that follows, and de facto consist of judgments themselves. The very definition of "terrorist violence," for instance, holds that such violence is "patently unreasonable and non-debatable"; it is not just unjustifiable but, indeed, is incomprehensible (2009, 154). The meaning of the term "terrorist violence" determines in advance not only that such violence is wrong but further that its wrongness is not even a matter of debate. There is no understanding "terrorist violence" because as it is defined there is nothing to understand. The consequence is that there is no impetus to make our use of the term more precise or to follow its "semantic sliding"; the definition of the term makes it almost impermissible to do so (2009, 153). Butler expresses this concern by noting that "it may well be that definition has been substituted for description, and that both are, in fact, judgment—at which point judgment, and the normative, have preempted the descriptive altogether. We judge a world we refuse to know, and our judgment becomes one means of refusing to know that world" (2009, 155–156). The problem is not that the line between the normative and the descriptive is blurred, but rather that the blurring of this line is not acknowledged and normative judgments are allowed to masquerade as description. By supplanting description and understanding with judgment and justification of that judgment, we "refuse to know" and persist in non-thinking. Only by refraining from judgment can one begin to see and bring to light the ways in which moral judgment is implicit in description and definition.

A normative theory with critique at its center is one that questions this habit of a non-thinking invocation of the normative. The emphasis is placed not on judgment, which is univocal and unable to see its own foundations (let alone problematize them), but on evaluation, which is comparative and self-reflexive. Prescription and normativity, however, are not abandoned with a suspension of judgment. What is abandoned are the security and ease of relying on a normative framework as if it were a given, and the certainty with which judgment is made within that framework. The critical and comparative evaluations Butler has in mind are ones that go beyond weighing different possible moral responses (different possible judgments) and their outcomes and rationales. Instead, "the practice of critique . . . focus[es] on the violence effected by the normative framework itself"; one interrogates the moral framework for what it conceals, assesses and seeks an understanding of what lies outside the given framework, and does so not just with respect to the normative frameworks of others but with respect to one's own (2009, 150). The point, as Butler puts it, "is not to dispense with normativity, but to insist that normative inquiry take on a critical and comparative form so that it does not unwittingly reproduce the internal schisms and blind spots inherent" in the presumptions of our moral frameworks (2009, 162).

As the foregoing discussion sought to emphasize, Butler's view of norms and normativity is a complex one that significantly departs from more conventional conceptions of the normative in ethics and social and political thought. To summarize, this sense of normativity involves (1) a dedication to the suspension of judgment, (2) undertaken in order to facilitate the practice of critique, which (3) takes as its target the normative frames that appear to us as givens and (4) seeks to lay bare the judgments implicit in definition and description, which (5) reveals taken for granted normative frameworks to be ones that shore up their own authority and status as unquestionable. This understanding of normativity regards critique as central to normative theory and thus as an ethical practice in its own right. Butler's account likewise reverses the priority of judgment and understanding by according understanding greater significance in normative theory. This shift—from "judging a world we refuse to know" to seeking to know a world by refraining from judging—is important for making sense of the normative import of vulnerability. Experiencing vulnerability and apprehending the precariousness of all life affords us the ability to understand better the way in which we are related to others in a social world and the nature of ethical responsibility.

In the remainder of this section, I turn to the relationship between vulnerability and normativity, elaborating how vulnerability functions as a basis for certain kinds of normative claims. These claims, as should be clear from the above account of the sense of normativity, have a different status from many normative claims: the fact of shared vulnerability does not *necessitate* a particular ethical response, making it objectively required, nor does an experience of vulnerability necessarily motivate ethical response. Rather, vulnerability is at the heart of a normative theory that prioritizes understanding and critique, and an adequate apprehension of shared precariousness and vulnerability forms the basis for certain normative aspirations.

One way to begin to describe the normative significance of vulnerability and precariousness is in terms of an expanded sense of community. The aim, Butler writes, is "reimaging the possibility of community on the basis of vulnerability and loss" (2004a, 20). There are at least two ways in which we might understand the meaning of community here. In one sense, Butler refers to an ethical and a political community, the community in relation to which one is responsible. In another sense, this community as she reenvisions it is simply that of those who share a common vulnerability and, in this respect, of being with others in that shared milieu. As with MacIntyre and Goodin, an expansion of the former—the community of those responsible to one another—in light of the latter—the community of all who share in vulnerability—is one of the key aspirations of Butler's ethics of vulnerability. What is distinctive about this second sense of community, however, is that it is not a community of individuals but one premised on an unwilled, prior, and constitutive relationality. Such a community is one we did not choose, just as we did not choose the site of our birth or the parents who engendered us, and one we cannot escape or avoid insofar as we cannot choose not to be in (some kind of) relation to others. We are necessarily vulnerable precisely because we are beings who are what they are in relation to others, who are in basic community. In its normative dimension, this community emerges not from individuals setting aside self-interest to work together or forming pacts that regulate their self-interest for the greater good, but from the recognition that I am in, have always been in, and, indeed, *am* only in virtue of community with others. For this reason, the term 'interdependence' seems insufficient to capture the kind of being with others that is at stake when speaking of vulnerability. As Butler notes, "if, at the beginning . . . *I am only in the address to you*, then the 'I' that I am is nothing without this 'you,'" (2005, 82). Where interdependence might imply that we are separate and isolatable individuals who depend on one another, the idea here is that interconnectedness goes all the way down and is prior to the establishment of individuals who can be said to depend on one another. It is through relations and in virtue of interdependence that we become such individuals. This mode of being with others implies that "my existence is not mine alone, but is to be found outside myself, in this set of relations that precede and exceed the boundaries of who I am" (2009, 44). Interdependence and community, thus, are not just matters of solidarity of interest but of shared history of and potential for self-dispossession, that is, being undone by the ties that of necessity link us.

It is in this context that Butler believes we should consider violence anew. In so doing, we should consider it not just as a wrong, a harm, an injustice, or a violation of rights, but, more fundamentally, as "an exploitation of that primary tie" of relationality, shared precariousness, and vulnerability (2004a, 27). Hence, her work in *Frames of War* and *Precarious Life* takes as its focal point war and violence, but also grief and loss. As previously discussed, grief indicates that a loss has been felt and the lost life was valued. In this way, the experience of grief is also a form of dispossession, a way of being undone by loss; to grieve is not only a sign that one loved and valued the one who is lost, but is also an indication that the other was (and is) part of who one is. The loss is not just a loss of the other, but a destabilization of the self in relation to that loss. Thus grief reveals the truth of these ties of interconnection and their power to shake the stability of our sense of self. Grief, and the violence that may lead to it, has normative salience because of what it can enable us to recognize: our ontological reality, to put the point abstractly, as interdependent and vulnerable.

At the same time as grief can refer us back to a fundamental feature of our existence, it can also be a starting point for more substantial ethical engagement. Butler contends that by "tarrying with grief" and the vulnerability it lays bare, by refraining from getting over it too quickly, by not eradicating the unsettling emotion, it is possible to create the basis for an expanded ethical community (2004a, 30). In particular, we may "develop a point of identification with suffering itself" (ibid). The suffering with which we may identify is, importantly, not just our own. Rather, it is "suffering itself" with which one must identify. By inhabiting the space of grief, one might identify not only with one's own individualized, private suffering but begin to apprehend suffering as a common ground. A new sense of responsibility and community can be gained only "if the narcissistic preoccupation of melancholia can be moved into a consideration of the vulnerability of others" (ibid). In contrast with melancholia, which involves both a refusal of grief and mourning by repudiating the loss and so entails never getting over loss, "tarrying with grief" entails staying with loss and going through mourning rather than making grief the jumping off point for other responses. Letting grief linger, Butler avers, occasions understanding whereas removing grief, as an obstacle of sorts, leads only to unthinking and unknowing judgment. Grief, loss, and the effects of violence can lead to ethical practice (rather than narcissism and fear of persecution) only if they do not remain experiences that are self-contained and privatized. When loss is used to create boundaries—for example, between the ones who have lost and the ones who have caused the loss—rather than allowed to dissolve them, such a reception of loss denies what would be revealed by experiencing it fully: the implication of the self in others and of others in the self, and the pervasiveness of vulnerability. If loss, grief, and vulnerability instead invite awareness of the ontological truth of precariousness as equally shared, of suffering as more than just one's own, and of vulnerability as universal, then, in this way, vulnerability—that "unwilled susceptibility" that binds us to others—can be made an ethical "resource for becoming responsive to the Other" (2005, 91).

Although a comprehension of the way in which precariousness and vulnerability are fundamental shared conditions is necessary for ethical response, Butler makes clear that such awareness—"of the injurability of all peoples"—is not sufficient: instead, an ethics of nonviolence must "take its departure . . . from an understanding of the possibilities of one's own violent actions in relation to those lives to which one is bound, including those whom one never chose and never knew" (2009, 179). In the first place, only by understanding one's own capacity for violence can one struggle against expressing oneself violently. Knowing that one possesses this capacity enables one to channel aggression into nonviolent forms. Such understanding is crucial to contesting and breaking with what Butler calls the "postures of sovereignty and persecution" (2009, 181). The ethical importance of vulnerability becomes most clear in relation to these two attitudes, which echo Winterson's diagnosis that the problem with now is that we are sharded people, either vulnerable or insolent but failing to be both.

The sovereign self or sovereign state is one who shifts injurability onto an other by doing violence to that other in order to secure its own impermeability, invulnerability, and defense against violence. The position of persecution is one in which the subject defines itself as injured and persecuted, and thus justifies its own violence; its status as injured party entails that the subject "is, by definition, precluded from doing anything but suffering injury" and thus cannot be seen to *do* violence or to do violence *unjustly* (2009, 179). Although in persecution vulnerability is avowed as definitive of the self whereas in sovereignty it is denied as a possibility for the self, the postures of persecution and sovereignty often coincide. The movement by which a sovereign subject "denies its own constitutive injurability" and "locates injurability with the other" (178) can align with the movement by which a persecuted subject rationalizes its violence in light of the perceived injustice and horror of its persecution (also see Jenkins 2007, 164–166). As both persecuted and sovereign, one can at the same time deny injurability—and vulnerability in general—and position oneself as the injured, vulnerable party.

The logic of this coincidence depends upon the (faulty) sense of vulnerability presumed by these postures. Rather than apprehending precariousness as definitive of all life and vulnerability as a fundamental and shared condition, vulnerability is thought to be localized, either in injurable others or in the persecuted subject. Rather than understanding vulnerability as an openness basic to human existence that unites self and others in a prior interconnectedness, vulnerability is understood only as a condition in which injury and harm is possible. The first point, that vulnerability is localized and localizable, entails that isolating it in one subject precludes it from pertaining to others. The second point entails that vulnerability is understood in a reductively negative way, as tantamount to harm and as a form of weakness that is to be eschewed or, at the very least, justifying a defensive posture. Together, these two points form the flawed conception of vulnerability upon which sovereignty and persecution are both premised. Thus, we can now see what is problematic about Goodin's account. The persecuted subject identifies with vulnerability only as the suffering of injury and the sovereign subject disidentifies with vulnerability for the same reason, because vulnerability is equated with being harmed. There is, thus, a unproblematic transition from a position of persecution to a pursuit of sovereignty—one identifies as persecuted in order to justify the pursuit of sovereignty—and from sovereignty to persecution—the failure to achieve complete mastery and impermeability, an impossible aim, can only lead to a heightened sense of vulnerability as liability to harm. These postures are misguided responses to vulnerability and our fundamentally precarious condition. The persecuted self preserves vulnerability as a kind of privilege for itself, denying it to others, while the sovereign self repudiates vulnerability as a condition that pertains to itself, projecting it onto others. Both fail to apprehend shared vulnerability and the way in which such vulnerability is the condition of our existence.

For Butler, the problem posed by these postures, and thus the problem for which ethical and political response is called, is that of self-justifying destructiveness and violence. The problem is the coincidence of aggression and non-thinking judgment, which turns aggression into preemptive violence and which is the practical outcome of judging a world we refuse to know. Even as aggression may be "coextensive with being human," "destructiveness forms the problem for the subject" (2009, 176). Thus, as noted above, the ethical problem to which answers are sought is how to deal with the primary impulse to aggression so that it does not produce the destruction of those others to whom we are bound and exploit the vulnerability that we share.

Yet, this problem is only one half of the formula that Butler has offered us. In the preceding paragraphs, I have sketched a picture of Butler's ethics of vulnerability that is defined chiefly by two aspects: (1) a comprehension of equality in precariousness and (2) a comprehension of both one's own capacity to act violently and the possible consequences of such actions. These two requirements are necessarily linked, and are connected to the aforementioned criteria for a normative theory that places critique at its center. First, awareness of one's own potential for violence is predicated on "the apprehension of a generalized condition of precariousness" (2009, 183). An awareness of vulnerability as fundamental and common, as a condition that binds one to others, is a more primary apprehension that allows one to understand that one's possible violent actions would affect others; only in the context of an apprehension of their vulnerability and precariousness as on par with one's own, does understanding one's capacity for violence begin to have ethical salience. Second, the willingness to suspend judgment, the capacity for greater understanding, and the undertaking of critique are only possible given comprehension of these two specific dynamics.

The positions of sovereignty and of persecution, however, deny shared precariousness from the beginning. They both deny that it is the case by simply failing to comprehend it and deny that there is injustice in redistributing precariousness in an inegalitarian fashion. These denials are rooted in a reductively negative understanding of what it means to be vulnerable, which both reduces vulnerability to susceptibility to violation and makes of vulnerability an isolated, private experience. Thus, these postures grow out of an ontology that rests on pervasive illusions; they may, for instance, operate on the basis of a liberal individualist conception of the human person, "an ontology of discrete identity [that] cannot yield the kinds of analytic vocabularies we need for thinking about global interdependency" (2009, 31).[13] Therefore, the ethical and political problems lie not only in the failure to reckon with one's tendency toward aggression and turn it away from violent destruction, but also in the deficient understanding of vulnerability that accompanies and sustains violent action. Comprehension of precariousness and vulnerability as conditions that are shared and common is connected to awareness of one's capacity for violence; the latter has little ethical and political significance without the former. When the ethical and political problems are the failures of comprehension and the absence of awareness, then we should emphasize this connection all the more rather than privilege one aspect (grasping one's capacity for violence) over the other (awareness of vulnerability as shared) as Butler appears to do. In particular, in analyzing the problem of non-thinking judgment that may produce various forms of violence, we should ask what conditions give rise to violence, examine the sources of the inability to check one's own tendency to violence, and consider how this inability may grow out of the failure to comprehend the nature of vulnerability and precariousness.

In light of the foregoing discussion, it is clear that an ethics that grows out of an ontology of vulnerability must be a critical one. That is, if vulnerability is to be an ethical resource, our practical thought and action with respect to it cannot consist merely of avowing vulnerability in response to pervasive denials of vulnerability. We cannot imagine that responsibility simply follows from an avowal of shared vulnerability. Indeed, critical investigation of why responsibility does not follow and of the conditions that prevent responsibility from being assumed is crucial. As I will argue in the next chapter, practically engaging vulnerability—our own and that of others—and engaging ethically with others on the basis of vulnerability must involve a critique of the norms that produce vulnerability as something either to be eschewed or to be avowed only defensively. Although avowal of vulnerability does not infallibly generate responsibility, it does present us with a context in which to create new norms that facilitate being together as vulnerable persons.

CRITICAL COMMENTS

I concluded the previous section with the contention that in order to develop the kind of normative theory that Butler proposes it is necessary to examine the ways in which vulnerability is conceptualized negatively as a state to avoid and fear. Such a normative theory is one that withholds judgment so as to seek understanding, that centers on critique so as not to perpetuate the oversights and exclusions of accepted normative frameworks, and that is founded on grasping both our own capacity for violence and the way vulnerability is a generalizable condition relevant to all beings. If it is necessary not just to comprehend our capacity for violence but also, and perhaps more fundamentally, to comprehend and experience vulnerability as a shared condition, then our concerns must turn also to the roots of what I have described as a reductively negative view of vulnerability. It is this view of vulnerability that hinders that basic aim of "the apprehension of equality in the midst of precariousness" and so we must seek to understand the practices, patterns of thought, structures, institutions, etc. that give rise to it (2009, 181). Such a consideration will involve analysis of the concrete practices through which vulnerability is eschewed as well as of the norms, both social and moral, which support this way of thinking about and experiencing vulnerability. Thus, the role given to critique becomes even more significant. We must turn our attention toward a critical understanding of the conventional reception of the concepts, like that of vulnerability, that form the core of this normative account.

In this concluding section, I will briefly raise some concerns about the scope and tenor of Butler's account in light of the requirements for an ethic rooted in vulnerability. I suggest, first, that in specific respects Butler's account of the normative dimensions of vulnerability and precariousness remains too theoretical and, second, that it is overly focused on a conception of vulnerability that is intrinsically linked to violence. The first concern is, in some sense, one about scope whereas the second is one of tenor.

With respect to the question of scope, there is a certain breadth to Butler's account that I believe is most fruitfully accompanied by an analysis with a more concrete and narrowed focus.[14] This kind of analysis is necessary for a couple of reasons. In this first place, if the normative account provided—an account of an ethics of nonviolence and/or an ethics rooted in vulnerability—is one that primarily seeks to respond to pervasive ethical failures and lapses, then it needs to involve a thorough account of the social and cultural genesis of those failures. Butler explains how when we adopt the postures of persecution and sovereignty we fail to refrain from destructive violence and fail to respond ethically when rendered vulnerable through violence, but does not describe why these postures are adopted, and how they are generated and perpetuated. The emblematic instance of these postures is the preemptive violence of the United States in the wake of the events of September 11th, 2001, yet this example only facilitates a certain degree of understanding. Attitudes of sovereignty and persecution did not emerge suddenly at this historical moment, to be consolidated only in its aftermath. Rather, in order to understand the conditions that give rise to failed ethical response it is crucial to investigate the perhaps more mundane ways in which we take ourselves to be sovereign and/or persecuted. In such an account, we—we, relatively privileged, left-leaning academics, for instance—might begin to see reflections of ourselves rather than only sovereign boogeymen like Bush, Cheney, and Rumsfeld.

In the second place, merely being aware of, avowing, or otherwise affirming vulnerability and, likewise, acknowledging one's capacity for violence rather than denying it or failing to be aware of it is ethically inadequate on its own. Awareness or avowal instead of disavowal and repudiation is inadequate because it does not necessarily lead to ethical responsiveness. As Catherine Mills notes, "the recognition of vulnerability and relationality does not itself guarantee ethical responsibility. [Although it] might be a necessary condition for responsibility, it is not sufficient in itself . . ." (2007, 153). In this type of normative account, of course, nothing guarantees or necessitates responsibility and ethical action; the acknowledgment of shared vulnerability and the demand not to exploit such vulnerability does not have the force of a categorical imperative. How to make possible ethical responsibility becomes one of the most pressing questions. Thus, it is all the more necessary to articulate what precludes ethical response, how the sense of responsibility that might grow out of awareness of common vulnerability is truncated, how the actions and attitudes that might fulfill responsibility are inhibited, and how the ways in which we live channel our energies away from ethical responsiveness. One may be aware of the ontological reality of a common vulnerability—one may have read Butler!—but without a consideration of the concrete ways vulnerability is repudiated or appropriated as a form of privilege, it is difficult to translate that awareness into ethical response.

Lastly, although Butler's emphasis on the framing is vital, the absence of an emphasis on practices renders it especially theoretical. The concrete conditions—"the conditions for responsiveness"—of which Butler requests we take stock are, on her account, primarily "the various mediating forms and frames that make responsiveness possible" or impossible (2009, 180). That is, we must critically bring to light those framing norms "that differentiate between those lives that count as livable and grievable and those that do not" (ibid). What is particularly interesting about this move is that the call for concrete critical analysis remains at the level of the frames that structure comprehension and apprehension. This level of analysis is of vital importance, so what I suggest here is not intended to undermine the importance of a critical interrogation of the frames that shape our perception and understanding. One consequence of this emphasis, however, is that the level of analysis remains that of discourse and ideology rather than that of practices, and the normative claims are oriented toward comprehension rather than engagement and action. In articulating my concern in this way I likewise do not mean to suggest that there are firm or clear separations between materiality and representation, between discourse and practices, or between comprehension and action. Rather, I wish to emphasize the other dimension—materiality, practices, and action—in order to demonstrate their intertwining more completely. So, for instance, when Butler prescribes "an understanding of the possibilities of one's own violent actions[,]" the form of comprehension she advocates is conceived as one that is itself a mode of engagement; arriving at and proceeding with this understanding is itself a struggle and a matter of constant practice (2009, 179). But, pressing questions remain about what types of action such an understanding might produce (what modes of action accompany this understanding of one's potential for violence?) and how we might bring this understanding to bear on our activities in our daily lives. How do we translate this understanding into practice? For instance, what form does it take in an existence in which mundane acts have pernicious and even violent consequences? If the violence is not our own but we participate in institutions and structures that facilitate and support it, then how must a comprehension of our capacity for violence be altered? Does awareness of our capacity for violent action includes an understanding of how our seemingly unproblematic and normal consumer activities have broader negative detrimental consequences, for example?[15]

So, following Butler's reservations about the abstract nature of ontological-ethical pronouncements," a similar concern can be raised about her own very compelling and valuable account of ethical practice. The conditions that would enable (1) comprehension of one's constitutive connection to others, (2) responsiveness to the address, the needs, and the vulnerability of others, and (3) awareness of one's own propensity for violence are sorely lacking. The absence of the conditions that facilitate ethical response requires us to examine the conditions from which our failed attempts at response arise so that we may begin to understand how to remedy them. In a criticism of the relationship between the ethical and the social in Butler's work, Moya Lloyd echoes the view that Butler's account would be well served if it were supplemented by an account of the concrete conditions that form the context for the ethical and political problems of destructive violence. She maintains that Butler's shift to the ethical from a more overtly political orientation is accompanied by an account of "how power circumscribes the kinds of ethical encounters that take place" but also "appears to take for granted the existence of the ethical imperative . . . argu[ing] *as if* the ethical imperative is *apolitical*" and prediscursive (Lloyd 2008, 103).

Lloyd attributes this assumption—of a prediscursive ethical imperative to respond to others—to the insufficient historicity of Butler's understanding of the social sphere, suggesting that the social is only an abstract term in Butler's work.[16] Instead, we must give due consideration to the particularities of "the historical practices that themselves generate the social" as well as to the development of social dynamics that shape desires, norms, and ethical imperatives (Lloyd 2008, 104). It is only through attention to the specific historical, social, economic, and political conditions and practices that produce the faulty postures of sovereignty and persecution that we can venture an understanding of more adequate conditions that might give rise to more adequate ethical response.

Ethical practice will require a transformation in our ontology, but such transformation will have to be undertaken both at the level of thought and at the level of occasionally mundane practice. Indeed, as much as we theorize a relational ontology—an ontology of vulnerability, precariousness, and interdependence—we still, for the most part, operate in accord with dominant liberal norms of personhood and individuality, norms that urge us to disregard the bonds that shared vulnerability forges among us. Our world is undeniably structured in such a way that makes it very difficult not to do so. Thus, we will not just have to articulate and find a language for this "new bodily ontology" that centers on vulnerability and precariousness, but find ways of practicing it and disseminating these practices.

The second point I wish to raise concerns the tenor of Butler's understanding of vulnerability.[17] If frames delimit how we perceive and understand, then what I seek to investigate is how Butler's texts enjoin us to understand vulnerability. The specific question I raise is whether vulnerability can be an ethical resource if there is a privileged relationship between vulnerability and violence. If vulnerability is always bound up with violence, as it seems to be in Butler's work, can we conceive of vulnerability apart from violence? What impact does the conjunction of vulnerability and violence have on how we conceive vulnerability?[18] Does thinking of vulnerability primarily in relation to violence lead to a reductively negative understanding of vulnerability, one that is linked to weakness, injury, and powerlessness, and thus one it feels imperative to eschew? If vulnerability is framed by conditions that make possible its recognition, what does it mean that we are most capable of recognizing vulnerability when it is manifest in violence, injury, and suffering? Can this fact reveal something to us about how vulnerability is framed? What purposes—political, economic, and social—can such framing serve? Moving beyond these frames, can we conceive vulnerability as having normative significance otherwise than as what is exploited by violence or that which we ought to apprehend as shared so as to induce us not to act violently? More basically, precisely how are vulnerability and violence related?

Often, on Butler's account vulnerability is laid bare by violence: violence, she notes, "delineates a physical vulnerability from which we cannot slip away" (2004a, 101). Violence is central to knowing, recognizing, and experiencing vulnerability. Incidences of violence are the privileged, if not the only, conditions of our awareness of vulnerability. Thus, violence provides one of the main contexts in which we experience and understand, or at least begin to understand, vulnerability. Yet, although violence is structurally linked to vulnerability, it is not *necessarily* linked. That is, occasions of violence may be the ones through which we often become aware of vulnerability, but they need not be the only occasions for such awareness; as Butler emphasizes, vulnerability is not reducible to injurability (2009, 34). Violence serves to show us what makes it possible—vulnerability—but this link does not exhaust the meaning of vulnerability. Rather, a particular normative dimension of vulnerability comes to light when considered in relation to violence: vulnerability is exploited by violence; vulnerability (of self or other) is denied by sadism, mastery, domination; avowing vulnerability—allowing oneself to experience vulnerability rather than fear and avoid a hyperbolic projection of it—can restore connection with others. Destructive violence and violent reactions to violence reveal the wrong, the harm, and the danger of dominant actions, attitudes, and perceptions concerning vulnerability.

While expressing the importance of attending to the thought of vulnerability, Butler wonders, "if we stay with the sense of loss, are we left feeling only passive and powerless, as some might fear?" (2004a, 30). It is wise to take this fear seriously, not because loss, grief, and experiences of vulnerability lack the power to precipitate thoughtful transformation and enhanced responsibility, but because of the way in which vulnerability is framed. Frames shape the contours of vulnerability, delimiting what we think about when we think about vulnerability, what we feel when we are in a vulnerable position, how we regard 'vulnerable others,' and so on. We are often "left feeling only passive and powerless" because loss and the vulnerability to which loss returns us are experiences whose limits are circumscribed and the meaning of which is annexed by the frames of a simpler ontology. In particular, the framing of vulnerability as negative—a condition of susceptibility to harm, one that is revealed by violence—is a framing that encourages us to eschew and avoid vulnerability. For this consequence not to be an inevitable one, we must begin to break these frames.

We are often vulnerable without therefore being susceptible to violence. Our vulnerability allows us to experience reassurance, sustenance, love, and even courage. For how can one be daring and courageous if one does not experience vulnerability, openness to the uncertain outcome of what one does? In connecting vulnerability with violence, we also connect it with the loss that is the consequence of violence. Yet, as I argued in the first section of this chapter, vulnerability need not always be linked to loss. In its more fundamental sense vulnerability may be understood as an openness to being altered and, more specifically, being altered in ways that destabilize a previously stable, or seemingly stable, state. For instance, although certain intuitions might lead us to believe that the emotional vulnerability of love boils down to a fear or acute awareness of loss—loss of the loved one, loss of the self one is in relation to the loved one, loss of love itself—Butler's own account, despite its emphasis on loss, reveals that this vulnerability is a more basic one. The vulnerability of loving lies in the way the self is made what it is through such relations. Since "vulnerability . . . precedes the formation of the 'I'" [and is the] condition of being laid bare from the start[,]" it places one outside of and *"beside oneself"* insofar as one's self is made, and unmade and remade, only in virtue of its permeability and is interwoven with the selves of others (2004b, 23, 20). So, what renders one uniquely vulnerable in the experience of love is not the possibility of loss but the exceptional openness that characterizes the relationship and, indeed, the expectation that one will change in unforeseen ways in relation to the loved one. In relationships between intimates, the unpredictability and uncontrollability of other beings has a heightened effect on the self; one is more vulnerable because one is more open to this other. Vulnerability, thus, may include being affected by loss, but this particular kind of event is not the constitutive dimension of the vulnerability.

Why, if the links between vulnerability, violence, and loss are contingent ones, do we accede to the framing of vulnerability as susceptibility to violence? What function might this framing serve? I focus on these questions more substantially in the next chapter, but here offer some preliminary thoughts. Butler herself remarks on the problem of the relationship between vulnerability and framing, emphasizing that recognition of vulnerability depends on how it is framed: "vulnerability is fundamentally dependent on existing norms of recognition if it is to be attributed to any human subject" (2004a, 43).[19] Her focus is on the relationship between vulnerability and humanization, and how the recognition of vulnerable others humanizes those who are perceived as vulnerable. In contrast, the failure to recognize the vulnerability of others is a consequence of dehumanizing frames that set those others outside the realm of perceptual awareness and concern. Also important for Butler is the way that "recognition wields the power to reconstitute vulnerability" and alter its meaning (ibid). In the simple act of recognizing vulnerability—even here and now in our thinking about it—we shape what it is taken to be. Following from this crucial point, I am interested in how we frame vulnerability itself so that our perception of it is variable in this way, so that some beings are apprehended and recognized as vulnerable while the vulnerability of others is unperceivable and unrecognizable. The differential and unequal apprehension of vulnerability is a product not just of frames that present some lives as livable and valuable, devaluing others, but also of the way in which we think about (frame) vulnerability in general.

So, what does it mean that we apprehend vulnerability most easily and recognize it most readily when it appears in the guise of violability, injurability, and suffering? Why frame vulnerability in this way and who is positioned as vulnerable according to these frames? One answer lies in the passages from Jeanette Winterson with which this chapter opened. When vulnerability is coupled with violence, it is easier to fragment the community of the vulnerable into "sufferers" and "darers," to cover over the ambiguity of vulnerability, and to make use of implicit assumptions about the meaning of vulnerability to establish clearly who is vulnerable and who is not, and what their respective vulnerabilities mean. If, in our reductively negative view, vulnerability is associated with weakness, passivity, being harmed, as well as with stereotypical ideas about femininity, then it becomes implausible to conceive certain people and groups of people as vulnerable. For example, prison inmates, despite the fact that they are incarcerated and entirely at the mercy of the prison staff, are widely regarded as the antithesis of vulnerable. The dehumanization of prisoners grows out of an inability to recognize them as vulnerable and the pervasive failure to recognize them as vulnerable is rooted in how we think of vulnerability (and how we connect it to gender, race, and class, and the cultural meanings that are associated with these aspects of identity). On this understanding, those who are generally perceived as physically strong, active, stereotypically masculine, and the agents of harm cannot also be vulnerable. Supreme Court Justice Antonin Scalia's dissenting opinion in *Brown v. Plata,* a 2011 case in which the court determined that severe overcrowding in California prisons constituted a violation of the Eight Amendment right not to be subject to cruel and unusual punishment, illustrates this perception. In his dissent, Scalia calls the court's decision "perhaps the most radical injunction issued by a court in our Nation's history" and describes the prisoners who might be released as a result of the decision as "fine physical specimens who have developed intimidating muscles pumping iron in the prison gym."[20] With exaggerated rhetoric, Scalia casts the prisoners as imposing figures, dangerous "specimens" rather than people, muscle-bound degenerates whose release back into the general population will imperil us all and is the most radical act in U.S. legal history. In his own dissent, Justice Samuel Alito reaffirms the belief that prison inmates are not vulnerable but are an inevitable threat whereas, in the wake of their release, the safety of "the public" is imminently vulnerable and requires safeguarding at any cost. They are dangerous, we are in danger; we are vulnerable, they are not. This logic is premised upon a reductively negative view of vulnerability and the persecutory posturing that is made possible by such a view of vulnerability.[21] Framing vulnerability in this way allows us to ignore the vulnerability of those who are socially devalued and thus justifies our failure to respond to it.

As long as we think vulnerability in conjunction with violence—the violence of war, the violence of crime, the violence of gender norms, the violence of the conditions of cultural intelligibility—we bring into being a thought of vulnerability that is bound to notions of infringement, violation, and destruction. Although there is truth to this connection—insofar as there is violence, there is vulnerability—it is a one-sided truth. Linking vulnerability with violence encourages understanding vulnerability dualistically, as a property that can only be had by one party to an interaction, and leads us to a fragmented conception of our social world: there are vulnerable "sufferers" and invulnerable "darers," there are the weak who need defending and the strong who are capable of either defending or perpetrating harm. In a world where no one wants to suffer or be weak, our options with respect to vulnerability are to repudiate it—in order to dare, one must not be vulnerable—or to appropriate it from a position of privilege—in order not to suffer from one's vulnerability, one must make oneself invulnerable—which amount to the same thing. This conception thus prevents us from perceiving and imagining the vulnerability of those who are regarded as the doers of unjust violence such as prisoners. In order to begin to break with this framing of vulnerability, to facilitate the critique of the norms that encourage disavowal of vulnerability and the conversion of inevitable precariousness into unequal precarity, we must envision other occasions for experiencing and thinking vulnerability. That is, we must seek to recognize vulnerability in more unlikely places, to find other sites where vulnerability is linked not only to violence but to affection, creativity, resiliency, and, as Butler puts it, "the feeling of aliveness" (2009, 55).

CONCLUSION

Throughout this chapter I have endeavored to reconstruct the normative account of vulnerability contained within Judith Butler's philosophy. My aims have been threefold: to begin to elaborate a more complex picture of the nature of vulnerability, to draw from Butler's work a nuanced theory of the normativity that encompasses both the aspirational and the constraining dimensions of norms, and to articulate how vulnerability possesses normative salience. Butler's account, I have maintained, represents an advance over other accounts that recognize the normative significance of vulnerability in several ways. First, the way in which Butler theorizes normativity enables us to take a more critical look at all norms, including the moral norms whose status as ideals might otherwise exempt them from inquiry. In this way, critique is integral to a normative account based on vulnerability, which is only appropriate given the way in which openness characterizes both the activity of critique and the nature of vulnerability. Second, as I have proposed in the critical comments in this final section, ethical engagement thus becomes not only a matter of responding to others in need but also of critically examining the practices, conventions, norms, and social structures that are central to our formation as selves because they are the conditions that enable or preclude ethical response. Third, the sense of vulnerability presented by Butler's work acknowledges the variability of the meaning of vulnerability and the variability in how vulnerability is experienced. Given her account of the formative power of frameworks for understanding, she acknowledges that whether or not vulnerability is recognized and the ways in which it is recognized are complex matters. An ethics based on vulnerability cannot simply require that we respond to vulnerable others, attempting to protect them and minimize their vulnerability. We must ask the difficult questions about what kinds and whose vulnerabilities are perceived and recognized, why these ways of being vulnerable are available for apprehension while others are not, and how our common conception of vulnerability as susceptibility to harm contributes to framing vulnerability in inequitable ways.

The next chapter will take up again the issues I have identified in Butler's account as needing expansion. These issues include the specific ways in which postures of sovereignty and persecution are inhabited and perpetuated, how these attitudes are premised on and reaffirm a reductively negative view of vulnerability, and the norms in relation to which this view of vulnerability has become our common one.

NOTES

1. The distinction between precariousness and precarity parallels distinctions made by feminist care ethicists (see Kittay and Feder 2002) and feminist legal theorists (see Fineman 2008) between unavoidable, inevitable dependencies and constructed dependencies that are structural, the result of social, economic, and political organization.
2. Butler understands it to be a ground that is "ungrounding" both because precariousness is only an immanent basis for ethical obligation, and because it neither grounds nor stabilizes us or our ethical obligations; it is a condition in which one is *undone* rather than a solid basis.
3. Butler does not maintain that loss is always negative or undesirable, though. Indeed, loss has an important and positive role to play in ethics on her account.
4. The relationship between norms and violence, and the issue of so-called 'normative' or constitutive violence, is complicated for reasons beyond this tension. See Murphy 2012 for insightful reflection on this issue.
5. Butler's reply to this challenge is more extensive than I can recount here. On this point in particular, she emphasizes the difference between some notion of "ontological violence," which she takes to be a transcendental claim about the foundational nature of violence, and a (Foucaultian) conception of power, which operates in a far more mutable, differential, and less unilateral way, as well as reiterating her conception of norms as noncoercive and hence not traditionally violent. For the rest of her response to Mills, see Butler 2007.
6. Although Butler maintains the terminology of violence—even in the face of Mills' critique—to name both the way in which selves are brought into being in relation to norms and the harmful actions of those selves, I see no reason to do so. Although violence takes different forms—and indeed the contrast between physical violence and the violence of dehumanization is a good example of the range of these forms—to term 'violent' the diverse, complex, repeatable practices through which we become who we are seems to obscure the point (see Gilson 2013 on this point). If one of the ideas suggested by 'constitutive violence' is that we do not make ourselves consciously but are brought into being through relations that exceed us and are beyond our control, then we capture this insight better by supplanting normative/constitutive violence with an idea of constitutive vulnerability, and thinking the formation of the self

through the nexus of vulnerability and norms rather than that of violence and norms.
7. The work of those affiliated with the Vulnerability and the Human Condition Initiative at Emory University also pursues this kind of legal and political project, focusing on how the concept of vulnerability provides an alternative framework for thinking inequity and injustice.
8. Jodi Dean claims, "Butler's ethical sensitivity is purchased at the cost of politics" (Dean 2008, 109). Moya Lloyd argues that Butler needs to develop "a cultural politics of vulnerability" that attends to the historical conditions of the social in order to prevent ethics from eclipsing politics (Lloyd 2008, 105). In contrast, Mills notes Butler's wariness of "the ethical turn in contemporary theory" (2007, 133).
9. Butler draws her understanding of the norm not just from Foucault but also from François Ewald and Georges Canguilhem. See "Gender Regulations" in 2004b.
10. On the way the norm functions as a continuous corrective mechanism see Foucault 1990. For further valuable consideration of the norm and normativity in Foucault's work, see D. Taylor 2009 and Mader 2007.
11. On the self-reflexive nature of critique see Foucault's "What is Enlightenment?" (1997).
12. Critique also involves putting oneself in question since one's self is formed in relation to those ontological categories that comprise the frames through which we understand our world and our place in it. See Butler 2005, 22–26. The subsequent chapter also considers this dimension of critique.
13. See the consideration of autonomy in Butler 2004a and the analysis of the "traditional prejudices" of presence and discrete selfhood in Russon 2003.
14. When I state that there is a certain breadth to Butler's account of the normative dimension of vulnerability, I mean that the account has a broad, comprehensive scope. For instance, we are talking about a quality, precariousness, that characterizes life itself, and a condition, vulnerability, that defines existence in a fundamental way, and processes of exclusion, definition, and violence that are widespread. Such sweeping claims, broad and open-ended questions (whose lives are grievable and whose are not?), and "insurrection[s] at the level of ontology" require more specific, detailed, and historicized critical analysis (2004a, 33).
15. See Young 2004 and 2011 for an account of responsibility addressing this problem.
16. Jodi Dean (2008) makes similar points about Butler's conception of sovereignty (110), the implications of this view for her understanding of the law (115), and Butler's "avoidance of the economy."
17. Kelly Oliver's discussion of Butler's account of the formation of subjectivity implies a similar concern about the tenor of Butler's understanding of vulnerability, dispossession, and dependence (2001, see 67–68 in particular).
18. My concern here is different from Mills' critique of Butler's ethics of nonviolence. Mills argues that nonviolence is an aim that rejects its own basis (in the formative violence of norms on the subject, which create a subject able to take responsibility), and so contends that the ideal of nonviolence should be relinquished because it is inconsistent with Butler's own account of "the ambivalent violence of norms" and fails to live up to the challenges presented by that account (Mills 2007, 135). My concern is that the emphasis on violence colors the understanding of vulnerability with which the account operates, lending unintentional support to the reductively negative view (even as Butler overtly rejects that view).

70 The Ethics of Vulnerability

19. Throughout this discussion in *Precarious Life*, Butler uses the language of recognition and has not yet articulated the precise distinction between apprehension and recognition found in *Frames of War*. In my subsequent discussion, I use both terms when appropriate since both apprehension of and recognition of vulnerability is conditioned by perceptual/cognitive frames.
20. *Brown v. Plata* 131 U.S. 1910 (2011). http://www.supremecourt.gov/opinions/slipopinions.aspx (accessed August 2, 2011).
21. Yet, it was the vulnerability of the prisoners that motivated the majority on the court to decide the case as it did. Justice Kennedy notes that a "psychiatric expert reported observing an inmate who had been held in such a [toiletless, telephone-booth sized] cage for nearly 24 hours, standing in a pool of his own urine, unresponsive and nearly catatonic" because prison officials had nowhere else to put him while he awaited mental health treatment. The vulnerability of prisoners is not merely vulnerability to harm, though. Even more recently, prisoners in the Californian prison system undertook a hunger strike to protest the pervasive and extended use of solitary confinement to punish and prevent gang activity in the prisons. This undertaking indicates that the prisoners do not see their vulnerability as a form of weakness but as basis for political action. See http://www.prisons.org/hungerstrike.htm for more information.

Part II
Analyzing Avoidance and Disavowal

3 The Ideal of Invulnerability

At the close of the last chapter, I suggested that Butler's account of an ethics of vulnerability is an important corrective to some of the oversights in MacIntyre and Goodin's accounts but also requires supplementing of its own. Butler's critique of the postures of sovereignty and persecution reveals the ethical failure inherent in these ways of responding to vulnerability: they not only perpetuate violence but also partake in an ontologically erroneous division of vulnerability that produces an abdication of responsibility. It does not, however, interrogate the conditions that give rise to these kinds of responses. If an ethics of vulnerability is to be viable, then a consideration of the concrete social conditions that both make possible and preclude ethical response is necessary. An ethics of vulnerability is an immanent ethics, one that cannot bind transcendentally and necessarily, but rather compels only from within our own experience and grounded on a specific set of recognitions: that we all share in a common vulnerability; that particular forms of vulnerability, or precariousness, are often differentially distributed; that we possess a capacity for aggression that can lead us to abuse others in their vulnerability and the expression of which we must mitigate in order to conduct ourselves ethically; and that the vulnerability that we share binds us to one another in a way that we cannot undo or ignore. In seeking to enact an ethics of vulnerability, we must begin to understand where we go awry with respect to these recognitions. That is, the task is one of continuing to integrate ethics into social life, as feminist ethicists have frequently sought to do, exploring what in our social life makes ethics possible and what prevents us from engaging our and others' vulnerability ethically. The primary aim of this chapter, thus, is both to understand why culturally dominant reactions to experiences of vulnerability tend to be those of avoidance and disavowal not avowal and attentive response, and to understand the forms taken by those reactions.

The first section provides a conceptual framework for understanding denials of vulnerability by turning to the literature of the epistemology of ignorance. My general aim is to show how the relationship to vulnerability taken in the postures of sovereignty and persecution is a common rather than exceptional one. In particular, the repudiation of vulnerability we seek to understand is not a conscious, deliberate rejection but a matter of habit and enculturation; one does not come to inhabit these postures by acknowledging and comprehending vulnerability, and then disavowing it. Rather, an inability to perceive and apprehend vulnerability becomes the condition of one's social existence or, in other words, the basis for the development of one's sense of self. The framework of the epistemology of ignorance provides context for understanding the form taken by denials of vulnerability and why such denials occur. Specifically, I elaborate how this form of ignorance of vulnerability is tantamount to a pursuit of invulnerability—by pursing invulnerability, one becomes ignorant of vulnerability—and explain in what ways invulnerability is a form of ignorance. In the second section, I develop the claim that ignorance of vulnerability is a pervasive form of ignorance that underlies other oppressive types of ignorance. This contention establishes an ethics of vulnerability as an account that evinces serious concern for the political and social dimensions of ethical action. A failure to acknowledge and deal with vulnerability in its complex manifestations perpetuates oppressive social, economic, and political relations.[1] An ethics of vulnerability, thus, is crucial not just to living one's life well but also to instantiating more just and equitable social relationships. Considering the connection between ignorance of vulnerability and various forms of oppression will also enable us to see more precisely the forms of response of which we should be critical because they foster an unjust pursuit of invulnerability. One of the central arguments of this section is that ignorance is a form of closure, in particular, closure to being affected by others in ways that one cannot predict or control, and which challenge and destabilize one's socially established sense of self. Lastly, in the third section, I begin to put forth a way of thinking about vulnerability that departs from our reductively negative understanding of vulnerability. If denial of vulnerability is a common phenomenon, and an ethically and politically dangerous one, then awareness of vulnerability is central to undoing not just violence but oppressive social relations in general. Yet, awareness or acknowledgement of vulnerability is not a clear and simple undertaking. Indeed, the notion that we must avow rather than repudiate vulnerability remains quite general. As the reasoning of the second section indicates, awareness cannot be conceived as equivalent to embracing, welcoming, or assuming vulnerability. If we recognize the ways in which vulnerability is often an occasion for harm, then such demands (that one embrace one's vulnerability) are unreasonable and unjust in many cases. Rather, what is called for is an exploration of specific forms of vulnerability that we should cultivate and pursue in specific situations and in response to specific problems. I suggest, in close, that the perilous effects of ignorance can be attenuated through the cultivation of a certain kind of vulnerability, namely, epistemic vulnerability.

THE PURSUIT OF INVULNERABILITY

Recent work in the epistemology of ignorance provides valuable insight into the nature of the denial of vulnerability as well as how to go about analyzing it. Epistemologists of ignorance have made the convincing case that ignorance is no mere lack of knowledge but rather is actively produced and maintained. If, like knowledge, ignorance is "a practice with supporting social causes," then it also has conditions of creation and perpetuation, and these conditions merit close scrutiny (Tuana 2004, 195). Although it is clear that ignorance and not knowing can render one vulnerable, this kind of relationship between vulnerability and ignorance typically involves a negative sense of vulnerability: ignorance of potential carcinogens in one's environment leads one to be more vulnerable to these cancer-causing agents, for instance. This form of ignorance and these kinds of vulnerabilities are significant yet my concern here is what I take to be their more profound source: ignorance of vulnerability as a fundamental condition. Thus, I focus on ignorance of vulnerability itself and how it operates: the practices that constitute such ignorance, the social causes that may undergird it, and lastly, its relationship to other modes of ignorance. As should be obvious from the previous chapter, there are far fewer difficulties in perceiving negative forms of vulnerability, especially when they pertain to oneself and others like oneself. On my account, ignorance of the situational vulnerabilities of others who are perceived as 'other'—for instance, the vulnerabilities of prisoners to the physical control and violence of the agents of the state—is a product of this deeper ignorance of shared ontological vulnerability. The presumption here is that ignorance of vulnerability takes shape through an unthinking adherence to a negative conception of it, according to which vulnerability is a hindrance and weakness, and thus something to be repudiated and ignored.

Thus, an oppressive effect of the reductively negative understanding of vulnerability is that vulnerability is often disavowed and projected onto others with whom one disidentifies. The projection of vulnerability onto others and disidentification with those vulnerable others goes hand in hand with the idea of vulnerability as a negative state; only conceived thusly is vulnerability something one feels one ought to renounce. Conceiving vulnerability as solely negative, then, is part of maintaining ignorance of the more fundamental sense vulnerability, ontological vulnerability. Hence, the disavowal is double, comprising an ignorance of vulnerability as a shared, basic condition in favor of a more limited idea of it and a rejection of even that more narrow negative form of vulnerability in the form of an unwillingness to experience it, the posture of sovereignty. I contend that this disavowal is a form of cultivated ignorance rather than a conscious and deliberate rejection. In particular, ignorance of vulnerability is generated through the achievement of invulnerability as a desirable character trait and form of subjectivity. Thus, ignorance of vulnerability must be understood through an analysis of the practices and habits that propagate invulnerability. As a "substantive epistemic practice," ignorance is not just a defect on the part of the knower but is a structural, social problem (Alcoff 2007, 40).

In this section, therefore, I examine how invulnerability can be understood as a form of ignorance and consider the conditions that facilitate this ignorance of a fundamental and shared vulnerability. The denial of vulnerability can be understood to be motivated by the desire—conscious or not—to maintain a certain kind of subjectivity privileged in capitalist socioeconomic systems, namely, that of the proto-typical arrogantly self-sufficient, independent, invulnerable master subject (see Frye 1983, Plumwood 1993, Young 2002, O'Neill 2005). Invulnerability is a central feature of masterful subjectivity because it solidifies a sense of control, which is, indeed, an illusion. The achievement of full mastery, complete control, and utter impenetrability is an impossibility. The simple fact of the illusoriness of invulnerability and the inevitable persistence of vulnerability is key to understanding the nature of invulnerability. If vulnerability is openness to being affected and affecting, then invulnerability is closure to those modes of being affected that bring us into contact with our own vulnerability most vividly. Through pursuit of invulnerability, we seek not to experience vulnerability even as vulnerability as a condition cannot be evaded. Without the persistence of vulnerability, without the constant 'threat' of its openness, such closure is unnecessary. Because vulnerability is an unavoidable feature of our existence, however, invulnerability is continually sought and, since it is never adequately and securely achieved, masterful identity must be continually shored up. Invulnerability, accordingly, is a stance that enables us to ignore those aspects of existence that are inconvenient, disadvantageous, or uncomfortable for us, such as vulnerability's persistence. As invulnerable, we cannot be affected by what might unsettle us.[2]

The taxonomy of ignorance offered by Nancy Tuana presents a valuable lens for understanding the status of ignorance of vulnerability. Her taxonomy delineates four modes of ignorance: (1) knowing that we do not know yet not caring to know, (2) not even knowing that we do not know, (3) not knowing because (privileged) others do not want us to know, and (4) willful ignorance (2006). These four broad types of ignorance are differentiated by the conditions that give rise to them, namely, currently existing bodies of knowledge, sets of interests, and structural power dynamics both subtle and overt. In the first type of ignorance, knowledge concerning certain questions or issues is pursued at the expense of other knowledge, which is deemed irrelevant or unimportant; we know we do not know certain things but do not seek this knowledge because we do not consider it important. In the second type of ignorance, we utterly fail to recognize that we do not know certain things "because our current interests, beliefs, and theories obscure them" as objects of possible knowledge (Tuana 2006, 6). Once we become aware of our ignorance, we can either seek to know what we do not know or simply turn to the "not caring" attitude of the first kind of ignorance. In the third type of ignorance, the acquisition of knowledge is precluded by power relations; one is prevented, either overtly or indirectly, from knowing.

It might appear that ignorance of vulnerability is a case of not knowing in the second way, which might be overcome if only we were to become aware of our ignorance and desire to understand ourselves as vulnerable through and through. Yet, as we saw with Butler, ignorance of vulnerability is primarily operative at the level of self-formation and self-understanding: we shape ourselves and are formed as vulnerable or invulnerable subjects in various ways. Coming to be, and to conceive ourselves as, invulnerable is a process that is more slow, subtle, and subconscious. Therefore, ignorance of vulnerability is best understood as an instance of the fourth kind of ignorance: willful ignorance. Willful ignorance is actively cultivated, an ignorance that must be continually maintained and is maintained because it appears to be in one's interests to remain ignorant. In Tuana's words, "willful ignorance is a systematic process of self-deception, a willful embrace of ignorance that infects those who are in positions of privilege, an active ignoring of the oppression of others and one's role in that exploitation" (2006, 11). As Charles Mills demonstrates in *The Racial Contract* (1997), the white ignorance of the racial contract that ensures the persistence of white privilege and racism is a willful ignorance. One of the most important aspects of willful ignorance is that, like the existentialist idea of bad faith, it is not a matter of a conscious act of volition. It is not the simple chosen ignorance of 'not caring to know' but is a deeper form of ignorance, closer to a disavowal than a dismissal. In this way, willful ignorance is the consequence, one that is continually produced, of a whole history of choices and actions that have made someone the person that she is. Such a deeply rooted ignorance, moreover, is characterized by a fundamental uncertainty about what one believes. In her reading of James Baldwin, Elizabeth Spelman puts this point in a propositional form in which "W" is "Baldwin's rhetorically conceived white American" and "g" is the belief that "Black America's grievances are real." What is distinctive about willful ignorance is that it stems from not wanting to think about "g": "W does not think about whether g is true or false. And yet she is hardly indifferent to its being true or false. Her ignoring g allows her to stand by g's being false, to be committed to g's being false, without believing that g is false" (2007, 122). In this way, willful ignorance is not just the consequence of the omissions that stem from a particular set of interests, but also shapes those interests in the first place. That is, there is no direct line from interest to ignorance as there is with the other three types of ignorance; it is not the case that one ignores simply because it is in one's interest to ignore. Rather, ambivalence, and the absence of conscious awareness and commitment shape an ignorance that reinforces itself. Willful ignorance is perpetuated by the pain, discomfort, or disturbance that are attendant upon bringing it to light.

Existential accounts of bad faith, which are conceived as forms of ignorance, also develop this sense of willful ignorance. The descriptions of bad faith offered by Sartre and de Beauvoir foreground both the absence of conscious commitment to a belief or choice and the implications of bad faith for relations with others. Simply put, bad faith amounts to comporting oneself as if one were an object and one's future were determined, and thus to a denial of one's own freedom. More specifically, both Sartre and de Beauvoir describe bad faith as a way of conflating immanence, the domain of the fixed and given (one's physical being, for instance), and transcendence, the domain of freedom and future possibility. One may conceive one's transcendence as immanence by regarding one's freedom as something given rather than something undertaken and chosen, and thus as something seemingly easily achieved. One may conceive one's immanence as transcendence by considering concrete elements of one's being as so far from defining oneself that they no longer tie oneself to facticity. These two conflations are, of course, complementary. As we will see, this latter attitude often defines the perspective we take on the history that has shaped who we have become, especially when this history is replete with violence and injustice. Of even more interest for our purposes here, however, is the bad faith perspective on others. As de Beauvoir contends in *The Second Sex* (2011), bad faith is the condition of oppression. Whereas bad faith concerning oneself may take the form of experiencing one's transcendence as immanence, taking one's freedom as a given rather than a capacity that must be exercised, and so viewing oneself as only subject not object, as only transcendent not immanent, when it comes to others, it consists of reducing them to objects. Thus, common justifications for race-based and sex-based oppression rest upon descriptions of the oppressed group's supposedly natural inferiority. On de Beauvoir's analysis this move amounts to perceiving others solely in terms of their immanence and denying their transcendence, while at the same time postulating the pure transcendence of the oppressors. In fixing the other as an object, one correspondingly and oppositionally fixes oneself as a subject; one takes one's own transcendence as given by denying it to the other and taking his facticity as a reified given. What we fail to recognize when we are in bad faith, and the reason it is both an ontological and ethical error, is that we all are both immanent and transcendent, comprised of both facticity and the potential to move forward into the future, becoming other than what we presently are. Further, on de Beauvoir's account in *The Ethics of Ambiguity* (1976), we find this ambiguous condition of being simultaneously transcendent and immanent profoundly unsettling, and the various forms of bad faith are our attempts to deal with such uncomfortable ambiguity by resolving it into one or the other: immanence or transcendence, immanence as transcendence or transcendence as immanence. In the same way, willful ignorance is an avoidance of the complexity of ambiguity and its implications for one's self that is affected through a resolution of ambiguity in favor of the mastery of transcendence.

Ignorance of vulnerability is a willful ignorance, first of all, because the ambiguity of vulnerability produces deep discomfort and we feel compelled to resolve it in a way that eliminates this unease (by reducing it to its negative dimensions). Moreover, it is likewise something concerning which we do not take up an attitude of belief, precisely because of our unease. When we ignore vulnerability we do not devote ourselves to the falsity of a pervasive and common vulnerability. Rather, we repudiate vulnerability in both thought and practice such that we are committed not to the truth of invulnerability but to its social utility for us. We learn the habits of invulnerability in social contexts. I learn, for instance, that if I demonstrate that I am in control, self-possessed, then I get taken seriously. I might learn to exhibit this self-control in myriad ways, depending on context, ranging from suppressing emotion to manifesting a generally assertive, aggressive demeanor to engaging in all my activities in a competitive manner, to adopting a particular style of dress and speech. Invulnerability has social utility because we understand vulnerability in the conventional manner that collapses all forms of vulnerability into one negative conception and equates vulnerability with weakness, dependency, powerlessness, and defect: if to be vulnerable is to be weak and subject to harm, then to be invulnerable is the only way to be strong and competent. Invulnerability as a form of mastery is sought at the price of disavowing vulnerability and is sought because it is the paradigmatic characteristic of an ideal form of subjectivity in present socioeconomic conditions. As Nancy Annaromao claims, "[i]nvulnerability is the standard for successful humans in this society" (1996, 5). Thus, ignorance of vulnerability is produced precisely because we do know and experience our own vulnerability, yet disavow it as formative and significant because acknowledging it will hinder our attempts to achieve our diverse goals in a social world that has come to value the trappings of invulnerability. Susan Bordo's now classic work on the social meanings of gendered bodily ideals demonstrates this point quite clearly. Concerning women's "disidentification with the maternal body," Bordo writes, "taking on the accoutrements of the white, male world may be experienced as empowerment by women themselves, as their chance to embody qualities—detachment, self-containment, self-mastery, control—that are highly valued in our culture" (2003, 209). Feminine vulnerability, which is already redoubled because of its gendered specificity, must be renounced. This ignorance is established not by refraining from investigating certain questions or by directly withholding knowledge from certain groups of people, but through social practices and habits.

Bordo's more recent work also provides an effective example of such practices and habits. In *Twilight Zones*, she details the intersection of our preferences, desires, and aims and the images that pervade a Western consumer society like the U.S. To maintain the economic core of such a society—the production and consumption of products and services—consumers must be made to feel a need for new products. On Bordo's analysis, this need is produced—is made to be *felt as a need*—by inducing consumers to perceive themselves as defective and to believe that these defects (blemished skin, a "gummy smile," supposedly excess weight, a less than perfectly straight nose, wrinkles, etc.) ought to be corrected and can be corrected with the right products (1999a, 33–57). As one forum for conveying and shaping social meaning, advertisements appeal to the aversion to vulnerability by coding such physical 'imperfections' in terms of vulnerability: they are not just signs of less than photoshopped perfect good looks or aging but are read as signs of physical failure, of a lack of control and an attendant moral debility, and of an unstoppable slide into weakness against which we must continually struggle (1999a, 59). Beyond cosmetic surgery, fitness and diet routines and products, and beauty regimes, the recent phenomenon of "age-management medicine" likewise bespeaks the pursuit of physical invulnerability: middle-aged men flock to the Cenegenics Medical Institute company to undergo costly treatments that include not just the standard vitamins and supplements but also hormone treatments—involving anything from human chorionic gonadotropin, a hormone produced by pregnant women, to testosterone, to human growth hormone—designed to trigger an increase in the production of testosterone to prevent the slowing of the metabolism that comes with age (Dunkel 2010). Here, physical fitness has come to mean retaining or recovering the physical state of one's peak. It means shunning any physical change that hints of decline. It means, essentially, denying the universal process of aging because to age is to reveal vulnerability in the most manifest of ways. Whereas Bordo portrays the invulnerable body as one that is firm, taut, self-contained, and utterly under control, the more specifically masculine version is an image of muscular bodies, vigorous physical activity, as well as a return to sexual potency. Practices such as these are socially sanctioned for men and women alike but are quintessentially those expected of and accessible to the upper and middle classes whose disposable income enables them to spend thousands of dollars a year to monitor and modulate their metabolisms. The class and race specific nature of these bodily ideals is manifest when we recall the description of California prisoners proffered by Justice Scalia, and contrast the moral approbation that attends taking care of one's body in the aforementioned ways with the social panic similar bodies produce when they are not white or upper class. In general, these "age-management" techniques, however extreme, are instances of a more culturally pervasive disavowal of vulnerability via the pursuit of physical invulnerability.

The habits and practices through which we seek invulnerability are not mere superficial effects, as the example of ridding ourselves of wrinkles might imply, but rather contribute to constituting a norm of invulnerability that in turn supports the practices. Such norms are undergirded by patterns of thought that we can understand through the idea of reductionism. Following Maria Mies and Vandana Shiva's account, reductionism is neither the metaphysical reductionism of physicalism nor the methodological reduction of phenomenology. Rather, it is defined as a framework for both knowing and valuing that reduces what is known to its isolatable and manipulable parts, and what is valuable to its economic value. Shiva describes the epistemology of Western modern science as reductionist because "(1) it reduced the capacity of humans to know nature both by excluding other knowers and other ways of knowing; and [because] (2) by manipulating it as inert and fragmented matter, nature's capacity for creative regeneration and renewal was reduced" (Shiva and Mies 1993, 23). These paired reductions—of the richness of our knowledge and the richness of nature's processes—are the product of a reductionist method that is based on the premises of ontological and epistemological uniformity. A mechanistic perspective lends itself to considering all systems—natural and social—as comprised of the same uniform constituent parts. The presumption of uniformity leads us to consider things—nature, human persons, etc.—as manipulable because we are able to break them down into manageable, exploitable parts. Since on a reductionist model one can know a whole through its (uniform, manipulable) parts, these parts are alienated from the whole and objectified. Correspondingly, the knowledge that is produced is lacking in context, and objectivity is construed as "context-free abstraction" (1993, 23–24). This epistemological and ontological reduction is widespread: it pertains not just to objects but to processes, not just to knowledge but to value. Ecosystems, for instance, are commonly reduced "to a single component, and a single component to a single function"; productivity is generally reduced to economic productivity defined in terms of profit, and so value is attributed only to profit-generating activities (1993, 24).[3] As a dominant worldview, reductionism functions to narrow one's perspective, barring from view many salient features of the world; it is a pattern of thought based on closure. Thus, reductionism is a pattern of thought and practice that serves as an enabling background condition for willful ignorance about vulnerability. Indeed, reductionist practices are commonly ones that pursue invulnerability.

In Shiva's view, the dominance of a reductionist perspective is not an accident: "Far from being an epistemological accident, reductionism is a response to the needs of a particular form of economic and political organization. The reductionist worldview, the industrialist revolution and the capitalist economy are the philosophical, technological, and economic components of the same process" (ibid). Capitalism and the technological processes that have driven it make reductionism not merely a way of thinking or theoretical outlook (where thought is separate from practice), but a mode of operation that governs our practices. The import of Shiva's contention lies in the emphasis she places on the intertwining of theoretical, economic, social, and technological systems; it is through the concurrence of the theory, technology, economics, and politics of reductionism that the habits of invulnerability are reinforced, and are rendered pervasive and normal. Overall, reductionism is defined by the dominance of a uniform measure, and concern for predictability, measurability, and maximization of profit or return on investments of various types.

In her *Alchemy of Race and Rights* Patricia Williams provides a telling example of the social manifestation of a reductionist outlook and the way such a perspective contributes to the production of invulnerability. While tracking the way in which economic value has come to dominate modern life (to such an extent that other values such as freedom of speech are conceived in terms of monetary expenditure), Williams reiterates the idea that money is our uniform measure, through which we "express our valuation of things" and thus "the measure of our lives" (1991, 29, 31). To demonstrate the effect this measure has on our lives, she tells a story "of the deep-rooted commonplaceness of our economically rationalized notions of humanity": a father responds to his young daughter's desire to help a homeless woman in the subway station by explaining that "giving money to the woman directly was 'not the way we do things.' Then he launched into a lecture on the United Way as succor for the masses. It was a first lesson in distributive justice: conditioned passivity, indirection, distance—statistical need positioned against actual need. . . . [R]esponsiveness to immediate need was being devalued as wrong" (1991, 27). From this perspective, people in need are reduced to numbers—the numbers assisted by aid organizations, demonstrating the efficacy of those groups, the numbers increased or decreased by social policies, the amount of money spent to aid them—and empathy and responsiveness are twisted into an "economically rationalized notion of humanity." Having such a sense of humanity, the father is not unconcerned, not callous, but rather is concerned primarily with the efficient use of his, and presumably the state's, monetary resources. There is no assurance of a good outcome when one gives some money (or food or other resources) directly to a homeless person, but one can be assured that one's hard-earned money is put to good use if one gives it to the Red Cross or Oxfam or the United Way. Thus, the ethically right course of action is determined by what is most fiscally sensible. The result of this instance of reductionism is social distancing and detachment, which support an invulnerable stance. We need not interact with and be affected by the homeless woman sitting in front of us; we need not feel saddened by the woman's situation or ashamed of our own position, be struck by the inadequacy and futility of our actions, experience the insignificance of what we do (give her a few dollars perhaps) in the face of structural impediments, or deal with the frustration of such recognitions. We are safely, unresponsively but efficiently, ensconced in a world where she is just a number and where the 'best' response permits us never really to have to see her vulnerability or be vulnerable to such seeing. This "economically rationalized" sense of humanity is the form human virtue takes within a reductionist worldview.

Another element of reductionism suggested above concerns our experience of and perspective on embodiment. As the discussion of common bodily practices indicated, the management of the body's appearance and function is a prime site for the pursuit of invulnerability. As both MacIntyre and Bordo demonstrate, the body is regarded as a domain of particular vulnerability: our bodies change in unanticipated ways that we cannot control, physically manifest these changes, which bespeak our mortality, are the source of likewise uncontrolled desires, needs, and urges (which render us dependent on others), and also reveal our proximity to our nonhuman kin, above whom we have elevated ourselves. Moreover, and perhaps more to the point, it is through our bodies that we are most obviously affected and, specifically, wounded. The body is the most manifest locus of affectivity. As such, these tendencies of the body can be experienced as a source of fear, and the body becomes a prime object of our attempts to avoid and disavow vulnerability. Although the body cannot be made invulnerable (because we are mortal, because it is flesh and bone), the bodily pursuit of invulnerability involves managing the body so as to present and experience it as strong, controlled, fit, trim and taut, and youthful.

The pursuit of invulnerability thus presupposes a mind/body dualism and a relationship of control between the mind and body. The body can become the object of techniques of management and control through which we pursue invulnerability because the body is still conceived as conceptually distinct from the mind and the self. In classic dualist thinking, the body is thought as an object, inert matter rather than the active subject or author of our decisions and actions; the body is likewise aligned with nature and animality, and so conceived as that which the mind ought to be able to control and master just as humans endeavor to control and master animal life and the elements and forces of the natural world (Plumwood 1993). Such dualism reduces the ambiguity of human existence, separating the mind and body so the complex relationship between the two is reduced to a simple relation in which the mind attempts to exert control over and shape the body. In order to be the target of such control, the body is reduced from the locus of experience—that as which we feel, sense, remember, and so on, the site of our contact with the world and others (see Russon 2003, 21–22)—to an entity whose appearance represents the self to the external world. Rather than understanding the body as an opening to what is outside it and as something with "its own immanent sensitivity, its own perspective, and initiative, its own desires," the body becomes another object to be manipulated (Russon 2003, 25). In this way, the body's physical appearance takes precedence over the body's (externally imperceptible) capabilities and the quality of experience we have as embodied creatures. Moreover, contemporarily, mind/body dualism is supplanted by an inner self/outer appearance dichotomy whereby we seek to make our bodies' outward appearances correspond with our conception of our inner selves, endeavoring to shape the body so that it conveys an image of strength, competency, and impermeability. As Cressida Heyes concludes, "the picture of the inner image of oneself that can fit (or not) the outer reality of the body has been fully internalized and is . . . experienced as the truth of our subjectivity" (Heyes 2007, 25–26). In this way, the "inner self" is likewise reduced, boiled down to some kernel of immutable truth—an authentic essence—that must make itself known, and do so by mastering the body and transforming it so that it harmonizes with one's self-image (see Heyes, 2007, 36).

As John Russon explores in detail in *Human Experience,* this dualist conceptual framework—which, in Russon's terms, is composed of a series of ontological "prejudices" such as the mind/body, active/passive, reason/emotion, and subject/object dualisms—entails a conception of the self as a discrete, autonomous chooser who imposes both meaning and his will upon the world, including his body. The prejudice of "discrete selfhood" leads us to presume that we have the ability simply to choose and to exercise control willfully, and is integral to the prejudice of "normalcy," which amounts to a form of stoicism that renounces vulnerability (Russon 2003, 23, 89). It thus discounts the meaningfulness of the world in which we are situated and our implicit interpretative knowledge of it (in favor of the notion that we impose meaning upon it), the constitutive nature of relationships (in favor of a discrete self impervious to the effects of others), the embodied nature of the self (in favor of mind/body dualism), and the significance of habitual action (in favor of belief in independent and deliberate choice). These reductions generate frustration and dissatisfaction since it is primarily through habitual interpretations that we understand the world and comport ourselves in it. By rejecting these elements of a phenomenological account of experience and positioning ourselves as discrete choosers, we set ourselves up to fail in our attempts at self-transformation. Although we think it should be a simple matter of choice and will power, our patterns of thought and action—indeed, our very selves—are formed through habit, and without acknowledging the formative role of habituation with respect to both patterns of action and interpretative patterns of thought, we cannot alter these patterns. Thus, the pursuit of invulnerability is fantastical in an additional way; it is not only an impossible dream—a dream of controlled, dominated physicality—since we cannot overcome our finitude, but further the presumptions that underlie the dream continually frustrate our attempts to achieve it because of the way in which they are at odds with experience. The prejudices that mold how we think about and experience our selves, our bodies, and their contact with the world and others are simply forms of closure. The body is a way of being open—is defined by its vulnerability in this fundamental sense—and bodies are shaped as *ours* by the specific kinds of interactions we have as embodied beings. Mind/body dualism, then, shuts down our ability to understand the nature of our experience and thus to experience it fully. The reductionism inherent in mind/body dualism closes the circuit of relationship between self-world-others, first, by fragmenting self into body and mind, and second, by seeking to exercise control of the body with the mind and thus foreclose the openness to the world that would subvert such control.

Thus, thinking and operating in a reductionist fashion is part and parcel of pursuing invulnerability. As an attitude that isolates variables from their contexts and focuses on these isolated elements—stripped of all seemingly unnecessary and inessential connections and characteristics—reductionism is a way to achieve mastery and command. Through reducing an object or a subject to the properties that are essential to one's ends, which are likewise reduced by fiscal imperatives, one is better poised to know it and better equipped to manipulate it in the desired manner. One must be closed to those aspects of a situation, an object, a being, or a person that are seen as inessential or irrelevant. Moreover, one must close off those aspects of one's self that would undermine or call into question one's command and one's competence. One must command not only the objects that populate one's world, but oneself as well. Reductionism involves closure in advance and, thus, is a mode of willful ignorance. The subject for whom epistemic and axiological reductionism is a virtue is also a subject for whom vulnerability is an implicit vice: to be affected by what is irrelevant or what will create bias is to be a poor epistemic agent. Thus, the achievement of invulnerability is constitutive of what Val Plumwood has called the "master model" of subjectivity, which is effectively the cultural identity of those who occupy positions of privilege and/or participate in relations of domination (1993, 5). The "master subject" is the model of humanity that is implicitly presumed by the dominant culture, yet it is a model based on the "exclusion and domination of the sphere of nature [and those associated with that sphere, such as nonwhite people and women] by a white, largely male elite" (1993, 23). This model of subjectivity is purportedly neutral and is defined by values, such as those Bordo emphasizes ("detachment, self-containment, self-mastery, control"), that are purportedly neutral. Yet these values, and the attitudes and behaviors through which they are accomplished and established as central to self-identity have a history that is decidedly sexist, racist, classist, and ableist. The pursuit of invulnerability is at the core of masterful subjectivity and has as its consequence a pragmatic efficiency in accomplishing narrowly defined (reductionist) goals. When one's interests are narrowly construed on the basis of present socioeconomic exigencies and ideologies, it appears in one's interests to develop such a self-identity and, thus, to eschew and ignore the vulnerability of the self in all its permutations. Yet, these interests, goals, and desires emerge from a social world in which inequity, bias, and oppression persist, and the values of the dominant hold sway; yet they do not advance even the perceived interests of all.

INVULNERABILITY AND OPPRESSION

The previous section focused on how invulnerability constitutes willful ignorance of vulnerability, and thus a closure to being affected and shaped by others. Willful ignorance is a kind of unconscious self-deception and, more specifically, a self-deception oriented toward retaining privilege and eschewing recognition of those facts that would destabilize privileged subjectivity. Thus, the other main claim established above is that the pursuit of invulnerability is central in the formation of masterful self-identity. This section extends that analysis to show how this ignorance lies at the heart of other forms of ignorance and oppression, for instance, as both Plumwood and Shiva are concerned to emphasize, in the domination and exploitation of nature and the nonwhite people of 'developing' or formerly colonized parts of the world. Developing the ideas of vulnerability and invulnerability in this direction is one way to begin concretely to expand the political and social dimensions of an ethics of vulnerability. That is, an ethics of vulnerability is not just one oriented toward protecting the vulnerable or even establishing sounder communal ties based on our shared vulnerability, per Goodin and MacIntyre, but also necessarily engages in critique of the forms of life that rest upon a rejection of vulnerability and a pursuit of invulnerability.[4] Here I argue that the pursuit of invulnerability grounds and perpetuates various forms of oppression. This connection between denials of vulnerability and the perpetuation of oppression strengthens the rationale for an ethics of vulnerability. Resisting and overcoming oppression in its myriad forms, I contend, requires a critical refusal of the pursuit of invulnerability and a renewed experience of vulnerability in specific ways.

The central claim developed in this section is that ignorance of vulnerability functions as the basis upon which we build many other kinds of ignorance. If the impetus for willful ignorance is an attempt to avoid what might unsettle us, when we ignore we are necessarily avoiding our own vulnerability. We ignore because to know might disturb us and even disempower us, rendering us vulnerable (see McHugh 2007). A denial of vulnerability, then, underlies other types of ignorance, such as the ignorance of one's complicity in racial oppression, because to admit such complicity is to open oneself to features of one's social world and one's way of inhabiting that world that are discomfiting and thus to make oneself vulnerable. To know in this sense is to be vulnerable, to be susceptible to being altered by others, whereas to ignore is to seek invulnerability. Consequently, it is only upon the grounds of invulnerability that ignorance can be constructed.

When considering the role of invulnerability in perpetuating oppression, we are afforded an opportunity to make the foregoing conception of invulnerability more specific. It is a closure to a certain understanding of the nature of relations with others as well as to features of the self; it is a closure to change that alters the meaning of the self and the interpretations we have formed of ourselves. As I have portrayed it, vulnerability is openness to alteration and to being affected in ways that cause such alteration. Understanding oneself as vulnerable therefore involves an understanding of the self as being shaped through its relationships to others, its world, and environs, as Butler's account in particular emphasizes. Concomitantly, in seeking invulnerability we specifically ignore the constitutive aspect of vulnerability, the way in which we become who we are through our openness to others. Disavowals of vulnerability, thus, are not only repudiations of the perception and feeling of weakness, passivity, and dependency, but are also repudiations of such openness. Furthermore, disavowals of vulnerability are also ways of remaining ignorant of how our own invulnerability is a constructed attitude and position rather than something that is given or necessary. From the perspectives of sovereignty and persecution, invulnerability is what one must seek and establish; its value is taken for granted. From the critical perspective of an ethics of vulnerability, the value of invulnerability is contingent, a product of particular socioeconomic and political conditions. In bare-bones terms, if vulnerability is openness to unplanned and unanticipated change, then invulnerability is closure to such change, which entails a generally ahistorical and atemporal perspective. By seeking to attain invulnerability, we fail to comprehend both the processes through which we become allegedly invulnerable subjects and the very fact that there are such processes to which we might attend (and through attending to them, understand ourselves and others better). Thus, invulnerability is made an unacknowledged norm, the standard mode of existence, rather than a value that can be acknowledged, contextualized, interrogated, and contested. Following Butler's formulation, we might say that we embrace non-thinking in the name of invulnerability.

Upon this fundamental ignorance, we layer other modes of ignorance. Failing to comprehend that one's knowledge and one's knowing attitude, indeed, one's self, has a history—has been constituted in and through that history—is to lay the groundwork for ignorance of all stripes. To return to Spelman's case of a white American's ignorance of the grievances of Black America, we can understand the ignorance of "W"—her simply not wanting to think about these grievances—as intrinsically tied to a desire not to think about her *self* in the context of these grievances. The need to preserve the invulnerable self supersedes and effaces the possibility of contextualizing the formation of that self, a contextualization that might call into question the contours of this self. In his essay "White Ignorance," Charles Mills affirms the importance of historical contextualization in combating white ignorance about race and emphasizes the role of historical decontextualization—historical ignorance—in perpetuating racial oppression:

> If previously whites were color demarcated as biologically and/or culturally unequal and superior, now through a strategic 'color blindness' they are assimilated as putative equals to the status and situation of nonwhites on terms that negate the need for measures to repair the inequities of the past. So white normativity manifests itself in a white refusal to recognize the long history of structural discrimination that has left whites with the differential resources they have today, and all of its consequent advantages in negotiating opportunity structures. If

originally whiteness was race, then now it is racelessness, an equal status and a common history in which all have shared, with white privilege being conceptually erased. (2007, 28)

A refusal of historical context constitutes ignorance about race and facilitates an ignorant preservation of white privilege under the guise of color blindness, which is simultaneously a way of remaining ignorant about oneself, one's share in that history, and the way that history has shaped one's present. It is a rejection of particularly difficult elements of one's facticity in favor of facile transcendence.

To claim that invulnerability as a form of willful ignorance paves the ground for oppressive types of ignorance, however, is not to claim that all eschewals of vulnerability and all forms of closure operate in this way. That is, just as it is vital not to generalize about vulnerability—assuming it to be equivalent to harm—but to understand the different forms it may take, so it is necessary to recognize that one may reject the experience of vulnerability and seek to shield oneself from greater vulnerability for different reasons and in different ways depending on social and historical circumstances. Such closure can be pursued for other purposes and in other forms, which make it not a form of invulnerability but the product of strategically adopted ignorance: a rejection that functions to resist rather than collude in oppression. As a result, we must see ignorance not as an unequivocally negative phenomenon but recognize that when it takes certain forms it can also operate as a vital tool in resistance against oppression. Therefore, we must distinguish between invulnerability as a constitutive attitude that is practiced as willful ignorance—as it is for those aspiring to the position of "master" subject—and a knowingly undertaken refusal of vulnerability through which one seeks to protect the self. As willful ignorance, invulnerability grounds oppression. Pursued in other ways, in other contexts, attempts to prevent oneself from being vulnerable may stand in a different relationship to oppression precisely because they effect a different kind of closure.

In her essay "Denying Relationality," Sarah Lucia Hoagland delineates two distinct kinds of ignorance of the relationality and interdependence that exists between "competent practitioners of a dominant culture" and oppressed people within that culture (2007, 96). As noted above, ignorance of relationality—of the constitutive nature of relations with others—is a core feature of invulnerability. On Hoagland's account, an ignorance of relationality can function as a part of both a logic of resistance and a logic of oppression. Such ignorance on the part of those "competent practitioners" maintains the status quo, denying dependence on and relation to those who are deemed marginal because to acknowledge this dependence is to diminish their status (as "master" subjects) within the culture. This denial of dependency clearly falls within the domain of willful ignorance; it is a particular form of the more encompassing ignorance of vulnerability. For instance, to deny a very real dependence on immigrants working both legally and illegally in the United States (as those who provide the vast majority of us with food, for example), as anti-immigration rhetoric does through the common accusation that immigrants are 'stealing jobs,' is to inhabit a posture of invulnerability. From such a position of persecution, one acknowledges one's own vulnerability in only a limited way—acknowledging the harm inherent in the loss of jobs and livelihood—and focuses on isolating those who can be blamed, feigning ignorance of their more imminent vulnerabilities. Thus, underlying this rejection of relationality is a repudiation of vulnerability in its more fundamental sense as a shared condition and a willful ignorance of the particular situational vulnerabilities of those who cross national borders to find work. The invulnerable stance is central to this kind of ignorance of relationality: as impermeable, self-sufficient, and in control, one does not need those people who enter one's country illegally to perform the low-wage labor one's compatriots no longer want to perform. Not only is one not related to them, not connected to them either simply as living beings or as individuals whose lives are constrained by socioeconomic factors beyond one's control, but moreover they do not even figure into making one who one is.[5]

This connection between denials of relationality and ignorance of vulnerability, and the contribution of both to oppressive social relations is also manifest in many other cases. Susan Wendell's analysis of the social meaning of disability demonstrates clearly how a willful ignorance of vulnerability underlies the oppressive denial of relationality:

> The disabled are not only de-valued for their de-valued bodies (Hannarod 1985), they are constant reminders to the able-bodied of the negative body—of what the able-bodied are trying to avoid, forget and ignore (Lessing 1981). For example, if someone tells me she is in pain, she reminds me of the existence of pain, the imperfection and fragility of the body, the possibility of my own pain, the *inevitability* of it. The less willing I am to accept all these, the less I want to know about her pain; if I cannot avoid it in her presence, I will avoid her. I may even blame her for it. I may tell myself that she *could have* avoided it, in order to go on believing that I *can* avoid it. I want to believe that I am not like her; I cling to the differences. Gradually, I make her 'other' because I don't want to confront my real body, which I fear and cannot accept. (Wendell 2008, 832)

On Wendell's account, the imperative to avoid one's own vulnerability—the potential susceptibility of one's body to pain, to less than 'ideal' functioning—precipitates a denial of relationality in which one dissociates oneself from an other who is a reminder of this vulnerability. Her bodily presence and pain epitomize the opposite of the invulnerable self one seeks to be, and one's response of avoidance and disidentification is intended to shore up that sense of invulnerability. Thus, ignorance of relationality, of relations with others as being constitutive of the self, is at the core of ignorance of vulnerability. Moreover, Wendell's analysis extends the points made by MacIntyre about the link between embodiment and vulnerability. For MacIntyre, denials of vulnerability find their root in our rejection of our embodied and animal nature. We perceive ourselves to be most vulnerable, most subject to injury, least in control of ourselves and our fates, most at the mercy of others, and most like other nonhuman animals as corporeal beings. As Wendell indicates, fear of our embodied being manifests in the abjection of those others who remind us of these dimensions of ourselves. Underlying this fearful response, however, are deeply-rooted social norms about competence and perfection that facilitate this abjection and 'othering.' To the "master" subject who aspires to such norms, the disabled person represents not only the possibility of pain and the absence of control over one's own body but also the loss of capacity and esteem in accord with social norms. As MacIntyre suggested with respect to vulnerability, disability represents a loss of continuity with one's social world. What Wendell highlights, though, is that the loss of continuity is not inherent in physical impairment but in the social norms that structure how that impairment is perceived and that lead to it being perceived as an object of pain, fear, and avoidance.[6]

In contrast to ignorance of relationality that stems from a logic of oppression, the other type of ignorance of relationality Hoagland identifies stems from a logic of resistance. It is a kind of knowing ignorance, a strategic denial through which one refuses not relationality itself or the forms of relationality that would lay bare one's vulnerable state, but the dominant forms of relationality, the roles that are prescribed or expected in relation to those who maintain an oppressive status quo. Thus, the repudiation of vulnerability that is sought appears quite different from that sought as part of a logic of oppression. As explored above, the denials of relationality that come from a logic of oppression ultimately constitute a willful ignorance of ontological vulnerability. The denials of relationality that come from a logic of resistance do not repudiate ontological vulnerability—vulnerability as a fundamental shared condition—but rather involve closure to particular situational forms of vulnerability. Moreover, as Shilliam notes, "to find one's vulnerability is already a privileged pursuit" (2013, 141–142). As oppressive relations, the dominant forms of relationality rendered individuals and groups vulnerable in certain negative ways. For instance, the stereotypical gender norms that prescribe activity and dominance for men and passivity and submission for women clearly make women vulnerable to harm in various ways. For women to reject relations that follow such patterns is an act of resistance rather than a total repudiation of relationality and the vulnerability it represents. Maintaining a protective stance as part of a strategy for resistance to oppressive conditions is necessarily the pursuit of *a certain form* of closure: protection against violence, against economic vulnerability and attendant social vulnerabilities (for instance, diminished access to the health care that would ensure bodily health or to the educational opportunities that might provide a route out of poverty), and against the emotional vulnerability that comes from occupying a traditionally inferiorized role. In seeking to deal with and prevent one's vulnerability from being exploited, one must know why and in what ways one is vulnerable, and how and why one seeks to neutralize this particular form of vulnerability. This refusal of vulnerability and certain forms of relationality, thus, requires knowledge instead of precluding and suppressing it. Managing one's vulnerability in this way differs significantly from pursuing invulnerability as a characteristic essential to one's subjectivity. It does not entail valuing invulnerability as a context-free, unequivocal good, but rather involves understanding the repercussions of closing oneself to certain kinds of relations and situations and judging such closure to be a necessary tool of resistance. The closure of the self is not constitutive but selective and strategic. One does not ignore and deny vulnerability per se, but refuses the experience of vulnerability in particular cases. In contrast, the invulnerability that constitutes willful ignorance is an epistemic and ethical closure of the self to that which challenges it, one that involves a (tacit) refusal of historical contextualization, wards off challenges to the coherence of one's self-interpretation, and entails a wariness of unforeseen and uncontrolled modes of change.

Two additional points can help to clarify further the connection I am seeking to draw between ignorance of vulnerability and the persistence of oppressive social relations. As noted above, underlying and supporting such oppressive relations is a denial of vulnerability in its most fundamental sense: vulnerability as openness to being affected and affecting in relation to others. In the context of such ignorance, one may make use of knowledge of who is particularly vulnerable in the sense of susceptible to harm to exploit that vulnerability; overt forms of oppression entail such exploitation. The knowledge had in this instance is a simple knowledge that someone is situated so as to be especially vulnerable. It involves no deeper comprehension of vulnerability as a shared ontological condition, but rather is predicated upon denial of this condition with respect to oneself and others. In this way, exploitation of vulnerability is in bad faith: it involves reading the other's vulnerability as solely negative, exploitable—solely as a factical condition—and repudiating one's own ambiguous vulnerability. Thus, oppressive exploitation of vulnerability is an expression of the belief that vulnerability is a negative condition and the desire to continue to avoid, ignore, and repudiate vulnerability by projecting it onto others. Although they do not always go hand in hand, exploitation of vulnerability and ignorance of vulnerability are bound together insofar as the latter is the condition of the former.

The second point is that the ignorance of vulnerability that is constitutive of oppression is often deployed in more subtle ways. It is presupposed in the norms that pervade our culture, making invulnerability an ideal.

Feminist analyses of the nature of oppression, such as those offered by Marilyn Frye (1983) and Iris Marion Young (1990), emphasize the structural nature of oppression; oppression is not an irregular occurrence, is not the product of a discrete set of choices and actions, and is not "the result of a few people's choices or policies" (Young 1990, 41). Rather, oppression involves systematic obstruction and operates on groups (rather than individuals) through the intersection of social, economic, political, and cultural structures. Thus, oppression takes a variety of forms—five of which Young classifies as exploitation, marginalization, powerlessness, cultural imperialism, and violence—and is not always overt. Moreover, as Foucault's understanding of power has indicated, oppression not only works through rejection—rejection of "foreign" and devalued others, rejection of relation and connection to these others, rejection of their impact on the self and the self's formation in relation to them—but through the production of and adherence to norms that structure such repudiation, inciting us to attain the normative ideal. One key feature of this ideal of invulnerability, as has been noted, is ignorance of the relational dimension of vulnerability. To deny vulnerability and its inherent relationality, is thus also to deny the power of one's own actions to affect others, to stand as an example for others, to contribute to a culture in which the norms of the invulnerable self are those upon which so many of us model ourselves. This ignorance means that we do not conceive of ourselves as "culture makers as well as culture consumers," that we abdicate responsibility for the selves that we make, and thusly perpetuate oppressive ideals by denying our complicity in doing so (Bordo 1999a, 50).

One consequence of the foregoing discussion is that ethical failures regarding vulnerability are far from exceptional. If, as I have argued, the pursuit of invulnerability amounts to ignorance of vulnerability and involves common practices and habits that solidify such ignorance, then disavowal of vulnerability is deeply embedded in our daily activities and modes of comportment. The consequence is that our projects of critique should take as their target the mundane and everyday as much as they do that which appears exceptional, striking, and uncommonly atrocious. My aim here is not to suggest that our critical attention is misdirected—toward the significant and large-scale violence of war, terrorism and counter-terrorism, for instance—but rather to argue that the mundane, the minor, and the everyday merits just as much scrutiny and concern since it is the ground upon which more weighty denials and abuses of vulnerability are built. It is through mundane and daily acts, habits, and patterns of thought that we create and maintain a climate that, for instance, persists in conceiving color-blindness as our aspiration for a 'post-racial' world and thus ignoring the way the assumption of color-blindness serves to obscure racial reality and history, as Mills and many others indicate. As a consequence, any attempt to avow vulnerability rather than repudiate it must involve thoughtful deconstruction and reconstruction of our more mundane modes of interaction and daily patterns of thought and action.

EPISTEMIC VULNERABILITY

As detailed in the previous sections, persistent disavowal of vulnerability in the form of the pursuit of invulnerability is integral to oppressive social relations because it operates as a form of epistemic reductionism and ethical closure. Yet, the appropriate response to the ethical failures of avoidance and disavowal is clearly not simple avowal or acceptance of vulnerability in all its forms. Indeed, as Hoagland's suggestions about resistance to logics of oppression demonstrates, denials of relationality and the particular forms of vulnerability it entails can be necessary and desirable in order to combat oppressive relations. Since denials of vulnerability often lead to the exploitation of those who are vulnerable, it is clearly unreasonable and unethical to suggest that the solution to avoidance and disavowal is, generally, embracing one's own vulnerability. If we are to call for more adequate recognition and response to vulnerability, we can do so only by delineating particular forms of vulnerability and particular situations in which these forms of vulnerability should be cultivated, and by taking into account whether they exacerbate or mitigate the potential for violence and harm.

If invulnerability as willful ignorance is the basis for the forms of ignorance that make possible oppression precisely because it enables one to isolate and close oneself off, then an essential part of overcoming these pernicious types of ignorance is fostering a specific type of vulnerability, namely, epistemic vulnerability. Only by departing from a solely negative understanding of vulnerability, though, can we conceive of vulnerability as being a resource for ethical response and political resistance to oppression. The presupposition that vulnerability is negative construes it as something to avoid, and leads to rationalizations for willful ignorance and closure to those individuals whose vulnerable conditions recall the fact of one's own vulnerability. Refusing to conflate vulnerability in its most profound and general sense—openness to being affected and altered—with specifically negative forms of vulnerability makes room for positive and constructive attitudes with respect to this the fundamental condition of our existence. Advancing such attitudes is vital if a disavowal of vulnerability is formative of oppressive types of subjectivity and, consequently, oppressive social relations. Accounts of situational forms of vulnerability that are positive are particularly necessary. A notion of epistemic vulnerability is one example of a positive type of vulnerability.

In brief, epistemic vulnerability is what makes learning, and thus a reduction of ignorance, possible. Undoing ignorance involves cultivating the attitude of one who is epistemically vulnerable rather than that of a masterful, invulnerable knower who has nothing to learn from others or for whom others are merely vehicles for the transmission of information. Given that the previous section recognized the necessity of strategic invulnerability in resisting oppression, it may seem incongruous to prescribe a form of vulnerability as a means to combat oppression. Yet, epistemic vulnerability is not incompatible with the selective and strategic adoption of invulnerability;

invulnerability as a protective mechanism can create the conditions that allow for greater epistemic vulnerability within a community. In any case, epistemic vulnerability is indispensable, albeit in different ways, not only on the part of those who are relatively privileged but also on the part of those who are relatively oppressed or do not stand to benefit from the status quo. Because theories of oppression have come to encompass an understanding of the intersectional nature of difference and the interlocking nature of oppressions, it seems reasonable to propose that epistemic vulnerability is vital for all; we all have lapses, gaps in our experience and attunement that demand alterations in our knowing attitudes, which the cultivation of epistemic vulnerability can ameliorate. Evidence for this claim can be found within feminist theory itself, which, as a movement intending to oppose the oppression of women, has not been without its own forms of ignorance and oppression (see Lorde 1984, Collins 2000, hooks 2000, Mohanty 2003).

So, in conclusion, I sketch five defining aspects of epistemic vulnerability in order to begin to describe what is involved in this kind of attitude. If invulnerability is, first and foremost, closure (not wanting to know), then epistemic vulnerability begins with being open to not knowing, which is the precondition of learning. This stipulation may sound simple, yet it is all too clear that openness to not knowing is culturally considered a form of weakness and thus is a form of being vulnerable out of which we are trained at an early age, for instance, through the way in which we are educated, evaluated, and ranked as children.[7] Second, it is an openness to being wrong and venturing one's ideas, beliefs, and feelings nonetheless. As Tuana suggests, "there are modalities of being that exceed our own and cannot be fully comprehended" and, yet, we can and should still interact respectfully with that which we cannot understand (2006, 16). To refrain from interaction, to abstain from dialogue because one fears that one does not know is simply another way of closing oneself off. Third, epistemic vulnerability entails the ability to put oneself in and learn from situations in which one is the unknowing, foreign, and perhaps uncomfortable party. This criterion in particular is necessary in order to avoid what Mariana Ortega calls "loving, knowing ignorance" and, instead, enable one to engage in "world"-traveling "as a concrete life activity" (2006, 69). Without an acceptance of the genuine value of discomfort and the real necessity of immersing oneself in situations in which one does not normally find oneself, learning does not happen. As implied above, not all of these elements of epistemic vulnerability need be undertaken at the same time or in every situation; this third facet, for instance, is one that is more appropriately demanded of those who are relatively privileged precisely because they have likely not already found themselves in situations in which they are the unknowing, uncomfortable, and nondominant party. Additionally, these first three dimensions of epistemic vulnerability build on one another; without the first two criteria—being open to not knowing and nonetheless venturing one's thoughts in the context of not knowing—the third fails to be an element of epistemic vulnerability.

Fourth, the concept of epistemic vulnerability calls attention to the affective and bodily dimensions of knowledge. If the ignorance one seeks to dispel is often a deeply rooted, willful form of ignorance that entails not just beliefs but unconscious commitments and habits, then it must be destabilized at this level. To be epistemically vulnerable, therefore, is not just to be open to new ideas, but to be open to the ambivalence of our emotional and bodily responses and to reflecting on those responses in nuanced ways. This stipulation draws upon the idea that vulnerability is significantly corporeal, and thus emphasizes a more holistic picture of what it means to have knowledge and allow that knowledge to impact action. We might know the facts of racial discrimination and oppression, for instance, but to allow that knowledge really to 'sink in' means to have it sink into our bodies, into our emotional responses, into our more basic interpretation of the world and ourselves and not just to incorporate it into a set of beliefs we hold. In this way, the fourth criterion builds on the third since it is only by immersing oneself in unfamiliar situations that one can begin alter habitual unconscious commitments. Altering bodily habits and the forms of knowledge that are ingrained into the body (not just had in the mind as beliefs) also clearly requires attention to mundane daily activity. Simply put, habits become habits—in particular, habitual forms of interpretation—through repetition, so rehabituation requires that same repetition. Moreover, if we reject the dualistic view of mind (subject) controlling body (object), then change can only happen through embodied habituation and immersion in alternate patterns.

The last dimension of epistemic vulnerability follows directly from the fourth: consequently, one must be open to altering not just one's ideas and beliefs, but one's self and sense of one's self.[8] If one changes only what one believes but does not allow this alteration to go all the way down, to affect what one does (those mundane practices that shape self-identity), how one thinks about and defines oneself, then the power of vulnerability is limited. As Spelman writes, "In W's case, her not wanting to believe that g [Black Americans' grievances are real] is true has to do with her not being able to face the consequences of its truth for *her understanding of herself* and her country" (2007, 123; my emphasis). W not only cannot entertain the reality of racism, but further cannot do so because this reality undermines her conception of herself (as someone who is basically a good person, hardworking and diligent, as someone who has achieved what she has fairly and justly rather than partly due to white privilege). The problem is not simply that she cannot allow herself to be affected by the reality of racism (to feel guilt, for instance) but also that she cannot conceive of herself *as having already been* affected by this reality, having had it be a part of what made her who she is, and cannot reconcile herself to the ambiguity in self-identity that this reality produces (she is both a good person and someone who has benefited from white privilege). Yet, as Kimberly Hutchings proposes, taking "seriously a challenge to *who* one is, as opposed to *what* one says, is profoundly disturbing and painful. It is, however, the only way to shift the ground of ethical debate" in a more just way (2013, 40).

Adopting epistemic vulnerability requires dispelling some of the formative "prejudices" that help shore up willful ignorance and the ideal of invulnerability. If epistemic vulnerability is defined by openness to changes in the self in light of coming to perceive what one does not know and has prevented oneself from knowing, then it entails a different perspective on change, permanence, history, and the formation of the self. In allowing the self to change, one likewise allows change in what one knows, how one knows, and in relation to whom and what one knows. Thus, epistemic vulnerability entails rejecting the closure of the self that defines invulnerability. Instead, one begins to comprehend oneself as a being who has come into being and is continually evolving, one positions oneself as one who has been and will continue to be affected by others; one perceives oneself as vulnerable and conceives this vulnerability as the condition of one's knowledge since it is only by being affected by others that one knows and is. As suggested throughout this chapter, the ideal of invulnerability is defined by the sense of immutability that attends it, the sense that this state of affairs is 'just the way things are' and will always be, that being impermeable just is what it means to be autonomous, active, in control, successful, and good. In contrast, to be epistemically vulnerable is to be open to the revision of the self and conceptions of the self—past, present, and future—since such alteration both comes from changes in what one knows and precipitates such changes in knowledge. Thus, it is through the cultivation of habits of epistemic vulnerability that we begin to dissipate those deeply ingrained habits of invulnerability. Crucial to dispensing with the ideal of invulnerability is an awareness of processes of constitution because such awareness is an avowal of vulnerability itself and an avowal of the self as a vulnerable one, susceptible to being affected and affecting in relation to others.

The next chapter continues the exploration of the ideal of invulnerability begun in this chapter by considering an important nexus of concepts—risk, control, danger, and responsibility—that contribute to making invulnerability an aspiration and vulnerability an object of avoidance. In particular, I seek to draw a more precise picture of the type of subjectivity cultivated through the pursuit of invulnerability. In this chapter, I sketched the notion of a "master" subject described by feminist and ecofeminist theorists; this conception of the subject remains somewhat one-dimensional, however, and has been described primarily in terms of its relationship to a dominant dualist history of thought. In the next chapter, I turn to Michel Foucault's work on normalization, biopolitics, and neoliberalism in order to flesh out the form taken by the subject pursuing invulnerability in a more complex social, economic, and political scene, and explore the greater ambiguity of this form of subjectivity. The specific focus will be what Foucault describes as entrepreneurial subjectivity, which, I contend, is the form taken by the contemporary pursuit of invulnerability.

NOTES

1. See Annaromao 1996 for discussion of how patriarchy in particular is sustained through denial of vulnerability and pursuit of invulnerability.
2. Attempts to secure invulnerability through ignorance of vulnerability can make us more vulnerable (in the sense of open to harm) because they involve ignorance of the real conditions that give rise to particular patterns of vulnerability. Examples might include ignorance about the correlation between high rates of gun ownership and high rates of gun violence, and the waging of a 'war on terrorism' that ignores, among other things, the diverse causes of 'terrorist' activity, likely making many people more susceptible to violence.
3. This account of reductionism is similar to the critique of instrumental reason offered by Adorno and Horkheimer in *The Dialectic of Enlightenment* (1972), and more recently by Axel Honneth in *Reification* (2008).
4. See Beattie and Schick 2013 for a discussion of how "rationalism" in international relations facilitates denials of vulnerability.
5. The rationale behind Arizona Senate Bill 1070, conventionally known as the "Support Our Law Enforcement and Safe Neighborhoods Act," illuminates whose vulnerability is ignored and whose is of concern. The law aims to "discourage and deter the unlawful entry and presence of aliens and economic activity by persons unlawfully present in the United States," focusing on the economic vulnerability of the citizens of Arizona manifest in the perceived loss of jobs to undocumented immigrants and the expenditure of state revenue on social services for them. The permeability of the U.S.-Mexico border is also regarded as making U.S. citizens vulnerable by exposing them to the violent activity of drug cartels and cross-border drug trafficking. Ignored is the vulnerability of those who cross the border, live near the border in Mexico, or live without documentation in the U.S. Only the vulnerability of a specific group of U.S. citizens is acknowledged and their vulnerability is perceived as justifying the exacerbation of vulnerabilities of others. Only negative vulnerability is recognized and only in order to secure a more invulnerable position, which is thought to be in jeopardy. See www.azleg.gov/legtext/49leg/2r/bills/sb1070s.pdf *and* www.azleg.gov/legtext/49leg/2r/.../s.1070pshs.doc.htm.
6. On the relationship between vulnerability and disability, and the 'othering' of those who do not fit the norms of invulnerability see Shildrick 2002.
7. See, for example, Kathryn Schulz's TED Talk "On being wrong": http://www.ted.com/talks/lang/en/kathryn_schulz_on_being_wrong.html
8. These last two dimensions of epistemic vulnerability are what distinguish it from what we might call epistemic humility, being humble and modest with respect to what one knows and does not know. Humility is a virtue oriented toward admission of ignorance, comprehension of the limits of one's knowledge, and an unassuming disposition, but epistemic vulnerability entails recognizing the production of ignorance and its role in the constitution of the self, and, then, actively seeking transformation of the self in light of recognition of this willful ignorance.

4 Risk and Control
The Formation of Entrepreneurial Subjectivity

In Western neoliberal societies and, increasingly, globally, risk management has become an imperative both at the level of institutions and policies, and at the level of individual action. Examples include risks as diverse as terrorism, the national debt, food safety and security, text messaging while driving, antibiotic resistant disease, and even the extent of government intervention itself. The assessment and management of risk affects not only policy, and political discourse and rhetoric, but also the relationship and attitudes individuals have to themselves. This chapter builds upon the account of the ideal of invulnerability developed in the previous chapter by incorporating an additional set of concepts into the analysis: ideas of risk, danger, control, and management, which enhance our picture of invulnerable subjectivity. In the previous chapter, the ideal of invulnerability was primarily discussed in terms of a kind of closure; through the pursuit of invulnerability we close ourselves off from alternative modes of experience, from the perspectives of others who are perceived as different from ourselves, and thus from challenges to the self-conceptions we have devised in order to understand our place in the social world. Here, I aim to account for the allure of the ideal of invulnerability, contending that culturally prevalent conceptions of risk and danger contribute to its appeal. I focus on how a particular sense of self and mode of subjectivity—entrepreneurial subjectivity—is forged in relation to broader social meanings and norms concerning responsibility and risk-taking. The overarching argument is that entrepreneurial subjectivity results in two ethically damaging consequences: (1) since entrepreneurial subjectivity relies on the reductively negative view of vulnerability, individuals become increasingly averse to vulnerability, regarding it not just as a condition to avoid but also as a bad character trait to possess, and (2) accordingly, responsibility for risk and for common human vulnerabilities is increasingly privatized rather than shared. Thus, entrepreneurial subjectivity contributes to our inability to recognize the full normative significance of vulnerability and respond ethically to both the vulnerabilities of others in adverse conditions and vulnerability as a common feature of life.

The first section of the chapter charts the evolution of our ideas of risk and danger through two of Michel Foucault's most relevant texts on these themes: *Discipline and Punish* (1975) and the 1978–79 lecture course at the Collège de France, *The Birth of Biopolitics*. Foucault's work is of particular interest because it provides a subtle account of danger, risk, and the development of social control. Foucault offers insight into how the construction of danger and risk, and their changing social meaning leads to the demand for control and management at the institutional and individual levels (biopolitics). Of particular significance is how, in his analysis, certain dangers and risks come to be allowed, encouraged, and eventually construed as desirable because, for instance, their existence is a precedent for increased surveillance or because inciting such risks generates forms of subjectivity that are economically or socially advantageous. Section two expands this Foucaultian analysis by drawing on Foucaultian-inspired work in the sociology of risk to make sense of the way in which risk is not just an object of avoidance for individuals but, simultaneously, something to be embraced in specific contexts. Management of risk, thus, involves both avoiding certain risks and actively courting other kinds of risk in order to form oneself as an ideally entrepreneurial subject. The third section considers the communal and social implications of the entrepreneurial mode of subjectivity. I take stock of the parallels between concepts of risk and vulnerability, suggesting that the idea of being 'at risk' is often synonymous with vulnerability but also entails reducing vulnerability to its negative sense. In the context of this view of vulnerability, I analyze the implications of the increasing privatization of many risks and vulnerabilities. By privatization is meant both how vulnerabilities are rhetorically deemed an issue of private individual responsibility rather than public concern and how responsibility is actually shifted from the public, collective sphere to the private sphere of the corporate world and individual choice. The privatization of risks and responsibility for those risks, I contend, shores up entrepreneurial subjectivity as an ideal mode of comportment. At the same time, entrepreneurial subjectivity and risk privatization facilitate disavowal of vulnerability as a more fundamental and ambiguous condition, and abnegation of responsibility for shared vulnerability. To exemplify these claims, in the last section I consider one complex case of such privatization of vulnerability and responsibility: the issue of food production and consumption in the contemporary U.S.

DANGER AND RISK THROUGH A FOUCAULTIAN LENS

Michel Foucault's classic text *Discipline and Punish* offers insights crucial for understanding how contemporary forms of power shape the subjectivity of individuals through the organization of space and time, and individuals' activities in their milieux. One main aim of Foucault's overall project is to delineate a shift in how power was conceived and practiced from the 'classical' age to the 'modern' age, or, in more familiar terms, from the modern period (the 16th through the 18th centuries) to the beginning of the contemporary era (the 19th century onward). Although *Discipline and Punish* is primarily a study of historical shifts in the power to punish, penal practices, and the discourses surrounding the penitentiary, the text develops a conception of modern power—bio-power—elaborated in Foucault's subsequent work and reveals important features of the dynamics of power that are formative of individual subjectivity. Most notably, Foucault advances the thesis that new techniques of institutional management, control, and organization, which he labels 'discipline,' lead simultaneously to an increase in efficiency and capacity, and to an increase in docility and subjection in individuals. Such an analysis of how subjects are shaped—in relation to the institutions in which they participate, the spaces they occupy, the modes of relationship in which they engage, and the activities they take up—is integral to understanding both the production of forms of subjectivity that eschew vulnerability in favor of invulnerability and how to challenge such forms of subjectivity. Only by understanding how increased capacity comes to be paired with normalizing practices can we understand the precise appeal of ideals of invulnerability in contemporary life. The pursuit of invulnerability is conceived widely as a pursuit of enhanced capacity and this notion—that by maximizing one's abilities, one will render oneself invulnerable—supports the overvaluation of invulnerability and the association of vulnerability with weakness and incapacity. A more complete critique of invulnerability needs to take account of how increased capacity is achieved at the price of increased docility and obedience, that is, of the ways in which invulnerability actually involves subjection. Here I focus on how the particular ways danger and risk are constructed prompts discipline. Before turning to these themes, however, some background concerning how Foucault conceives contemporary forms of power is needed.

Foucault on Power

In volume I of *The History of Sexuality* (1990), Foucault elaborates on the conception of power outlined in *Discipline and Punish*. Foucault's main thesis about power holds that it has been thought of as repressive and understood in terms of a legal model. When law is the paradigm for how power functions, power is imagined as deductive and negative, and generally takes a single form; it prevents us from doing certain things. Yet, on Foucault's account, power is also productive, operating to produce knowledge, beliefs, behaviors, norms and customs, institutions, standards, and so on. Moreover, historically, the exercise of power has shifted from "juridico-discursive" power—the top-down power of a sovereign king, most notably exercised in the right to execute—to "biopower." Through the concept of biopower, Foucault analyzes how the processes of life itself become political matters, issues and objects of control and regulation: "methods of power and knowledge assumed responsibility for the life processes and undertook to control and modify them" (1990, 142). Whereas sovereign power could take life or let live, biopower operates in a multiplicity of ways in order to "foster life or disallow it" (1990, 138); it instigates, manages, controls, monitors, organizes, optimizes, encourages, regulates, reinforces, and so on. Thus, whereas the mode of sovereign power is the law, which prohibits, the mode of biopower is the norm, which allows for measurement, evaluation, and hierarchical ranking, all of which constitute more meticulous mechanisms of control. The norm is a continuous corrective mechanism, and so makes it possible to capture and implicate all the minute aspects of daily life in relations of power. Thus, where our traditional "juridico-discursive" view of power takes it to be a substance of a sort, something that can be had and held, Foucault proposes that power is relational. Power simply names a collection of relationships situated in a particular sociohistorical context.

Foucault also distinguishes between two dimensions of biopower that are joined in practice but indicate how biopower operates at two different levels (at least): through discipline at the level of the individual body and through regulatory control at the level of the social body or population. As noted above, disciplining the bodies of individuals aims to make them simultaneously more efficient and productive, and more obedient. Regulatory controls are interventions at the level of the body of the species; such controls take the biological existence of the population as their object, seeking to increase both knowledge of that population (via demographic studies, for instance) and control of that population (via policy, for instance). Both take as their object biological existence in all its facets and have as their aim the maximization of that existence in terms of health, well-being, longevity, and a more 'desirable' composition within the population. So, when considering mechanisms of control and management at the individual level, the discipline to which this individual is subject or to which she subjects herself is also always part of a broader web of relations of power that link the individual to the social milieu (via norms and location in relation to institutions) and politico-economic imperatives enacted through regulatory controls. In the context of the discussion that follows, the depiction of danger and the delimitation of what counts as risk operate both to manage populations and, in so managing them, to instigate particular behaviors and attitudes in individuals within those populations. Individuals are disciplined and exercise self-discipline, but such discipline cannot be severed from broader socio-politico-economic objectives it may serve.

Danger in Discipline and Punish

In *Discipline and Punish*, danger is thematized, in brief, as either localized in dangerous, abnormal individuals or as inherent in social dynamics such as the increasing popular support for instances of illegality. What is dangerous is what may precipitate disorder and instability, and so comes to be managed through disciplinary and normalizing practices. Yet, toward the end of Foucault's story of disciplinary power, we see that a certain mediated form of danger—delinquency—is tacitly permitted and so even danger has a role to play in the management of modern life. This understanding of both danger and risk—which take on distinct senses—is picked up and elaborated in *The Birth of Biopolitics,* the lecture course from two years later.

The first major turning point in the history of penal institutions offered in *Discipline and Punish* is the danger of execution as public spectacle (*supplice*). The concept of danger initially appears as a "double danger": with the *supplice* there is a "double danger" insofar as "tyranny confronts rebellion; each calls forth the other" (Foucault 1995, 74). Here, danger lies in the instability of the situation, in the rebellious potential of the crowds forming to witness elaborate public executions, and in the possibility that the tyrannical penal power of the sovereign will be deemed excessive enough to merit insurrection. In light of this danger, a new economy of punishment—a semio-technique—emerges that seeks to achieve stability by quashing rebellion, taming the excessive forces of the masses. It must also deal with the danger of tyranny, the excessiveness of the power to punish, which if wielded would provoke the masses. Aimed at preventing future crime and maintaining stability and order, punishment becomes subject to calculation and an economic rationality that seeks the maximum deterrence for the minimum expenditure of force; instead of excessive, it becomes moderate. Punishment wards off danger—specifically, the danger of disorder—and is itself no longer a danger since it has become judicious, "an art of effects" (1995, 93). Although discipline as a model of punishment supplants the semiotics of punishment in which these ideas arise, both are "utilitarian" and calculative, and have an increasingly individualizing perspective concerning danger (1995, 130). In both techniques of punishment, danger is located within the individual. With disciplinary power, however, the dangerous individual is conceived as part of a "dangerous multitude" that, in accord with economic rationality, is dealt with best as part of a totality. Thus, the dangerous multitude, an unordered multiplicity, must be transformed into an ordered, organized multiplicity: segmented, ranked, evaluated, and monitored. This taming of unordered forces takes place via both individualization and totalization; that is, individuals are segmented, ranked, evaluated, and monitored both as individuals and as part of a unit. Qua individualizing, disciplinary power regulates the movements, positions, and use of time of the individual intensively and in detail. Qua totalizing, disciplinary power simultaneously fits this individual and all his minute activities into a larger machine composed of other individuals, their spatial location and physical site, and temporal imperatives (speed).

The oft-noted unique feature of disciplinary power is the way it both maximizes obedience and maximizes the capacity and efficiency of the individual body: discipline "increases the forces of the body (in economic terms of utility) and diminishes those same forces (in political terms of obedience). In short, it dissociates power from the body" (1995, 138). Thus, disciplinary power is especially successful in mitigating danger. Any increase in aptitude is achieved in tandem with an increase in domination, submission, and obedience. Bodies' energetic capacities are diverted from rebellion but amplified in the service of an externally imposed end. For Foucault, one of the paradigmatic forms taken by modern power relations is panopticism. Foucault's account of panoptic power has its origins in Jeremy Bentham's descriptions of the ideal prison: one in which a tall guard tower is positioned in the center of a circular building containing the prison cells, rendering the prisoners always visible while the guard is invisible to them, and thus precipitating self-discipline and self-surveillance on the part of the prisoners who would never know if or when they were being watched. The conjunction of visibility and invisibility defines the model of the Panopticon and ensures order:

> If the inmates are convicts, there is no danger of a plot, . . . if they are patients, there is no danger of contagion; if they are madmen, there is no risk of their committing violence upon one another; if they are schoolchildren, there is no copying, no noise, no chatter, no waste of time; if they are workers, there are not disorders, no thefts, no coalitions, none of those distractions that slow down the rate of work, make it less perfect or cause accidents. (1995, 201)

The virtue of this paradigm of disciplinary power is the near elimination of danger and risk. To do away with danger and risk, panopticism eradicates doubt. The Panopticon is "'a house of certainty'" (1995, 202). In this "house of certainty," there is no question about what is happening because it is known and thus there is no threat of danger. Certainty about the activities of the prisoners or workers or students or patients, and the implantation in them of the seed of self-discipline, eliminates the possibility of unruliness. Furthermore, because it is merely a technology, a mechanism built into the structure that is itself examined and evaluated rather than a power emanating unchecked from the sovereign, "[t]here is no risk . . . [that panoptic power] may degenerate into tyranny" (1995, 207). Consequently, as indicated in the previous chapter, there is a connection between epistemic certainty and disciplinary control. Epistemic certainty—or the pretense of it—makes disciplinary control possible, and disciplinary control is effected through epistemic certainty. The nature of this connection shifts as epistemic certainty, the knowledge that ensures that there is no risk, becomes increasingly difficult to achieve. Disciplinary control will proliferate and diversify, but there will be no corresponding increase in epistemic certainty or security. Thus, the pursuit of epistemic certainty is heightened; we wish to know all the risks we face so that we might protect ourselves against them, but their unknowability is precisely what renders them dangerous.[1] What remains crucial, however, is the closure that is affected through the presumption and pursuit of epistemic certainty. Only with security of this type and a concomitant deactivation of danger, is discipline enabled to do more; it not only "neutralize[s] dangers" but can positively "increase the possible utility of individuals" because such increase no longer poses a threat (1995, 210).

With this panoptic intensification of power, the object of penal concern becomes delinquency as a way of being that characterizes the entirety of an individual's life rather than just the criminal act; accordingly, experts must seek to know the individual's life history, especially including the "dangerous proclivities" of the individual's psychology (1995, 252). The delinquent is "a kernel of danger" that can and must be dissected and known (1995, 254). Yet, in this model, delinquency also becomes a form of "controlled illegality" (1995, 279). The delinquent is a knowable object, is manipulable and manageable, and, because the delinquent is "reduced to precarious conditions of existence," delinquency is a "less dangerous" form of illegality (1995, 278).[2] Yet, in the various crime stories of the 19th century, the delinquent is portrayed "both as very close and quite alien, a perpetual threat to everyday life" (1995, 286). The danger is controlled while still rhetorically positioned as a danger, facilitating greater control and management. Here we can hear hints of the depiction of and relation to danger that will come to feature prominently in neoliberal modernity.[3]

Danger and Control in *The Birth of Biopolitics*

I turn now to Foucault's 1978–79 lecture course *The Birth of Biopolitics*, an extended analysis of liberal and neoliberal economic thought, from which I extract three key ideas: (1) the intertwining of risk and control, (2) the economization of the social sphere, and (3) the entrepreneurial mode of subjectivity that accompanies them both. Before turning to these topics, however, a brief word about the differences between liberalism and neoliberalism is needed. In general terms, economic liberalism is considered to have its origins in Adam Smith's formulation of the idea of the free market as the best route for progress, development, and human liberty. Liberal economic thought went on to develop in a Keynesian direction that allowed a significant role for the state in ensuring employment and regulating inflation. Contemporary neoliberalism rejects this substantive role for the state. It might be summed up through an inventory of political and economic policy directives that include trade liberalization, comprehensive deregulation, privatization of public services with the aim of shrinking the public sector, and the implementation of such policies globally. Thus, a contemporary example of neoliberal intervention is the structural adjustment policies imposed by international financial institutions such as the World Bank and the International Monetary Fund on so-called developing countries. Such policies require a country to scale back its public services and to implement austerity measures among other things in order to qualify for loans for development from said institutions.

More specifically, according to Foucault's analysis, neoliberalism is distinguished from classical liberalism in virtue of the role attributed to the market in relation to the state. Whereas liberalism seeks to demarcate space for a free market, that market still falls under the supervision of the state. This supervisory relationship is reversed in neoliberalism and the free market is considered to act "as the organizing and regulating principle of the state" (2008, 116). This shift takes place in the context of concerns about the legitimacy of the state, thus, in particular, in German neoliberalism post-WWII (ordoliberalism). Features of this shift include corresponding doctrinal changes that result in differing governmental rationalities: departing from the liberal view that the key feature of the market is free economic exchange, which is based on the assumption of equality, the neoliberal view holds that the key feature of the market is competition, which rests upon inequality. Following from this change, in contrast with the liberal idea that the free market is best achieved through an absence of regulation, *laissez-faire*, neoliberalism maintains that the conditions for the market to flourish require "an active policy [of intervention to create favorable conditions for competition] without state control" (2008, 132).

In the context of these shifts, of particular interest is, first, the relationship Foucault perceives between, on the one hand, culturally conditioned ideas of risk and danger, and, on the other hand, the new techniques of control and management to which these ideas lead, in particular techniques of *self*-control and *self*-management. Danger emerges as a defining factor in the governmental rationalities of liberalism and neoliberalism because of the constant interplay of freedom and security. Danger and risk assume significant rhetorical functions in maintaining the balance between freedom and security. Freedom is not simply the absence of interference, but is a space demarcated by governmental rationality in which a set of allowable activities can occur. Liberal governance simply is "the management of freedom[,]" which it "proposes to manufacture . . . constantly" (2008, 65, 63). Rather than simply giving free reign to freedom, liberalism manages it and, in so doing, produces freedom. More specifically, freedom is produced in relation to that which threatens it. Since it is always threatened—since there is always something "in the production of freedom [that] risks limiting and destroying it"—it is ensured through "the establishment of limitations, controls, forms of coercion, and obligations relying on threats, etcetera" (2008, 64). As a consequence, control and freedom are intertwined insofar as freedom is understood to be possible only in light of the management of risk and the achievement of security. Yet, as was apparent in Foucault's account of the power to punish, these methods of management and control represent a potential danger themselves; they may overreach, overextend themselves, unduly interfering with zones of liberty. Thus, there is a constant need to balance the competing but complementary imperatives of freedom and security so that danger does not arise in the form of an excess or an absence of either, imperiling their tenuous interchange. Risk thus operates as the basis for control. Without danger, without risk, there is no impetus to control and nothing to manage. Thus, Foucault concludes rather presciently, "there is no liberalism without a culture of danger" (2008, 67). The presence of danger and risk renders necessary, rational, and acceptable the techniques of management aimed at achieving security and freedom within secure bounds. Danger, consequently, is an omnipresent potential but its ubiquity is a consequence of, and necessarily paired with, management. Just as liberalism produces freedom—setting the terrain of liberty—so it produces danger. Accordingly, individuals "are conditioned to experience their situation, their life, their present, and their future as containing danger" (2008, 66). Examples of such anticipation of danger are numerous. For instance, women are taught to fear and seek to protect themselves against rape, whether by carrying their keys so they can use them to ward off attack or by not venturing out alone at night or by second-guessing their choice of clothing.

Second, neoliberal thought generalizes "the 'enterprise' form," conceiving both economy and society as composed of "enterprise units," and inverting "the relationships of the social to the economic" (2008, 225, 242, 240). Social issues such as education, child-rearing, and health care are interpreted and understood in primarily economic terms, and, specifically, in terms of the greater or lesser risk (or cost) posed to individuals (and society as a composite of said individuals). Thus, with neoliberalism the domain of management and control on the part of the state shifts to the social sphere, which is ordered so as to serve and preserve—but not interfere with—the freedom of the economic sphere. In the specifically American form of neoliberalism, Foucault contends that economization—an "economic analysis of the non-economic"—operates as a "grid of intelligibility," rendering comprehensible a whole range of behaviors, activities, and relationships (2008, 243). Such an economized framework of intelligibility entails not just that "[t]he individual's life must be lodged ... within the framework of a multiplicity of diverse enterprises ... which are in some way ready to hand for the individual" but also that the individual must understand herself both tacitly and consciously within this framework such that she makes herself "a sort of permanent and multiple enterprise" (2008, 241). Within this framework, Foucault notes, "the individual becomes governmentalizable, ... power gets a hold on him to the extent, and only to the extent, that he is a *homo œconomicus*" (2008, 252).

Crime and punishment also become intelligible in a new way through an economic frame; the criminal is no longer a dangerous person per se, but rather is indistinct, a person like any other who weighs the risks, and calculates the costs and benefits of his action (2008, 253). The system of punishment thus has only "to react to the supply of crime" by increasing the risk associated with it, thus diminishing demand for crime (2008, 253). But, in accord with economic rationality, complete eradication of crime is not conceived as a desired or possible goal. Instead, a certain mean of compliance, a certain "balance between the curves of the supply of crime and negative demand" is sought (2008, 256). Thus, "society appears as the producer of conforming behavior with which it is satisfied in return for a certain investment" in, say, law enforcement, antidrug campaigns, and so on (ibid). As a consequence of the imposition of an economic grid of intelligibility rather than one specific to criminality (since the criminal is no different from other actors), this notion—that society produces and consumes conformity—can be extended to individual behavior in general: economized, managed in line with economic rationality, society produces "conforming behavior" on the part of individuals insofar as they are *homo œconomici,* insofar as they take themselves as enterprises.[4]

Third, the aforementioned presuppositions of the neoliberal terrain concerning the relationship between freedom, danger, and security set the stage for a particular type of relationship to self on the part of the individual inhabiting this terrain. This mode of subjectivity, Foucault suggests, is one defined by entrepreneurship. One consequence of understanding of one's environment as imminently dangerous is that one not only accedes to being managed and controlled, but also enacts self-management in an exemplarily panoptic manner. Yet, within the rules of the neoliberal game, "each remains master regarding himself"; self-management is undertaken in the name of freedom and with the aim of enhancing one's capacities. So, when Foucault describes panopticism as "the very formula of liberal government" (2008, 67), the full implications of this description only emerge many pages later in the discussion of the individual as *homo œconomicus,* "an entrepreneur of himself" (2008, 226). If panopticism makes the individual his own disciplinarian, it is because whoever is subject to it "inscribes in himself the power relation in which he simultaneously plays both roles [, that of observer and observed, trainer and trainee, teacher and student]; he becomes the principle of his own subjection" (1995, 202–203). As an entrepreneur of himself, therefore, the individual governs himself, ostensibly freely, in accord with the prevailing politico-economic ideals. He disciplines himself, producing not just goods and capital through his work, but, further and perhaps more significantly, producing himself as the bearer of human capital. As enterprise units, individuals are tasked with increasing their capital via their skills and abilities, their "capital-ability," as Foucault puts it (2008, 225). Thus, as Lois McNay notes, "Individual autonomy becomes not the opposite of, or limit to, neoliberal governance, rather it lies at the heart of its disciplinary control" (2009, 62). For the entrepreneurial subject, freedom and autonomy are found within the subtle mechanisms of social control that characterize neoliberal governmentality, but since these encourage "active differentiation" and "regulated self-responsibility" rather than homogeneous submission to an external authority, the entrepreneurial subject feels himself to be exercising and even expanding his autonomy (McNay 2009, 63). Yet, as an entrepreneur of oneself, when one disciplines oneself in order to develop one's capital enhancing capacities, one in effect engages in conforming behavior. Indeed, those behaviors that increase one's "capital-ability" are necessarily conforming ones because they are accepted as economically beneficial.[5]

SHAPING THE SELF THROUGH THE MANAGEMENT OF RISK

Although in *The Birth of Biopolitics* Foucault sounds neutral and even at times hopeful about the relationships and possibilities neoliberalism entails, contrasting it with disciplinary and normalizing mechanisms of power, more recent work in the sociology of risk demonstrates how entrepreneurial subjectivity links up with the normalizing and disciplinary workings of power. A governmentality approach to risk follows a broadly Foucaultian trajectory and explores how risk is at issue in the rationalities of governance and management, and how governmentality entails particular relationships to risk.[6] The questions that orient much of this literature focus on how risk functions as a tool in a biopolitical regime, asking "what is done *in the name of* risk?" (Baker and Simon 2002, 18). Following this orientation, I focus on the following questions: How is risk formative of subjectivity? How do we create ourselves as subjects in relation to risk? How is the differential framing of both risks and the parties taking on or securing themselves against risk conducive to entrepreneurial subjectivity? And, overarching all of these, how does the disposition toward risk cultivated in the contemporary neoliberal context facilitate abnegation of responsibility in relation to vulnerability?

In relation to risk, an entrepreneurial subject is one who becomes adept at personal cost-benefit analyses concerning the risks she takes, adopting a calculative attitude about how potential risks might affect her individual human capital. As sociologists of risk illuminate, however, it is not the case the some risks are inherently desirable and others are inherently undesirable; indeed, what is conceptualized as 'risk' is itself sociohistorically contingent. As a consequence, attitudes toward and management of risk are complex and ambivalent. Risk is something that we simultaneously eschew and embrace, both as individuals and as members of a social body. Given the social shaping of the meaning of various risks, distinctions between the kinds of risk considered appropriate to embrace—stock market speculation, for instance—and the kinds considered appropriate to eschew—unprotected sexual activity, for instance—indicate less about the nature of the risk itself and more about social and cultural values. The framing of actions as risks, and as either risks worth taking or risks to avoid, indicates what kinds of activities are considered worthy, what character traits are regarded as estimable, and what goals and aims are deemed realistic and desirable, and for whom. Thus, risk is an implicitly value-laden notion that appeals to presuppositions about individual responsibility and morality (for example, how taking responsibility for the risks one faces makes one morally praiseworthy), the value of security from different types of risks, and the appropriateness of individual or communal assumption of the burden of risk.

In the context of neoliberal values, entrepreneurial subjects must both boldly court and assiduously avoid risks of different sorts. Although one takes certain risks because they are likely to pay off, figuratively and literally, one also deliberately avoids or refrains from taking others either because they lead to probable harm, decreasing one's human capital, or because they are too risky and not a good investment, so to speak. From the perspective of this economized frame of intelligibility, dangers are omnipresent, thus it falls to the individual to ward off these dangers and negotiate the varieties of risk she encounters. Risk avoidance in particular involves both developing capacities of prevention through which one controls one's situation, a central part of one's set of "capital-abilities," and exercising precaution in the face of uncertainties that cannot be mastered.[7] For example, one exercises not just to be fit but also to prevent various health problems, and one eats well not just because high quality food tastes good but also because it might protect against various diseases. Avoiding negatively coded risks in this way positions one as a responsible moral agent, as does assuming such responsibility as an individual rather than awaiting and depending upon the social distribution of risk. Yet, embracing risk is equally necessary for the individual who is an entrepreneur of herself since it is only through courting certain risks that she can increase her human capital. In the remainder of this section, I briefly sketch an example of courting risk drawn from Jonathan Simon's study of the ethos of mountain-climbing—a paradigmatic risk-taking activity—in order to show how this kind of interaction with risk is formative of entrepreneurial subjectivity and, as such, facilitates ignorance of vulnerability and concomitant repudiations of responsibility.

Simon's analysis centers on "the relationship between new governmental rationalities that urge the embrace of risk . . . and the discourses of extreme sports[,]" and rests on a distinction between mountaineering and summiteering (2002, 180). Popular depictions of mountain-climbing typically focus on summiteering, which is defined by a "fetishization of the summit," a focus on the "unmediated adversity" faced by climbers, aspirations to set records of various sorts, and the belief that reaching the summit of a mountain is a form of redemption, "a test that marks the participant as among an elect" (2002, 190–192). Mountaineering, in contrast, is defined by a broader understanding of what one does and what is required when climbing mountains; it involves "an ethical and communitarian ethos[,]" an emphasis on the technical skills necessary for ascending and surviving extreme conditions, and a more developed understanding of the interdependence crucial in successful climbs (181–182). As mountain-climbing expeditions have become more commercialized and consumer-oriented, Simon notes, the summiteering dimension has prevailed. In essence, one can buy access to a summit; depth of skill and understanding, and interdependence and cooperation are superfluous.

These two perspectives on mountain-climbing are characterized by different ideas about what one does when one embraces risk. The summiteering perspective leads to a privatization of one's project, of responsibility, and thus a concomitantly narrow understanding of struggle and adversity, which is thoroughly externalized, "reduced to a singular and natural force [the mountain] with which negotiation and compromise are impossible" (191). Risk is embraced by the person who seeks to ascend to the summit as "a device for proving and redeeming the self" (198). Taking this risk is a way to demonstrate one's mastery of a mountain and, by extension, one's "mastery in the world of the marketplace and the home" (190). Thus, risk is conceived as a thoroughly individual matter, a personal choice to better oneself, and the ways in which the summiteer depends on others—sherpas and guides, most obviously—are conveniently ignored as summiting is construed as an act of individual will and accomplishment. The entrepreneurial subject undertakes the risk because the project of climbing a mountain "promise[s] a new subjectivity" via an increase in one's capital and status (190). It is a risk worth taking only because it is formative of subjectivity, because it is regarded as a way "to bring about personal growth[,]" and does so because it results in a calculable payoff (192). That is, it connotes something recognizable in our social milieu: individualized mastery, achievement, and victory over challenges, and the establishment of self via the conquering of risk, all forms of invulnerability.

The calculation that such a risk is one worth embracing—one that will indeed lead to an increase in one's human capital and a new, improved self who radiates self-sufficiency, self-control, and achievement—can only be made in a social context in which these values of invulnerability are esteemed. Using risk-taking as a means to self-enhancement requires a social context in which invulnerability is valued and vulnerability is devalued, deemed a failing and weakness. Thus, although it might seem intuitive to associate the pursuit of control with the *avoidance* of risk, even when embracing risk the entrepreneurial subject seeks control by endeavoring to manage her human capital, maximizing it by taking certain risks and minimizing its reduction (or stagnation) by avoiding other risks.

It is crucial to note, however, that only *privatized* risks afford entrepreneurial subjects this kind of opportunity for self-enhancement. In this context, privatization refers both to the increasing economic privatization that occurs when the provision of services and resources is shifted from the public sphere to the private sphere, as well as to the ideology and rhetoric of privatization that necessarily accompanies it. The former takes two complementary forms: as necessary services are taken over by the private, corporate domain, responsibility for securing these services falls to individuals. The rhetoric that attends economic privatization emphasizes individualism and personal responsibility for obtaining such needed services and resources, and presumes the isolated, self-sufficient, masterful subject much critiqued by feminist thinkers. This rhetoric thus neglects the reality of dependency that persists even in the context of economic privatization. Both are manifest clearly in the aforementioned example of summiteering: ascent to the peak of a mountain becomes a matter of purchasing services, but is not reduced to the ability to render payment since the ideology of privatization allows the summiteer to construe his act as that of a self-sufficient individual. In the process, it elides the reality of financial privilege and inequity, and backgrounds the summiteer's dependency on the guides and sherpas who accompany him.

For risk-taking to contribute to the positive self-construction of an entrepreneurial subject, it must be privatized in both senses. Communal or socially distributed risks offer no such opportunities for increasing the capital-abilities of the entrepreneurial self. First, as it is conceived within the dominant neoliberal paradigm, the social distribution of risks and their benefits and burdens is typically regarded as a way to avoid significant risk rather than a way to embrace it (e.g., social welfare programs), and avoiding risk seemingly contributes less to positive self-construction; it is construed as an evasion of personal responsibility. Second, given an ideal of the self as an isolated, invulnerable individual, one can only enhance one's self by choosing to take a given risk, using one's own abilities to conquer it, and thus having one's own abilities, effort, and success recognized by others. The social distribution of risk does not allow for this valorization of individual mastery and capacity. Thus, if subjectivity is understood and experienced as entrepreneurial subjectivity idealizing invulnerability, then there is little incentive to distribute risk, take responsibility for shared vulnerabilities, or avow and understand one's own vulnerability.

RISK, PRIVATIZATION, AND RESPONSIBILITY

Entrepreneurial subjectivity, the comportment toward risk that characterizes it, and the ideology of privatization that supports it thus all have a significant impact on our ability to reckon with vulnerability and take responsibility in relation to it. This mode of subjectivity, furthermore, is premised on inequity: it takes resources both to avoid and to embrace risk, and given the increasing privatization of many risks, most chose to deploy their resources to ward off detrimental risks by meeting basic needs. Thus, those who stand to benefit most from embracing capacity-increasing risks are those who already possess the economic and social resources with which to take such risks. So, the successful entrepreneurial subject benefits from the increasing privatization of risk because he is already positioned in such a way to increase his status, self-conception, and "capital-abilities." Those who lack the requisite economic resources and the social benefit of privileged status in the dominant culture are hindered when much risk is considered to be most appropriately assumed by private persons rather than by collective institutions. The privatization of risk and responsibility stabilizes and enhances the self-conception of those entrepreneurial subjects who are perceived as taking risks, enabling them to appear masters of their fate, but it simply exacerbates the vulnerability of those who are perceived to be *at* risk and lack the resources to assume active control of their situations.

In this section, I explore the consequences of the differential privatization of forms of risk and vulnerability for human subjectivity and ethical relations, contending that such privatization prevents us from acknowledging vulnerability in a way that enables ethical relationships with others. This chapter has focused thus far on the concepts of danger and risk, and how our perceptions of dangers and risks are socially shaped, in particular, by the exigencies of the presently dominant neoliberal politico-economic framework. Of crucial import, however, is the relationship between the concepts of risk, danger, and vulnerability. Indeed, the intimate connection between vulnerability and risk is an integral part of the rationale behind both risk-avoidance and embracing risk. Risks are avoided and are coded negatively as presenting danger when they are believed to render one vulnerable to harm. Risks are coded positively, and pursued and assumed when they present an opportunity to pursue invulnerability. Yet, it is frequently the case that the two concepts are conflated with one another, and vulnerability is often thought to be an especially negative form of risk; when persons are positioned as vulnerable, they are regarded as *at risk*. In the discussion that follows, I differentiate the two concepts but also chart their overlap and convergence in order to comprehend how the social meanings of risk affect the perception of vulnerability and thus its normative salience.

Risk commonly tends to be understood more equivocally than vulnerability. Whereas vulnerability, when recognized, seems clearly to require the protection of vulnerable parties and the mitigation of their vulnerable condition, risk can be conceived as something that is *taken* (rather than being a given) or as a product of a situation that an individual has caused. That is, according to our common perceptions, we can avoid or seek risk whereas vulnerability is thought of as a given condition in which one already exists. So, responsibility for risk can be attributed to individuals whereas it is less common to hold individuals responsible for their vulnerability (unless, of course, it is a product of risk they have taken). Correspondingly, risk is the source of both worry and valorization: although many risks are avoided, taking certain kinds of risk is also socially esteemed. Risk-taking individuals are often regarded as self-determining individuals able to master their fate by forging it for themselves. Risk may be a conceptual stand-in for vulnerability, but it is one that is far more equivocal and one that facilitates an unequal distribution of responsibility: different social status and modes of subjectivity are attributed to those who are framed as actively *taking* culturally validated risks and those who are framed as passively being *at* risk. To be passively at risk is conceptually closer to being vulnerable to the extent that vulnerability is perceived negatively.

The connotations of passivity and incapacity that define being *at* risk, however, do not prevent individuals from being held privately responsible for the riskiness of their position. From the neoliberal perspective, being at risk may mean that one is passive and lacking in necessary capacities, but one can likewise be blamed for the failure to develop those capacities and to make oneself an active agent. Thus, when vulnerability is understood through the lens of risk, responsibility for it is often privatized. When we interpret vulnerability as risk, it is easier to hold individuals (rather than communities) responsible. One example of this phenomenon is the perception of health insurance in the U.S.: by understanding the issue of health care and insurance in either/or terms—of choosing either to take risks (by not obtaining insurance) or to adopt a precautionary attitude (by obtaining insurance)—rather than in terms of a fundamental vulnerability to physical illness, disease, and harm that all people share, health and responsibility for it is rendered a wholly individual matter and the shared condition that makes health insurance necessary—vulnerability—is obscured.

Thus, the conceptions of responsibility that underlie entrepreneurial subjectivity are framed in terms of the politico-economic suppositions of the ideology of neoliberalism. A core part of this ideology, which Foucault highlights, is a cultural overvaluation of economic ends and the actors who are seen as integral to achieving those ends. Another significantly overlooked dimension of neoliberalism is the way it allows for and, indeed, is premised upon, selective social distribution of risk. As Foucault's account indicates, neoliberalism entails increased management of the social sphere in the service of the maximum freedom of the economic sphere. The consequence of establishing economic ends as the most socially valuable ends is the differential and inequitable privatization of risk: the social sector activities and services needed by families and workers such as education, recreation, and childcare are increasingly privatized while the risks attendant on the economic sector, which is paradigmatically 'private,' are publicly distributed through 'corporate welfare' of various sorts.[8] As Martha McCluskey points out, the subsidizing of corporate needs and mitigation of corporate risk is framed as an issue of efficiency and thus contrasted with the subsidizing of caretaking through social welfare policies, which is framed as a form of redistribution. Such framing, McCluskey argues, construes corporate subsidies as neutral, objective, and in the public interest (because aimed at efficiency) whereas subsidies for caretakers are construed as partial, subjective, and only benefiting particular interests (because aimed at redistribution) (2002a, 118). This framing of the issue is, of course, far from neutral, resting instead on a "double standard for moral hazard" according to which social welfare leads to the moral hazard of increased reliance on public assistance but the comparable reliance of corporations on subsidies is not even conceived as a moral hazard but rather an inevitability and "a price worth paying" (2002a, 126).

Thus, what is at stake in the differential privatization of risk is not just the needs of the social sector versus those of the economic sector, but also estimations of the worth of those who benefit from the collective distribution of risk: when one's worth is equated with one's ability to bring economic gain, privileged entrepreneurial subjects win out. Risks are privatized for those who are not regarded as economically valuable (e.g., laborers, caretakers), rendering their position more precarious, and publicly distributed for those who are regarded as economically valuable (e.g., those who produce capital, CEOs and corporations who ostensibly create jobs). This framing of human worth and moral status by an economized grid of intelligibility shapes our assessment of risk and risk-taking:

> ... border-crossing undocumented immigrants who defy heavily armed government authority in pursuit of personal economic gain could, in theory, personify the values of neoliberal risk taking. However, in mainstream U.S. politics and culture, even if immigrants' pursuit of gain in the global market requires entrepreneurial, anti-bureaucratic nerviness, their behavior is typically understood instead as base recklessness; not as self-reliant glory seeking but as parasitic evasion of responsibility (McCluskey 2002b, 164–165).

As McCluskey illuminates, the solely economic lens through which we understand risk, social value, and the public good enables us to ignore the falsity of common apprehensions of character and value. According to neoliberal ideology, we ought to esteem border-crossing immigrants for their initiative and willingness to embrace risk. From a reductive economic perspective as well as a xenophobic one, though, the undocumented immigrant contributes little of value to the public good and is even depicted as draining resources whereas corporate executives are thought to provide jobs, industry, and economic growth. Thus, we are inclined to see their activities as active, self-sufficient forms of risk-taking even though "multinational corporations that represent the triumph of free-market risk taking inherently depend on socialized risk spreading for their success" (McCluskey 2002b, 165). These are the estimations of worth that undergird entrepreneurial subjectivity and account for its appeal. One implication of this (il)logic of privatization is that it insulates those who are privileged from vulnerability—by spreading the risk of their endeavors—and so reinforces two misperceptions about risk and vulnerability: (1) that vulnerabilities and undesirable risks are individual matters and, consequently, (2) that risk can be avoided with just a modicum of precaution because it is a matter of what one chooses to assume, and not equally a matter of that to which one is subject. So, engagement with risk is perceived to be either wholly active—one takes it, one avoids it—or wholly passive—one fails to exercise precaution or take advantage of a risk-taking opportunity—rather than an engagement undertaken in the context of complex socio-politico and economic structures.

While shielding corporate "risk-takers" from risk, the trend toward privatization exposes most others to increased risk and vulnerability. Maurizio Lazzarato proffers the example of "workfare" or "welfare-to-work" programs as an instance of increased risk:

> Contemporary policies regarding employment, for example 'workfare', which forces those in receipt of assistance to work, are policies that introduce degrees of insecurity, instability, uncertainty, economic and existential precarity into the lives of individuals. They make insecure both individual lives and their relation to the institutions that used to protect them. It is not the same insecurity for everyone whatever the level and conditions of employment, yet a differential of fear runs along the whole continuum. (Lazzarato 2009, 119–120)

The production of increased insecurity for welfare recipients exacerbates the precarity of their position. Here we see an extension of Foucault's notion of discipline as maximizing submission and obedience while developing capacities and efficiency. If welfare recipients are inadequately entrepreneurial subjects, "workfare" compels them shift to an entrepreneurial mode of self-relation by making benefits contingent upon work or self-'improvement' of some sort. Thus, insecurity precipitates concession to self-management in line with neoliberal norms; it produces docile but capable bodies. The insecurity that stems from the risk of losing one's benefits is one particular kind on the continuum of fear to which Lazzarato refers. More generally, the omnipresent danger in this economized frame of intelligibility is economic slowdown, loss of jobs, and diminishment of profits. Therefore, another point of insecurity in relation to this danger and the fear it provokes is the risk of being unemployable and the sense of inferiority such risk involves. To avoid such risk one must be employable and "[t]o be employable one must conduct oneself and have a lifestyle which is in harmony with the market" (Lazzarato 2009, 127). Yet, given that the demands of the market are unpredictable and continually changing, being a good-enough entrepreneurial subject entails constant awareness that one is never good enough and must also be increasing, maximizing, and developing one's capacities. Even for the most aspirational of entrepreneurial subjects, the danger that accompanies neoliberalism inculcates a sense of insecurity. One's sense of one's own vulnerability—experienced negatively as being at risk and susceptible to harm—is thus heightened, and the simultaneous individualization of and intensification of vulnerability prevents recognition of shared vulnerability.

Thus, the kind of preoccupation with risk that characterizes entrepreneurial subjectivity buttresses the reductively negative view of vulnerability. This relation to risk—one in which we manage it, or believe we manage it, by avoidance and precaution, and simultaneously by pursuing it—shapes our attitudes toward vulnerability and prevents vulnerability from becoming an ethical resource. For the entrepreneurial subject, vulnerability is coded as weakness and hence as something to avoid because it undermines rather than enhances human capital. Vulnerability is not a risk that "pays-off." Within our economized grid of intelligibility, it is merely a cost and rarely a benefit. By definition, entrepreneurial subjectivity is vulnerability-averse; an enterprise protects itself from conditions of vulnerability rather than seeking to avow, experience, or respond sensitively to them. The *modus operandi* of entrepreneurial subjectivity is control, both over the self and, as explored in the previous chapter, over the effects others may have on the self. Indeed, control of others can be a vehicle for achieving self-control; there can be no upheavals within the self if others fail to affect it in unpredictable ways or if those effects are denied. Entrepreneurial subjectivity thus masks the unavoidable vulnerability that characterizes life, covering it over with an illusory ideal of self-made individuality. By entrenching this solely negative view of and attitude of aversion to vulnerability, entrepreneurial subjectivity facilitates repudiation of responsibility for vulnerability both by fostering disavowal of vulnerability instead of reckoning with it as a fundamental condition we cannot evade and by devaluing those who are vulnerable to harm as deficient and weak.

AN EXEMPLARY CASE OF THE PERILS OF PRIVATIZATION: VULNERABILITY AND FOOD

As a concrete contemporary example of these ideas, I examine a particular domain recently understood as a site of heightened risk and vulnerability: food production and consumption. Myriad concerns about food—ranging from food safety and quality, food security, hunger, the ecological consequences of industrial food production, and the gendered social meanings of eating and cooking—make food a site of increased vulnerability. People may be vulnerable because of the poor quality of the food they eat, because of the pesticides used in the fields in which they work and on the food that they consume, in virtue of lack of access to food or adequate nutrition, and so on. When analyzing food-related vulnerabilities in this fashion, food is seen as a source of numerous risks that must be managed and/or averted.

How these risks are understood and responsibility for them is allocated illustrates how risk and vulnerability are privatized. Food related vulnerabilities and risks are commonly privatized even though these risks are widely dispersed and shared. Ensuring food safety, for instance, is regularly a burden placed on consumers rather than on the industries that produce potentially contaminated food products (Moss 2009). This shift in responsibility is attributed to the complexity of supply chains, which makes it increasingly difficult for producers to chart the sources of their ingredients and verify their safety; it is simply easier to transfer responsibility to consumers. Two additional examples, which I explore in more depth, demonstrate the consequences of privatizing responsibility: the 'obesity epidemic' and the use of agricultural chemicals.

Rising rates of obesity in the U.S. have provoked the worry that the population hovers on the edge of an 'obesity epidemic'—nearly 35% of the population is classified as 'obese,' having a BMI over 30—that is having and will have significant consequences for overall health, stretching the limits of an overburdened health care system and raising health care costs.[9] Thus, increasing attention is paid to responsibility for one's health, especially to the importance of a healthy diet for maintaining a 'normal' weight. This attention has taken the form of a flurry of anti-obesity campaigns and significant media focus on individual responsibility for health and diet. This attention, however, has focused on urging change in individuals' eating habits and levels of physical activity. Although some strides are being made in increasing access to healthy food,[10] structural impediments to healthy eating are neither widely acknowledged nor commonly taken into account in attempts to address the 'obesity epidemic' (see Patel 2007, 276). Personal health is regarded as a largely private matter notwithstanding widely disparate and inequitable access to healthy foods, and research that indicates that unhealthy junk food functions on the body in a quasi addictive way (see Kessler 2008). The reality of "food deserts" and the "grocery gap" may be acknowledged, but is not conceived by many as a legitimate obstacle to pursuing good health. Even Mark Bittman, a *New York Times* food writer who should know better, questions the complaint that healthy food is more expensive and thus inaccessible to those with lower incomes, titling a recent article "Is Junk Food Really Cheaper?" The increased risk of heart disease and Type II diabetes that accompanies a diet high in processed foods and sugar, fat, and salt (e.g., in soda, fast food, and processed foods) is thus attributed to personal choice and a failure to engage in the appropriate preventative activities. These particular vulnerabilities—ones we all share in virtue of being bodily beings—are privatized regardless of how they are constructed and exacerbated by social and economic conditions. Further, the privatization of responsibility preempts structural change: as Gottlieb and Joshi note concerning the privatization of anti-hunger work, "middle-class participation in antihunger acts of charity and volunteering were seen as an alternative for a targeted policy and political change" and "helped reduce the explosiveness of a core food justice issue—the failure of the system to provide food for all" (2010, 95). By construing both healthy diets and the provision of food to those in need as private matters the extent to which this vulnerability is shared, yet differentially experienced given social conditions, remains obscured. The individual who requires assistance in accessing food is "portrayed as victim and often stigmatized" while the individual who consumes unhealthy food is portrayed as unable to take responsibility for herself (ibid). If these problems are regarded as the result of a crisis in personal responsibility, then the entrepreneurial subject can sit in judgment or provide help, and furthermore can remain convinced that her healthy habits are a product of her free choice (rather than, say, made possible by the family and social circle with which she grew up, the media she consumed, the places she lived and their proximity to supermarkets, farmers markets, parks and recreation areas, and so on).

Moreover, the obese person is an easy target given the deeper significance of social norms concerning physical appearance and fitness. As Raj Patel points out, "[w]e are encouraged to understand obesity to be . . . an individual failing, an inability to deal with the farrago of choices offered to us, a deficit of impulse control" (2007, 273). The physical appearance, size, and shape of the body are continual sources of complex meaning. As Susan Bordo indicates, bodies are read for what they reveal about both social status and position, and moral character. In a socioeconomic context that valorizes control and masterful competence, a firm, taut, slender body is desired not just because it is deemed aesthetically appealing, but because it is interpreted as a sign of corresponding internal qualities such as the ability to manage oneself and control desires (Bordo 2003). Conversely, an overweight body is interpreted to signify the absence of those qualities: the wiggles, jiggles, and very fleshiness of our flesh are symbols of our failure to manage ourselves and exercise personal responsibility, of moral inadequacy. So, from the standpoint of an entrepreneurial subject, such moral condemnation of those who are overweight is the logical flipside of the praise and self-enhancement of those who properly manage their health; the obese are those in contrast with whom the 'healthy' define themselves and obesity operates as an ever-present, ever-increasing danger that spurs continued self-management. In addition to obstructing necessary structural change, the privatizing attitude of the entrepreneurial subject renders those who are overweight more vulnerable to ill health: dissatisfaction with one's body and weight is more positively correlated with ill health, both mental and physical, than is one's weight itself (Meunnig et al. 2008). The privatizing response isolates those who are overweight, labels them unhealthy, and deems them irresponsible for failing to improve their health through weight loss. Such a response is stigmatizing and shame inducing, and thus more likely to exacerbate health problems than to induce healthy behavior. The failure to grasp shared vulnerability leads only to an increase in the differential and inequitable experience of negative forms of vulnerability like mental and physical health problems.

Another arena of significant vulnerability and risk with respect to food is the use of agricultural chemicals. Accordingly, the rhetoric and practice of privatization is also found in the dominant response to increasing public knowledge of the detrimental effects of pesticides on human health. Many common agricultural pesticides are recognized carcinogens, and are linked to severe birth defects and other reproductive issues such as sterility. Direct exposure to these chemicals can cause pesticide poisoning, resulting in dizziness, nausea, difficulty breathing, and asthma. Long-term effects of exposure—direct and indirect—have not been studied systematically but potentially include neurodegeneration that leads to Parkinson's disease (Gottlieb and Joshi 2010, 26). Nonetheless, there is little to no momentum to enact a ban or even limit the use of such chemicals. Indeed, since the Kyoto protocol required the phase-out of methyl bromide—a particularly toxic soil fumigant used on tomatoes and strawberries—because of its effects on the ozone, methyl iodide, a chemical recognized to be even more toxic (it is used to create cancer cells in laboratories), is slated to replace it (Estabrook 2011). Avoiding exposure to pesticides, however, is primarily viewed as a matter of choice and broader change is thought to be best achieved through individuals' consumer choices.[11] Ultimately, this choice boils down to whether or not one wants to purchase and eat organic produce.[12] As with food safety, the burden of responsibility is placed on the consumer, yet in this case the consumer can pride herself on being knowledgeable and conscientious in her food choices and in exercising proper precaution. Vulnerabilities, therefore, are seen as private rather than shared—of concern is *my* exposure to pesticides—and responsibility for them as a route both to moral/social worth and to control over the effect one's environment has on oneself. Ignored in this response are those most susceptible to pesticide poisoning: farm workers who suffer the consequences of unenforced and inadequate regulation, and woeful negligence in compliance with safety measures in the fields. By privatizing risk and concerning myself with only my and my family's vulnerability, the widespread and systemic nature of the vulnerability is ignored. Moreover, the aim of some measure of control continues to be an illusion so long as responsibility is privatized. The simple fact is that as long as they are in use, exposure to pesticides cannot be controlled, even by the most cautious of entrepreneurial subjects. Overuse of pesticides contaminates ground water; pesticide drift from fields sickens those far from the fields (for instance, schoolchildren and teachers in Sarasota, parishioners at a church near Miami) (Estabrook 2011); and insects develop genetic resistances to the chemicals, requiring heavier application and the development of new concoctions (Kingsolver 2007, 164–165). The privatization of risks related to pesticide use enables some—select privileged consumers—to feel as if they are taking control of their lives and managing their health by making 'good' food choices. Yet, at the same time it precludes recognition of the effects of increasing and excessive pesticide use on all eaters (including those who cannot access or afford organic produce), on the workers who toil in immediate proximity to the chemicals, on the wild animals exposed during spraying, on the water system, and on ecosystems as wholes.

At issue in both of these examples is a particular but common conception of health, one that rests upon faulty assumptions. As they pertain to health, food choices are regarded as private choices that affect only the individual who makes them and thus are properly that individual's responsibility. This logic presupposes that individuals exercise direct control over their choices (that is, their choices are not constrained in systemic ways), that there is a direct causal connection between their choices and their health, and that the *only* significant or relevant impact of their choices is the impact those choices have on them. Accordingly, health is conceived as a state of an individual, one that entrepreneurial subjects ought to maintain and over which they can exercise control.[13] As Carole Counihan's study of college students' perspectives on eating shows, control is a focal point of entrepreneurial attitudes toward food and health: the students "are most concerned not with the food itself but rather with their behavior toward it . . . In the United States eating properly promotes individualism and personal power" (1999, 118, 121). The aforementioned examples indicate, however, that these presumptions about control and choice, the picture of health as an individual achievement, and the discourse of privatization with which they are intertwined rest on faulty ontological assumptions. These assumptions include the "prejudices" mentioned in the previous chapter, including that of conventional dualisms, which separate humans from the natural world and sanction mastery of it, and the image of the self as discrete, isolated individual chooser. As such they comprise a deep and pervasive ignorance of the nature of the self and the self's relationship to others, and thus of how one's actions are integrated into and compose a system that effects others. Just as in the example of summiteering, in contemporary discussions of food, eating, and health, control and management of one's desires, one's body, and one's environment are prized as a means for developing an invulnerable self.

CONCLUSION

In light of the concerns of this project, part of what makes this perspective on these cases particularly pernicious is the way they reduce vulnerability to its negative valence. Although the issues surrounding food production and consumption reveal the significant risk and vulnerability to harm inherent in our food system, there are real limitations in considering these issues in this way alone. Food is not merely a site of private moral and social choice but rather something that necessarily and unavoidably links us to one another and to our natural environment. For instance, though food choices have social and moral significance, they have these significances because of the cultural accrual of meaning around different dietary habits. The simple fact that a particular choice about food says something about one's disposition, character, and self—for instance, that choosing organic and eating fresh produce indicates that one cares about one's health, among other things—reveals that our choices are always made within a social context that shapes them. Food is one way we occupy a shared social world rather than existing as isolated choosers whose choices have little effect on anyone but ourselves. Beyond the social significance of eating, however, the nexus of relationships that comprise systems of production, distribution, marketing, and consumption also unavoidably link us to others and to the environment. As Val Plumwood demonstrates, ignoring these relationships and our participation in them results in a "denied dependency," whereby the dependency of the dominant party on the subordinate party—humans on natural systems, some humans (consumers) on others (workers), humans on animals—is denied in order to maintain the veneer of self-determination and control for the former (1993). Recognizing the extent of our dependency entails thinking more "ecologically" with awareness of how we are located within systems of relationships to which we contribute and which necessarily affect us (Code 2006).

If the example of food can call our attention to how our lives (and our very ability to persist in life) are intertwined with the lives of others and with natural systems, it also demonstrates that this interdependency and vulnerability is fundamentally ambiguous rather than inherently negative. As with the methods of food production that are currently dominant, vulnerability can mean harm: ill health due to poor diet, pesticide application that imperils workers' safety, and deterioration of soil quality. Yet, food also highlights the way vulnerability is fundamental, an unavoidable feature of life, a shared openness to affecting and being affected. As such, food also represents a site where vulnerability has not only a negative but also a positive meaning, where it can lead not just to harm but also to community and connection. A positive dimension of vulnerability is found in sensation and memory: in taste, touch, and smell we are affected by food in ways that we cannot conceive of doing without, and the intertwining of eating, special events, and history incorporates food into meaningful memories.

As I have sought to demonstrate, the equation of vulnerability with susceptibility to harm is a necessary move in the privatization of responsibility. The view that vulnerability is negative, coded as weakness and susceptibility to harm, is enshrined in entrepreneurial subjectivity. It is, de facto, a privatizing view of vulnerability because it breeds worry about dangers and risks, leading to a narrow focus on one's own precautionary activities and on cultivating a successful, healthy self. Because it functions as the basis for entrepreneurial subjectivity, this reductively negative view of vulnerability is also the basis for repudiation of responsibility for vulnerable others. Such a view of vulnerability entails that processes of food production and consumption are just occasions for potential harm, and so the target of techniques of management and control. Because the reductively negative view of vulnerability undergirds entrepreneurial subjectivity, emphasizing the positive dimensions of vulnerability—that is, the positive dimensions of our ability to affect one another and be affected—is one way to loosen the hold of entrepreneurial subjectivity. Emphasizing the positive valence of vulnerability is not intended to make vulnerability something easier to deal with since its ethical salience lies precisely in its difficulty and complexity, but rather to remedy a one-sided picture of an experience and condition that defines life. This emphasis counteracts the attitudes and assumptions of entrepreneurial subjectivity in a few ways. First, it diffuses the ethos of fear and wariness that accompanies the constant perception of danger and risk, and so breaks with the precautionary, calculative disposition that defines entrepreneurial subjectivity; the notion of epistemic vulnerability proposed at the close of the previous chapter encapsulates this aspect of the positive dimensions of vulnerability. Second, articulating the positive dimensions of vulnerability challenges the stereotypical view of 'the vulnerable' as lacking agency, which as we have seen is a significant worry about the language of vulnerability; it thus challenges the passive/active, weak/strong, pathetic/admirable, dependent/independent dichotomies upon which entrepreneurial subjects rely for their self-definition. Third, by reinterpreting vulnerability not as something that must be averted but as something multivalent and ambiguous, it can be felt as an experience that holds promise and potential rather than just probability of harm. In the next chapter, I expand on this view of vulnerability that I only mention here, developing a view of vulnerability that explicitly articulates the ambivalence of the concept.

In order to enable the assumption of responsibility for the perilous vulnerabilities, the positive dimensions of vulnerability cannot be limited to instances of individual sensation and memory, but must be expanded to include connections to land and plants, relationships of acknowledged and mutual dependency with those who grow our food, and effective community organization. As global food justice movements show, food is also a vital rallying point for pursuing "food sovereignty" in the face of the commodification of food, forging new community ties, and developing or regaining important agricultural and culinary knowledge, all of which are premised upon the reality of our interconnectedness and our ability to affect one another (our vulnerability). The interlocking systems of relations that make up our food systems thus offer a unique venue for disputing erroneous privatizing ideas about risk, responsibility, and vulnerability in favor of communally oriented ones that speak to how food connects us and demands shared responsibility.

Overall, therefore, entrepreneurial subjectivity, and the privatization of risk and responsibility that accompany it, presents an ethic of vulnerability with four distinct but interrelated challenges. This way of relating to risk and vulnerability leads us to become subjects who (1) have difficulty understanding ourselves as vulnerable (we'd prefer both to think and to make ourselves invulnerable), and (2) have difficulty understanding ourselves as participating in the social structures that create vulnerabilities (we'd prefer to privatize our activities, making them seem the pure results of our own effort, and ignore how our individual actions aggregate and therefore contribute to social problems). As a consequence, the prevalence of entrepreneurial attitudes produces (3) an unwillingness to share responsibility for vulnerable others and, underlying the three aforementioned problems, (4) an inability to conceive ourselves as sharing in a common vulnerability. In relation to these obstacles, an ethic of vulnerability must not merely stipulate responsibilities but further must seek to lay the ground for assuming those responsibilities. As I argued in relation to Butler's work in Chapter Two, an ethic of vulnerability must be a critical ethic that exposes the functioning of the norms surrounding vulnerability, especially those that favor invulnerability, control, and privatization. A key part of challenging entrepreneurial subjectivity is accounting for its appeal, as I have tried to do here. In a socio-politico-economic context in which dangers and risks are perceived as omnipresent, an entrepreneurial form of subjectivity is compelling because it promises control of ever-proliferating uncertainties by way of self-management and self-enhancement. It does so, however, at a price: increased capacity is accompanied by increased submission, and depends upon a faulty and inequitable form of individualism and privatization. We can only break with dominant ways of living, however, if we understand how they maintain their dominance and venture to offer alternatives that fulfill similar needs and desires in more ethically sound ways. The need for security, for instance, is a valid need, yet the means for attaining it need not entail fabricating perpetual insecurity or rendering the lives of others more precarious as one pursues personal invulnerability. We would do well instead to ask whether security and vulnerability are truly incompatible, and what forms a security compatible with vulnerability might take.

Thus, an ethic of vulnerability is one of targeted resistance, countering entrepreneurial forms of subjectivity as a way to resist the increasing privatization of vulnerability and responsibility, and revealing the reality of shared vulnerability that is belied by the rhetoric of privatization. A central part of this ethical critique, I have maintained, is rethinking how we talk and think about vulnerability so as to express its complexity and break with the reductive intuitions that construe it as something one must necessarily avoid. The next chapter develops just such a conception of vulnerability, an alternative vision of what it is involved in our basic capacity to affect and be affected by one another that can operate in the place of the reductively negative understanding.

NOTES

1. For this reason Ulrich Beck claims that our contemporary "world risk society" is ironic: "the irony of risk" is that "rationality . . . encourages anticipation of the wrong kind of risk, the one we believe we can calculate and control, whereas the disaster arises from what we do not know and cannot calculate" (Beck 2006, 330).
2. The difference between delinquency and illegality is that the prison produces delinquency (1995, 266) in various forms that are useful in distinct ways (1995, 272). Other forms of illegality are sanctioned and allowed to persist, not named and treated as "delinquency" (1995, 277, 279).
3. We might compare the figure of the delinquent to the figure of the 'terrorist' as contemporarily depicted; 'terrorists' occupy a similar rhetorical position but are also imagined as imminent threats that are not controlled and remain unknown, sanctioning covert and extensive surveillance and discipline of the population in general.

4. Foucault hypothesizes that this mode of power is quite different from disciplinary power, stating "... what appears on the horizon of this kind of analysis is not at all the ideal or project of an exhaustively disciplinary society in which the legal network hemming in individuals is taken over and extended internally by, let's say, normative mechanisms" (2008, 259; cf. 252–253). I part ways with Foucault on this point and seek instead to demonstrate the continuity between disciplinary power and neoliberal biopolitics.
5. Foucault himself dissents from this position, stating "... what appears on the horizon of this kind of analysis is not at all the ideal or project of an exhaustively disciplinary society in which the legal network hemming in individuals is taken over and extended internally by, let's say, normative mechanisms" (2008, 259). He regards neoliberalism as multiplying difference rather than enforcing conformity. How one interprets neoliberal power hinges on what is meant by conformity. Conformity need not entail homogeneity, or take the form of rigid normalization and exclusion of those who cannot be normalized as Foucault describes it (see 2008, 252–253). As I demonstrate throughout the remainder of the chapter, the norms in relation to which self-discipline is undertaken can be embodied in a multiplicity of ways yet this diversity does not alter the way in which, say, economic norms dominate social life, spurring particular modes of self-relation; there is, thus, conformity to a generally economized mode of self-understanding. See also McNay's characterization of this form of power as "profoundly normalizing" (2009, 64).
6. The sociology of risk includes two additional approaches with different foci: (1) a cultural-symbolic approach epitomized by the work of Mary Douglas maintains that risk is not an objective feature of the world but is culturally and symbolically framed; (2) the "risk-society" approach advanced by Ulrich Beck and Anthony Giddens considers how risk is increasingly a defining and dominant feature of global society. For an overview of these approaches see Lupton 1999, 1–11.
7. See Ewald 2002 for an analysis of three distinct approaches to uncertainty and risk: providence, prevention, and precaution.
8. For elaboratio of this idea see Lazzarato 2009, 124.
9. See Gottlieb and Joshi 2010, 65 for a critique of the terminology of 'epidemic' in relation to obesity. For a summary of the changes in obesity rates see the National Institutes of Health report: win.niddk.nih.gov/publications/PDFs/stat904z.pdf
10. Such as the Fresh Fruit and Vegetable Program, which was initiated as a pilot program in the 2002 Farm Bill and subsequently expanded. A full (all 50 states) version of the program could be funded in the future versions of the Farm Bill. Likewise, the expansion of the food stamp program (SNAP) to allow use at farmers markets aims to increase access to and consumption of fresh fruits and vegetables.
11. For an analysis of the way food politics and activism is itself a site of neoliberal engagement with a focus on individualism see Roff 2007.
12. Increasing numbers of consumers have turned to organic produce. 12% of the fruits and vegetables sold in the U.S. were organic. According to a 2010 Nielsen poll, over half of those choosing organic fruits and vegetables do so in order to avoid exposure to pesticide residue. See http://www.usatoday.com/news/health/story/2012-09-03/organic-food-health/57557912/1
13. An alternative picture would be the view of health as a matter of healthy relationships or being part of a healthy system (Pollan 2008), which serves as a counterpoint to the reductive individualist conception of health.

Part III
Rethinking Vulnerability

5 Vulnerability Beyond Opposition

Common experiences of vulnerability such as being in a foreign country, speaking in class, or being in love—just a few of the examples offered by my students—highlight one of the central challenges of vulnerability: that it is an experience born of discomfort with the unfamiliar, the uncontrolled, or the unpredictable and yet only through muddling about in this experience do we learn, change, and extend ourselves beyond our current limits. These examples neatly indicate why vulnerability presents us with such difficulty and generates such ambivalent responses: vulnerability is not, essentially, about suffering as MacIntyre's otherwise astute work suggests, nor is it, as I have taken pains to emphasize, merely a way of being susceptible to harm. The association of vulnerability with ideas of dispossession and exposure, however, indicates something vital about its meaning and significance: vulnerability is defined by openness and affectivity, and such openness entails the inability to predict, control, and fully know that to which we are open and how it will affect us. That kernel of the unpredictable, uncontrollable, and unknown can prompt in us alteration that is likewise unpredictable, uncontrollable, and unknown. In the previous chapters, I maintained that entrepreneurial subjectivity and the ideal of invulnerability effectively function as a facade, covering over the reality of vulnerability. The view of vulnerability that I have called a reductively negative understanding does likewise: by conceiving vulnerability as susceptibility to harm, weakness, passivity, and incapacity, we mask the ambiguous core of vulnerability and the potential it presents. Understanding vulnerability in this way has clear implications: we make it an object of fear and aversion, and in so doing, eschew not only affinity with those we socially stigmatize as 'vulnerable' but also the ways being vulnerable might affect us.

The viability of an ethic of vulnerability thus depends on what kind of conception of vulnerability it presupposes or expressly endorses. An ethic of vulnerability that retains a reductively negative understanding of what it means to be vulnerable will remain rooted in dichotomous categorizations of who needs and merits protection, who is suited to offering protection, whose existence is pervaded by risk, and whose is defined by the ability to assume risk. That is, it will fail to account for the complexities of both experiences of vulnerability and the nature of the relationship between vulnerability and responsibility. If, as I have contended, a negative understanding of vulnerability is both inadequate and ethically suspect, then an ethic of vulnerability requires an understanding of vulnerability that moves beyond this reductive view.

The task of elaborating a concept of vulnerability is a crucial one. If vulnerability does lie at the core of our ethical and political crises, at the core of subjectivity itself, then how we think and talk about it matters. If we are to respond well to vulnerability, then it is incumbent upon us to reflect on what we mean when we speak of vulnerability and to formulate a more developed account of the concept, namely one that does not rely upon uninterrogated presuppositions linking vulnerability with harm, affliction, and weakness, and thus opposing it to strength, agency, and ability. Such traditional and entrenched dualisms do little to reveal the nature of experiences of vulnerability or to enable us to comprehend the ethical difficulties surrounding it and disavowals attending it. If we are to reckon with vulnerability, we must also reckon with the cultural baggage with which the notion is laden. For instance, we must reject the idea that vulnerability is simply passivity. Vulnerability is not merely a way of being acted upon, and, moreover, such a conception of passivity is limited and reductive. Further, the association between passivity and vulnerability has implications for how we feel, act, and respond when we experience what we call vulnerability as well as for whether we understand a given experience to be one in which we are vulnerable at all.

The first two chapters explored the accounts of an ethic of vulnerability offered by MacIntyre, Goodin, and Butler, highlighting how vulnerability can operate as an impetus for ethical response in a variety of ways. Although none directly endorse the reductively negative view of vulnerability, I have suggested that it is present in their accounts as a non-logical implication. The assumption that vulnerability just is susceptibility to harm is central to both MacIntyre and Goodin's ethics, and its undercurrent runs through Butler's work given her focus on the tie between vulnerability and violence. In their work, however, we can discern core features of an ethic of vulnerability. Whereas Goodin's account focuses on the way vulnerability generates proportionate responsibility and MacIntyre advances a theory of the virtues that are needed in light of the recognition of pervasive vulnerability as a central feature of human existence, Butler elaborates a nuanced relationship between experiences of vulnerability and ethical response. An ethic of vulnerability thus has at least two dimensions that are emphasized to varying degrees: on the one hand, recognizing vulnerability as a fundamental and unavoidable feature of life necessitates more extensive responsibility for and responsiveness to others who are especially vulnerable; on the other hand, such ethical responsiveness is elicited through experiences of vulnerability and a process of reckoning with and/or assuming one's own vulnerability. For both MacIntyre and Butler, reckoning with vulnerability and becoming responsive to vulnerable others entails recognizing the extent to which vulnerability is a shared rather than exceptional state. Both of these facets of an ethic of vulnerability call for an alternative conception of vulnerability.

The criticisms of the concept of vulnerability discussed in the first chapter clearly delineate specific concerns that any alternative understanding of vulnerability must take into account. It must presume neither the fixity, homogeneity, or negativity of conditions of vulnerability, nor a hierarchical or inequitable distribution of vulnerability. These are the presumptions that generate patronizing, oppressive, paternalistic and controlling, and stigmatizing and exclusionary dispositions and treatment of others. In contrast, I contend that a viable understanding of vulnerability is one that breaks with oppositional, dualist thought by conceiving vulnerability in terms of potentiality (rather than fixity), ambiguity and ambivalence (rather than negativity), univocity (rather than inequitable distribution and hierarchy), and a diversity of manifestations (rather than homogeneity). These four shifts ameliorate the problems of a reductively negative conception of vulnerability both because they generate a more encompassing view of the experience of vulnerability and because they avoid making assumptions that facilitate the problematic avoidance of vulnerability and responsibility.

In the next sections I articulate the contours of an alternative understanding of vulnerability by drawing on conceptual resources found in the work of twentieth century French philosophers Maurice Merleau-Ponty, Gilles Deleuze, and Hélène Cixous. Although these thinkers are typically affiliated with distinct traditions in Continental European thought—phenomenology, post-structuralism, and deconstructive feminism, respectively—they are joined by concern for questions of difference, the formative nature of relations, and the constitutive openness that is the condition of such affective relations. In the first section, I seek to problematize one core opposition that characterizes our implicit conception of vulnerability—that between activity and passivity—and develop the idea that vulnerability is more fundamentally a form of openness than a form of passivity as it is conventionally understood. I find the basis for such a view of vulnerability in Merleau-Ponty's later ontology. The second section elaborates the four aforementioned features of a concept of vulnerability—univocity, potentiality, ambiguity and ambivalence, and heterogeneity—as well as returning to the proposal made in the first chapter for a distinction between "ontological" and "situational" vulnerability. I provide a theoretical account of an ontological concept of vulnerability with reference to core elements of Deleuze's philosophy of difference, and utilize this account to respond to central problems that stem from the reductively negative conception of vulnerability. Lastly, in the third section, I take up Cixous' expression of the idea that vulnerability is a virtue of sorts, one enabled by a "feminine economy" that departs from models of exchange that reduce difference to sameness, in order to explore the relationship between ontological vulnerability and specific, situational instances of vulnerability.

OPENNESS TO THE WORLD: RETHINKING PASSIVITY WITH MERLEAU-PONTY

According to the criticisms previously outlined, vulnerability is a concept of questionable value for ethics and public policy because it connotes passivity and weakness, and, as demonstrated in the foregoing chapters, thus is understood in ways that are conducive to varying degrees of oppressive treatment. Moreover, if our idea of vulnerability is defined by experiences of violence and infringement, it remains within the same dualist paradigm. These are experiences in which one is a recipient, the one who is acted upon, thus conceiving vulnerability predominantly in this way supports the idea that to be vulnerable is to be passive, *subject to* something. Here I propose that Merleau-Ponty's account of the structure of the flesh in *The Visible and the Invisible* provides a twofold rejoinder to this criticism by rethinking the relationship between activity and passivity (through the structure of reversibility) and by reconceiving passivity in particular (in terms of the receptive relationship between self, others, and the world). In what follows, I characterize Merleau-Ponty's ontology of the flesh, which Ann Murphy describes as "an ontology of passivity[,]" as one of 'openness' (2010, 444). I elaborate core features of this ontology with an emphasis on how they lend themselves to such rethinking. In order to begin to define vulnerability in terms of openness, I structure this explication in terms of a number of different forms that such openness takes in Merleau-Ponty's work.

The notion of openness that I seek to foreground finds its most prominent and central expression in Merleau-Ponty's view that our most basic relationship to the world must be described "simply as openness" (1968, 99/133). As perceptual beings, because we are continually engaged in interchanges with other bodies we are able to perceive, think, imagine, and feel. Indeed, what we are most fundamentally are openings to such interchanges. That is, our perceptual nature is defined and made possible by such openness, which is simply the porosity, impressionability, and receptivity of bodies. In this way openness to the world is a primordial and constitutive form of relationship; it is the condition of perception itself. The "openness upon the world" of which Merleau-Ponty writes is "a more muted relationship with the world" than our conscious, intentional attitudes and modes of engagement, and is so because it serves as their backdrop and necessary condition (1968, 35/56). For this reason, however, it is a mode of being that is ignored and taken for granted throughout the history of philosophy; because it is a background condition, the openness that defines vulnerability is overlooked.

If openness is a constitutive form of relationship, then it is also defined by continuity. From an ontological perspective, it is not the case that openness is greater or lesser, that one can be more or less open to the world in which one is immersed. On Merleau-Ponty's account, the flesh of my body is continuous with the flesh of others' bodies and the flesh of the material world in which I am located.¹ I am not homogeneous with the world in the sense that I am the same as it, but rather in the sense that I am of it, a part of it that cannot be extricated. This continuity of flesh—mine, others', nature's, that of objects and artifacts—composes the necessary condition of perception: "The visible can thus fill me and occupy me only because I who see it do not see it from the depths of nothingness, but from the midst of itself; I the seer am also visible" (1968, 113/150). Being of and in the midst of the visible world—being continuous with the world, of a piece with it—makes it available to me and enables my perception of dimensions of it, and makes me available to the others of my world. The chiasmatic structure of flesh is defined by a reversibility by which I am both seer and seen, sentient and sensible. Such reversibility is possible precisely because I am not detachable from what I see, touch, hear, etc.—a subject set apart from the world of objects—but am always a variable and impressionable part of it. Thus, experience is characterized not by an ability to receive impressions from and process the world, but rather by the way in which the world encroaches upon us. The relationship we have to our milieu is one of mutual imbrication. We are within it, it is within us: ". . . we are sensible-sentients . . ., insofar as we are within life, within the human being and within Being, and insofar as it is in us as well . . ." (Merleau-Ponty 1968, 116/154).

This idea of the continuity of flesh introduces a central point about the nature of passivity. The fact that perception requires that the perceiver be in the midst of that which she perceives shifts our understanding of the dynamics of experience. I am able to experience visible things in their depth and density "insofar as I am among them and insofar as *they communicate through me* as a sentient thing" (Merleau-Ponty 1968, 114/151, emphasis added). It is not simply that I can be alternately either seer or seen, that which is sensed or that which does the sensing, but further that my capacity for sensing demands that I can let the things I sense speak through me. Thus, my passivity and receptivity are integral to my sentient being, and are not simply dimensions of my sensible being. Passivity characterizes my active capacity for sensing as well as my capacity for being sensed. Thus, when Merleau-Ponty notes, ". . . he who sees cannot possess the visible *unless he is possessed by it*, unless he *is of it*," what he implies is not just that we must be sensible-sentients in order to perceive but further that we must find ourselves possessed by the world, receptively passive through and through, in order to perceive (1968, 134–135/175, first emphasis added).

Even as openness to the world involves continuity with the world, it is also characterized as distance. Thus, continuity is necessarily paired with distance, which takes varying forms (within the self, between self and world, between self and an other, between the things of the world) but is often described in terms of gaps, divergences, noncoincidence, and dehiscence.² As perceivers, we are continuous but not coincident with the things of world that we perceive. Only in virtue of our noncoincidence with or distance from the things of our world can they "communicate through us" and "possess us." Likewise, the reversibility that defines our experience requires a gap between touching and touched: "My left hand is always on the verge of touching my right hand touching the things, but I never reach coincidence" (Merleau-Ponty 1968, 147/191). The gap between touching and being touched is what makes manifest their overlap and partial coincidence, their intertwining. A total coincidence of the components of this experience, conversely, would preclude overlap. So, being in the midst of the world means being partially coincident with the things of it, being part of a system of intertwined relationships only segments of which are accessible to me. Thus, distance is integral to the aforementioned receptive passivity and, in this way, distance makes continuity and proximity possible: proximity, Merleau-Ponty says, is only found "through distance" (1968, 128/168).

> Consequently, the opening onto the world involves a relational ontology:[3]
> ... what merits the name being ... [is] the system of perspectives that open into it, ... at the intersection of my views and at the intersection of my views with those of the others, at the intersection of my acts and at the intersection of my acts with those of the others, [which] makes the sensible world and the historical world be always interworld [*intermonde*], since they are what, beyond our views, renders them interdependent among themselves and interdependent with those of the others... (Merleau-Ponty 1968, 84/114)

In being constitutively open to the world, we are constitutively and necessarily interdependent with others and so find ourselves defined by "essential relations of dependency" (1968, 12/28). By being defined relationally, by finding myself composed in relation to a world and others, "I am a field of experiences" within a broader "system of perspectives" and relationships (110/147). The key point here is that the constitutive openness of our bodies introduce us into spaces and temporalities—an "interworld"—that are shared in common because of the intertwining of the relationships that compose them. The interdependency of which Merleau-Ponty writes is a consequence of the overlapping made possible by distance. Any ontology of relations depends on distance, the gaps between things that make possible relation rather than coincidence. From the perspective of a relational ontology, Merleau-Ponty can characterize the body as a field of experience and "our living bond with nature" (27/46) rather than a particular kind of physical object. The body is the capacity for experience, for myriad connections to and relations with other bodies and the world, all of which define the openness it shares with the world.

These four points about openness to the world—that it is (1) constitutive of our ability to experience, (2) continuous and shared, (3) defined by distance and divergence, and (4) both the basis for and form of constitutive relations—enable a rethinking of the nature of passivity. The emphasis on the constitutive nature of passivity shifts our attention from its conventional focus, the activity of the constituted subject, to the way in which passivity lies at the basis of such activity. The formative nature of passivity is expressed in the idea that "my body does not perceive, but it is as if it were built around the perception that dawns through it" (Merleau-Ponty 1968, 9/24). Perception must "dawn through" the body in order for the body to accumulate memory and meaning. Although Merleau-Ponty's phrasing often seems to juxtapose passivity to activity, this juxtaposition serves not to entrench an oppositional view of activity and passivity but rather to displace the *de facto* privilege of activity. Perception "dawns through" the body rather than the body being the agent of perception not because Merleau-Ponty aims simply to reverse the opposition (between an active perceiver and a passively perceived world) by regarding the body as passive and the world as active, impressing upon the body, but because he aims to challenge the default view in which the subject actively perceives isolated, passive objects. This shift in focus is accompanied by a corresponding shift in the sense of passivity. In particular, the body's openness to the world calls our attention to the way in which passivity is receptive rather than just a way of being impressed upon. Passivity is not just 'being done to' but a way of 'taking in.' Moreover, the sense of activity is likewise revised since activity is not dualistically defined as action upon passive objects. On Merleau-Ponty's view, our openness to and in the midst of the world is such that activity and passivity intertwine. So, receptive passivity is necessary for the formation of the self and experience, and as such it is the locus of capacity and activity. As Kelly Oliver notes, "For Merleau-Ponty, we are connected to, and part of, our environment, not in a mechanical way but rather as a dynamic receptivity or responsiveness . . . [which] is our capacity for living in the world" (2004, 109). Passivity, therefore, is not a mode of weakness or even just susceptibility to the impressions coming from the world and others. Rather, it is an opening and a capacity for taking in, intertwining with, and connecting with other bodies. Moreover, this capacity is not one that belongs to the individual body but rather is emergent in relations between bodies. It cannot be said to be 'mine' in the sense of being the property of my body nor can I be said to be the author or creator of it given the "essential relations of dependency" that form me. Things communicate through me and I am possessed by them, and in being possessed I am able to interact. On this understanding, the dualistic line drawn between passivity and activity is blurred. Instead, " . . . my activity is identically passivity . . . so that the seer and the visible reciprocate one another and we no longer know which sees and which is seen" (Merleau-Ponty 1968, 139/181).

My aim in discussing these different dimensions of openness has been to indicate how vulnerability might be rethought in a way that preserves its essential meaning—openness to affectation—but does not presuppose a particular negative view of what it means to be vulnerable ("weak, passive, and pathetic"). From the perspective of Merleau-Ponty's ontology of the flesh in *The Visible and the Invisible,* vulnerability can be conceived as a specific, fundamental mode of passivity, which can be thought in terms of receptivity rather than simply as susceptibility. A secondary aim is to suggest that Merleau-Ponty's critical analysis can be used to challenge the ontology that underlies the problematic values associated with a dualistic view of vulnerability: i.e., the traditional liberal and neoliberal values that elevate independence, self-sufficiency, and mastery while devaluing connectedness, interdependence, and the absence of control. Merleau-Ponty's critique of surveying thought refutes not only the epistemic position it involves, that of a spectator, but also the ontology it presupposes in which subjects are detached from the objects and others that make up the world, and so can either know them from the distance of a spectator or, through this same distance, can completely coincide with, and thus master, them. This same ontology is presupposed when we regard vulnerability as antithetical to being capable, developed, and self-sufficient.

VULNERABILITY AS AN ONTOLOGICAL CONCEPT: RESOURCES FROM DELEUZE'S PHILOSOPHY OF DIFFERENCE

At the close of the first section, I proposed that a concept of vulnerability that did not fall into the pitfalls of the negative view would begin by understanding vulnerability in terms of potentiality rather than fixity, univocity rather than inequitable distribution and hierarchy, a diversity of manifestations rather than homogeneity, and ambiguity and ambivalence rather than negativity. These four dimensions of a concept of vulnerability have been foreshadowed by the emphasis on both continuity and difference in the Merleau-Pontian conceptualization of openness, and by Butler's characterization of precariousness as a shared, common feature of life. Here I elaborate the significance of these particular features and, in particular, explore how they comprise an ontological concept of vulnerability. This discussion draws resources for reconceptualizing vulnerability from the thought of French philosopher Gilles Deleuze, whose work on topics such as difference, affectivity, and becoming is rich and complex, and is conducive to understanding vulnerability as a fundamental openness to alteration.

In a somewhat confusing fashion, the term vulnerability is colloquially used to refer both to a possible state and to a particular type of reality; as a possible state, it is one in which one is susceptible to something else but this something else has not yet taken place and may not even occur (for instance, women are said to be vulnerable to sexual assault but such assault is just a possibility). Since the 'something else' need not happen for one to be vulnerable, the condition and experience of vulnerability is real and significant in its own way. Thus, vulnerability is real as a form of potential. Deleuze's understanding of potentiality can help us clarify the implications of these different senses of vulnerability and determine in what way we can regard it as a condition of potential.

In developing his concept of virtuality, Deleuze offers a criticism of the standard conception of possibility. His aim is to distinguish the relationship between his concepts of the virtual and the actual from that between the possible and the real, revealing possibility to be a derivative conception of potentiality. We can summarize this criticism by stating that the conventional idea of the relationship between what is possible and what is real is a reductive one; what is possible is considered as essentially the same as what is real, and is only different because it lacks existence. What we think of as possible is simply a nonexistent version of the real; when it comes into existence, it becomes real and is no longer possible. On Deleuze's account, this view is a defective one because it fails to offer an understanding of potentiality that is truly generative, that enables the existence of things. Understood in this way, the possible is not the true condition of the real—that which brings it into existence—but rather is retroactively postulated as such and thus merely mirrors what already exists. Thus, there is no real difference between what is 'possible' and what is 'real.'

The concept of potentiality Deleuze advances—what he calls the virtual—differs in important ways. First, it has a reality all its own; it is real *qua* potential. Second, it thus does not resemble or mirror actuality, but is heterogeneous with that which it conditions and produces. Third, although once something possible has been realized, possibility is eliminated, virtuality is not exhausted in the process of creation but persists as a reservoir of potential that enables continued change. To summarize, the main difference between these two versions of potentiality is that the possible is a homogeneous and general category that is dependent on the real and thus destined for realization in a certain form (its potential is to make that reality existent) whereas the virtual is itself a productive domain of reality that has its own movements and events, and retains its autonomy in relation to that which grows out of it.

As a form of potential, vulnerability ought to be conceived in terms of the virtual rather than in terms of the possible precisely because its meaning is not reducible to that to which one is vulnerable (in the way that the possible is reducible to a mere copy of the real). The sense of potential inherent in being vulnerable is not that of a simple 'could be' of some definite future state of affairs. That is, neither the condition of being vulnerable nor the experience of vulnerability is the same as or necessarily resembles what comes of this vulnerability. Indeed, what comes of vulnerability is not determined in advance unless we adopt an overdetermined sense of vulnerability. As a condition of openness to the world that is defined by an interwoven series of relationships of affectation, vulnerability is undetermined. Thus, our concept of vulnerability ought not to define it solely in terms of what is made possible because of it. Rather than being only a particular way of being affected or a specific pattern of change, vulnerability is a persistent openness to change and, as Deleuze contends of the virtual, is an openness that enables continuing transformation. Understanding vulnerability as a form of potential more in line with the virtual than with a conventional understanding of possibility averts the conflation of vulnerability with specific forms of vulnerability, namely, dependency and powerlessness, and certain consequences of vulnerability, namely, harm.

Conceiving vulnerability along the lines of the possible entails reducing it to an anticipatory state in a way that fails to be true to our varied and diverse experiences of vulnerability. For example, being vulnerable to sexual violence does not somehow mirror the real harm of sexual assault, nor is the experience of such vulnerability in any way equivalent to simple anticipation of the harm that may befall one. If we imagine, for instance, times at which we have felt particularly emotionally vulnerable—fragile even—we find that we cannot reduce that particular feeling to the pain or joy that may ultimately have come from it. Vulnerability itself is a distinctive experience. The 'vulnerable to' phrase, however, diminishes the autonomy of the experience of vulnerability by assimilating it to its outcome. Thinking about vulnerability in this way renders it merely a condition of possibility rather than one of potentiality. Conversely, understanding vulnerability as potential undermines the problematic presumption that vulnerability is fixed. As a distinctive condition of potential that is irreducible to that which comes of it, vulnerability is also attributed to all equally, which bring us to the second core feature of a concept of vulnerability: univocity.

One of the central postulates of Deleuze's ontology is the thesis of the univocity of Being, which provides a fruitful lens through which to understand the way vulnerability is a condition that pertains to all equally. The idea of the univocity of Being can be summarized with the simple phrase, Being is said of all things "in a single and same sense" (1994/1985, 35/53). With this notion, Deleuze sets himself in opposition to much of the history of philosophy, which has considered Being as a property that is distributed among beings, which possess it to a greater and a lesser extent. Rather than understanding Being as a thing to be divvied up among beings, he takes it to be "an unlimited, open space," "a space of play" throughout which beings distribute themselves (1994/1985, 36/54). Being is the openness of which Merleau-Ponty writes. In such an open space, beings distribute themselves by differentiating themselves from one another rather than having their differences attributed to them in virtue of how much reality they are said to possess.

With this alternative account of distribution comes an alternative understanding of hierarchy. Typically, hierarchy is established in terms of degree of being. The Cartesian distinctions, echoed by many other medieval and modern philosophers, between substances and modes, and finite and infinite substances are examples of this kind of ontological hierarchy. Substances are more real than modes, and infinite substances such as God more real than finite substances. Epistemic and axiological hierarchies accompany this ontological hierarchy: it is better to know (and to be) that which is more real. How such a hierarchy operates in terms of vulnerability is quite clear. When vulnerability is conceived as a property that is attributed to beings, some are deemed more vulnerable than others. The sense of potential inherent in vulnerability is purged because, when imagined as a property, it becomes fixed. Vulnerability is said of some in a different way than it is said of others—for instance, women as a class are categorically said to be more vulnerable than men—and the attribution of vulnerability qua property reifies and often naturalizes it. Yet, Deleuze proposes an alternative conception of hierarchy that better captures how vulnerability should be attributed: if Being, or vulnerability as a fundamental dimension of life, is said of all beings in the same way, then they cannot be measured by their proximity to the fullest degree of Being (or, in this case, invulnerability). Instead, hierarchy, in the sense of difference, is created between beings in terms of what they can do, the relationships into which they enter, the powers and capabilities they exercise, the affects of which they are capable, and the extent to which they surpass their limits and alter themselves. On this understanding, all are equally vulnerable—open to being affected and affecting—and differences are made by the ways we are affected and respond to this affection. Thus, in its fundamental sense as openness to the world, vulnerability is univocal. It is said of all in the same way insofar as what it means for us to be is for us to be open to affectation; to be is to be vulnerable. Yet, the relationships and various social, cultural, political, and historical processes of differentiation that are formative of human subjects constitute us as differentially vulnerable.

If vulnerability is this univocal form of potential—a fundamental openness that is said of all in the same way—it is quite clear that it is not actualized for all equally or in the same way; we do not all live our vulnerability in the same ways. It is only as an ontological condition that vulnerability is univocal. Since it is the ontological condition of openness to affecting and being affected, the experience of vulnerability is one of being affected and affecting in particular ways and in particular relations with others. In social life, patterns of affectation emerge and social positioning situates individuals and groups in ways that make them vulnerable to varying extents and in varying ways. As an experience and as a situational condition, vulnerability differs in virtue of these different relations of affectation; it has a diversity of manifestations. As Deleuze states, "it is we and our individuality which remains equivocal in and for a univocal Being" (1994/1985, 39/57). As potential, being is said of all beings in the same way, yet it is said of beings that differ and are always differing. Another way to make this point is to say that what is made of this openness, what is generated through it and what we experience in virtue of it, is equivocal. Whereas beings themselves, which differ and are differing, are said to be equivocal in Deleuze's *Difference and Repetition,* in his later work with Félix Guattari, they intimate that the value of what is created on the basis of such openness is also equivocal. The openness that defines vulnerability is not to be valued as unequivocally good but rather harbors dangers and requires caution. It is an univocal potential with uncertain and equivocal value. Accordingly, it ought neither be valorized as that which we must affirm at all costs as the key to ethical relation nor be warded off as a condition tantamount to injury and harm.

Thus, there are two distinct ways that vulnerability is equivocal, to employ Deleuze's terminology, and two senses of equivocity it manifests: vulnerability is both equivocal as experience and situational condition, and in the sense of being both ambivalent and ambiguous. It is an ambivalent condition of potential in the sense that it may produce results of uncertain value—harm or sustenance, affection or aggression, change or re-entrenchment—and in the sense that the differing relations in which individuals are affected vary both in their nature and in their value. Consequently, that which makes possible radical change also makes possible extreme re-entrenchment. Yet, vulnerability is not simply ambivalent—good or bad, negative or positive, beneficial or detrimental—and the task we face is not just that of discerning when it should be allowed and encouraged, and when it amounts to hazard. If part of what defines vulnerability as potential is its indeterminacy, then vulnerability is also ambiguous. Its effects and the ways we may experience it are uncertain. Whereas vulnerability's ambivalence speaks to its multidirectional potential, its ambiguity speaks to the way that we cannot disentangle these various dimensions from one another because they inhere in the same condition of potential, the same basic way of being open to the world, and the same capacity for affectation. Along these lines, de Beauvoir contends that ambiguity is the fundamental truth of the human condition; ambiguity lies in the simultaneous and intertwined "truth of life and death, of my solitude and my bond with the world, of my freedom and my servitude, of the insignificance and the sovereign importance of each man and all men [sic]" (1976, 9). Insofar as we are beings that are simultaneously mind and matter, dependent and independent, moving forward into the future and rooted in the reality of past and present, our existence is an ambiguously vulnerable one. We cannot separate our materiality from our intellectuality, our historicality from our futural orientation, our distinctness as individuals from our necessary sociality, and so on. Ambiguity, thus, is not vagueness but the indistinction and mixture of characteristics that are typically conceived as opposed. Vulnerability is ambiguous as a fundamental condition, but also can be ambiguous as an experience. These two ways that vulnerability is equivocal and two senses of equivocity, however, indicate that vulnerability cannot be fully understood either when viewed negatively as susceptibility to harm or when regarded as a homogenous property that manifests itself in basically the same way.

The last of the four Deleuzian concepts I invoke is perhaps the most familiar: becoming. Many European philosophers share the idea that the self is shaped through its constitutive exposure to alterity. The concept of becoming is one of the distinctive forms this notion takes in Deleuze's philosophy. For the purposes of this discussion, becoming can be defined as a process of alteration that takes place only through a relationship with another being (or, more precisely, another multiplicity). More specifically, a process of becoming occurs because of a connection between something in oneself and something in the other being that draws one out of oneself. The connection occurs at a sub-individual level rather than as a matter of subjective and conscious beliefs, feelings, or intentions and thus is a matter of affects. Accordingly, becoming is a process of transformation that exceeds the bounds of the activity/passivity dichotomy; it requires the kind of receptive openness described in the previous section. In becoming, one is neither active nor passive in the conventional sense. Rather, one experiences affects that one does not choose and undergoes changes that one does not will or plan. Becomings, however, are also characterized as movements of creative deformation: they undo set normative patterns and rigid ways of thinking and feeling, forming novel modes of living in their stead. Thus, becoming is defined as nonvolitional affective transformation that occasions new ways of feeling, thinking, and relating. As nonvolitional, it cannot be active in the conventional sense (because one undergoes something one did not choose) but as the spontaneous creation of new capacities, it cannot be passive in the conventional sense either (because one is not a mere object of another's willful action). That is, one is a participant in a process of which one is not the author. Jill Marsden argues in her essay "Deleuzian Bodies, Feminist Tactics," that Deleuze and Guattari's notion of becoming "amounts to . . . the claim that vulnerable and violated bodies can be reconfigured, that is, liberated from the defensive and defeated histories to which they have been consigned" (2004, 309). Becomings, thus, both presuppose the openness of vulnerability—they require the capacity to be affected and remain open to being affected—and are an example of the positive forms vulnerability can take. Yet, the proposal that the idea of becoming can help us understand the positive dimensions of vulnerability is far from simple. To say that becoming is a positive manifestation of a fundamental vulnerability is not to say that the processes of change called becoming are always 'good' or pleasant or unequivocally progressive.

Because the encounters that instigate becomings make their effects felt at a sub-individual level, meaning that they are neither chosen nor planned, becomings are necessarily unpredictable, uncontrollable, and their results unknown. Yet, because they are by definition creative deformations, becoming is a process of moving into unfamiliar territory. Because becoming requires openness to unknown others, uncontrollable and unpredictable change, it rests upon vulnerability. To become, one must be vulnerable. Thus, by taking steps toward the kind of epistemic vulnerability proposed in Chapter Three, one creates the conditions necessary for entering into a process of becoming, destabilizing and perhaps subverting the norms of entrepreneurial subjectivity. Although preoccupied with self-transformation and the development of new capacities, the entrepreneurial subject is so only to the extent that these capacities are conducive to increased invulnerability and maximize her human capital. In becoming, however, one precipitates a deformation or undoing of the self that would be in control of itself and cultivates the conditions for epistemic vulnerability.

To summarize, these four aspects of Deleuze's philosophy—potentiality, univocity, equivocity and diversity, and becoming—comprise an ontological concept of vulnerability. Understood in terms of these four features, vulnerability is, first, a condition of potential the experiential reality of which is undetermined; second, a fundamental and shared underlying condition of openness to alteration; third, a condition that cannot be characterized as homogenous, but is manifest in a diversity of forms and kinds of experiences; fourth, the nature and value of which are both ambivalent and ambiguous rather than determinately and inevitably negative. As such, vulnerability is the necessary condition of creative, critical, and novel becomings.

I have sketched a picture of these dimensions of Deleuze's thought both in order to refine and spell out some of the basic intuitions about the meaning of vulnerability (for instance, that it is a form of potential), and in order to clarify the problem with the assumptions (of fixity, negativity, homogeneity, and inequitable attribution) often made about vulnerability. In so doing, I hope to have delineated a concept of vulnerability that is of value for making sense of the diversity of experiences of vulnerability without shoehorning them into narrow and value-laden categories, and that provides resources for thinking about the relationship between vulnerability, invulnerability, and oppressive and/or normalizing social relations. As noted in the first chapter, the presumption that vulnerability is fixed, as a negative trait or susceptibility to harm, and fixes those who are deemed vulnerable results in a *de jure* inequitable understanding of who is vulnerable, how, why, and what that vulnerability means (being "weak, passive and pathetic"). The features of fixity, negativity, homogeneity, and inequity are fundamentally intertwined. Likewise, the alternative features of potential, equivocity, diverse manifestations, and univocity are mutually supporting. Supplanting fixity with an understanding of vulnerability as a shared condition of potential likewise shifts these related presumptions, precluding us both from reducing vulnerability to a solely negative condition of being open to harm and from conceiving the experience of this condition in a likewise homogenous way.

"FORCE IN THEIR FRAGILITY": THE EXPERIENCE OF VULNERABILITY IN CIXOUS

The aim of the previous two sections has been to articulate the contours of a concept of vulnerability as an ontological condition and, to that end, I have focused on outlining the characteristic features that define vulnerability in general. These features—constitutive openness that is characterized by the simultaneity of continuity with and divergence from other beings, fundamental and shared potentiality that is both ambivalent and ambiguous, and a diversity of expressions—structure the way in which vulnerability is experienced and, indeed, make those experiences possible. Defined in this way, vulnerability operates as a transcendental condition: being vulnerable, openness to being affected and affecting, is the basic precondition for experience in general. Accordingly, a central question, which I explore only briefly here, concerns the nature of the relationship between ontological vulnerability as defined through these distinct features and specific, situational instances of vulnerability: How is the openness that defines vulnerability experienced? What is it like to experience vulnerability as ambiguous potentiality rather than as already determined as negative and harmful? That is, how does vulnerability's ambiguity emerge in experience? Are there particular kinds of experiences that afford us greater appreciation of the fundamental nature of vulnerability? Is grief one such occasion as Butler suggests?

In what follows, I consider Hélène Cixous' account of experiences of vulnerability in order to explore how some of the definitive features of the concept of vulnerability translate into experience. Cixous' understanding of vulnerability is consonant with the outline of an ontological concept of vulnerability; vulnerability is conceived as a matter of affective openness, a form of ambiguous potential, and an occasion for becoming-other than what one is. Yet, her view of vulnerability also supplements the aforementioned conception of vulnerability in an important way: the sense of vulnerability she articulates is one that emerges from a complex sociopolitical context that includes concrete experiences of racism and sexism. Cixous' work enables us to grasp how features such as fundamental relational openness, potentiality, and ambiguity may be experienced in contexts of oppression. In her quasi-autobiographical essay "Sorties," translated as "Out and Out: Attacks/Ways Out/Forays," Cixous draws a picture of her own experience of vulnerability (1986/1975). The path of the essay shifts seamlessly from reflections on her coming of age in Algeria with a complex racial, ethnic, national, and linguistic identity and a keen attentiveness to injustice, to creative and fervent retellings of classic literary tales such as those of Cleopatra and Anthony, and Achilles and Penthesileia. Cixous meditates on her relationship to writing and literature in order to express her difficulty finding her own voice and place in the world, literary and social. In particular, she invokes many of the classic heroes of Greek mythology as a vehicle for revealing her desire for and struggle to find a literary figure with which she could identify, that is, one who exceeded the sociocultural norms for masculinity and femininity, norms with which she could not feel at home.

The difference between a 'masculine' and 'feminine' political economy is integral to Cixous' account, thus it is easy to misread her as a cultural or 'difference' feminist who seeks to valorize previously devalued stereotypically feminine traits.[4] Yet, Cixous is quick to note that she "makes[s] a point of using the *qualifiers* of sexual difference here to avoid the confusion man/

masculine, woman/feminine . . . Difference is not distributed, of course, on the basis of socially determined 'sexes' " (1986, 81). Not only does she reject the idea of innate sexual difference, but she also eschews the notion that difference stems from discrete gender identities that correlate with sex. Instead, the difference between 'masculine' and 'feminine' political economies is a difference in modes of relation, ways of organizing relationships, fundamental assumptions, and dispositions. It is connected to the sex/gender system but not essentially, naturally, or necessarily so; there are men who embody the 'feminine' way of relating and women who embody the 'masculine' way of relating. Labeling these modes of relation 'feminine' and 'masculine' indicates a contingent historical connection between gender and style of being. What Cixous describes as 'feminine' is a style of relating that is, in part, the product of the particular sociohistorical situations of many women. Some of the oppressive aspects of women's conditions—such as being consigned to embodiment, to passive receptivity, and to subordinating the self to the desires and needs of (male) others—can give rise to a 'feminine' form of subjectivity that is disposed to openness, generosity, and receptivity. The 'feminine' economy, however, involves both a transvaluation (rather than a mere revaluation) of typically 'feminine' modes of relationship and a repudiation of the norms of the 'masculine' economy that have produced 'feminine' subjectivity as complementary to 'masculine' subjectivity (e.g., with receptivity and passivity complementing assertiveness and activity). Accordingly, there are stereotypically 'feminine' patterns of behavior that ill-serve women. Cixous thus rejects and rebels against the sacrificial nature of "a certain passivity" that characterizes one who gives boundlessly to others who fail to value this generosity (1986, 77). Therefore, the 'feminine' economy and mode of subjectivity are not just 'feminine' ways of being; they are aspirational figures that are not fully realized, an imagined utopian 'elsewhere' rather than a given.

To understand the 'feminine' economy and the kind of vulnerability it involves, it is valuable to understand that to which it is a rejoinder: the 'masculine' economy. The 'masculine' economy is essentially the context in which entrepreneurial subjectivity emerges. It is characterized by oppositional thought, utilitarian calculation, a desire for mastery and control, the ability to manifest strength, and exchange that takes place through a system of quantifiable equivalences. The presumption of scarcity, and thus the fear of loss, organizes this political economy. Therefore, the exertion of energy is oriented toward what one can gain—"plus-value of virility, authority, power, money, or pleasure," human capital, in brief—and gain is the aim of relationship, exchange, and activity (Cixous 1986, 87). If value of various kinds is scarce, then one must accumulate it in order to make oneself secure, that is, in order to make one's self an estimable self. This pattern of relating is the dominant one: this "is what society is made for—how it is made; and men can hardly get out of it. . . . Masculine profit is almost always mixed up with a success that is socially defined" (ibid). If (social, emotional/psychic) resources are scarce, then one must build up the self continually in order to protect the self. Consequently, what one wants when one enters into an interchange with another is a return on one's investment.

In contrast, the 'feminine' economy is primarily characterized by openness rather than a closed circuit of exchange. The guiding presumption is abundance and plenitude rather than scarcity. As a consequence, vulnerability understood as openness is the starting point for encounters with others. Cixous describes vulnerability alternately in terms of fragility, receptivity, self-dispossession, and inclusiveness or nonclosure. By refusing to presume that others are threats to the self and that the self must thus be secured, one may embody a posture of "nonclosure that is not submission but confidence and comprehension" (1986, 86). The 'feminine' thus admits otherness into the self to a greater extent and enters into relationship without the expectation that what one gives of oneself will be returned. A particular kind of self-dispossession, which Cixous terms "de-propriation, depersonalization," is key to this receptive nonclosure (1986, 96): self-dispossession is defined not as letting oneself be possessed by another but rather as refusing to master and own one's self through centralizing and hierarchical organization of the self (e.g., the will, or conscience, or rationality as master) in the service of maximizing one's capital and demonstrating one's superiority. If the self is not experienced as a territory whose borders must be policed and maintained, then allowing others to affect the self is not *de facto* experienced as invasion. Cixous shares Deleuze's understanding of the level at which transformative relationships of becoming occur, the sub-individual level: although one may enter into relationship with another individual, it is something within the other that affects something within one's self. The other individual does not overtake the self, but rather some element of one's self is altered in relation to some element within the other.

Thus, by opening oneself up to others and their effects on the self, one is also open to transformation in relation to these others: receptivity, nonclosure, and self-dispossession endow one with a "gift of changeability" (1986, 88). Openness to experiencing alterity, and altering in relation to it, is the condition of invention. Mobility and inclusiveness make one stronger and yet more fragile at the same time: individuals become "much richer, more various, stronger, and—to the extent that they are mobile—very fragile" (1986, 84). An affirmative and generous response to the fundamental condition of vulnerability requires a new form of strength that is not mastery or dominance, but "force in . . . fragility" (1986, 95). Thus, a noteworthy feature of Cixous' deconstructive account is that vulnerability is both strength and dispossession, which are not mutually exclusive but necessarily intertwined; herein lies one dimension of the ambiguity of vulnerability. In order for receptivity and self-dispossession to be creative and active, and not to become forms of submissiveness, this form of strength is necessary. Outside of the activity/passivity dichotomy, strength is redefined neither as wielding power over another nor as enduring the onslaught of another. Instead,

Cixous asserts, "the only true strength . . . has no need to protect itself, or to flaunt or prove itself, the strength that makes no use of tools or arms and that is secure enough to be a source of peace; not the false strength which is only fear's other face, and which, in order to reassure itself, produces only deeds of death and aggression" (1986, 116). Thus, in the 'feminine' economy, vulnerability is a source of strength and creativity rather than just a danger to be averted.

Cixous describes the experience of this kind of vulnerability—"force in . . . fragility"—as one born of resistance. To be strong in this way, to need to be strong in this way, one must find oneself at odds with the dominant culture and its terms, challenging them. For Cixous, resistance to the 'masculine' economy is a creative endeavor, an outpouring of spontaneous activity. Her focus on creative expression and, specifically, writing stems from concern about the way the 'masculine' economy restricts 'feminine' modes of expression (e.g., nonquantifiable, affective, evocative, embodied expression). To resist, thus, is to let loose what the dominant economy seeks to constrain, what does not fit within it. Thus, the strength of 'feminine' subjectivity "jams sociality" by introducing discord into the calculable relations of exchange of the 'masculine,' neoliberal economy (1986, 96). In this way, the particular kind of strength that is found in vulnerability comes from the failure to fit in the dominant culture seamlessly and appropriately: "This power to be errant is strength; it is also what makes her vulnerable to those who champion the Selfsame, acknowledgement, and attribution [the norms of the 'masculine' economy]" (1986, 91). A central part of the errancy of 'feminine' subjectivity is the aforementioned receptive nonclosure and self-dispossession, which run counter to the dominant ideals of self-containment, self-mastery, and invulnerability.

This alternative, nondichotomous form of strength is, however, not unequivocally positive or pleasant. On Cixous' account, it is experientially ambivalent and ambiguous: vulnerability as strength brings with it vulnerability as exposure to those who would thwart one's attempts to undo the dominant order or undermine one's mode of being in general. Indeed, one is all the more vulnerable because one lets oneself be affected, admits others into the self, and not only accedes to but seeks the becoming-other of the self. The "peopling" of the self by elements of others, the openness of the self to alterity, "gives neither rest nor security, always disturbs the relationship to 'reality,' produces an uncertainty that gets in the way of the subject's socialization. It is distressing, it wears you out" (1986, 86). On this understanding, vulnerability can be exhausting, especially under less than ideal socio-economic conditions. When the sense of 'reality' and the standards for socialization align with dominant norms and these norms entail repudiating vulnerability, "it wears you out" to experience yourself as vulnerable. Moreover, the uncertain transformations that may come of being vulnerable are not "done without danger, without pain, without loss—of moments of self, of consciousness, of persons one has been, goes beyond, leaves" (ibid).

Cixous' exploration of the experience of vulnerability—'feminine' subjectivity—reveals that some of the hazards of vulnerability are likely pernicious but are also a product of a social context that aims to reproduce itself and its guiding norms. Vulnerability is most susceptible to exploitation in contexts where invulnerability is prized and vulnerability devalued. Yet, it also reveals that some hazards may come with vulnerability regardless of socio-cultural context. Danger, pain, and loss are not natural or inevitable consequences of vulnerability per se, but may accompany the alterations of the self that characterize vulnerability because they are unfamiliar. This dimension of vulnerability is not a pleasant experience—it may be distressing, disturbing, and tiring—but it is not exactly negative or harmful either. As explored through the idea of epistemic vulnerability in Chapter Three, changes to the self that entail breaking with familiar received understandings can be painful but valuable.

CONCLUSION

One reason for considering Cixous' account of vulnerability was to allay concerns that the ontological understanding of vulnerability sketched in sections II and III remains detached from the particularities of experiences of vulnerability. On the contrary, I have sought to show that Cixous offers a nuanced understanding of vulnerability, of "force in fragility," that is consonant with the concept of vulnerability I have sketched, but also firmly rooted in awareness and experience of injustice and oppression. Thus, her articulations of the 'feminine' economy illustrates well how vulnerability can be thought and experienced beyond the passivity/activity dualism, but also illustrates how this dichotomy along with others work to sustain dominant norms that devalue vulnerability and the various forms it takes (such as openness, inclusivity, relationality, and so on).

As I argued in conjunction with Hoagland's work on the denial of relationality, an ethics of vulnerability does not demand that all embrace vulnerability unqualifiedly and in all circumstances, but rather that habitual repudiation of vulnerability be renounced. Vulnerability is not an absolute value to be avowed, but a fundamental condition with which to reckon. To disavow vulnerability preemptively is to refuse to experience and take stock of something that is the condition of life itself, as well as of vital movements of intimacy, transformation, and learning. Although the ontological understanding of vulnerability proposed herein, and the view of vulnerability articulated throughout this work, does not require any particular relationship to vulnerability, it does position vulnerability as a condition that is fundamental. Positioning vulnerability thus implies that to deny or repudiate vulnerability is to deny and repudiate the nature of human reality. As de Beauvoir writes, "man [sic] must not attempt to dispel the ambiguity of his being but, on the contrary, accept the task of realizing it" and only in so doing is freedom, as a genuine value rather than as a given, realized (1976, 13). Thus, the value and distinctiveness of the 'feminine' political economy lies not only in the aforementioned virtues that are embodied in 'feminine' subjectivity—virtues of inclusivity or receptive nonclosure, openness to difference, generosity, and willingness to alter oneself—but also in how it affirms what is ontologically the case: vulnerability.

I have sought to show that oppression and injustice—in the forms that they currently take—rely upon the repudiation of vulnerability, upon the normative status of invulnerability, and upon practices (and the forms of subjectivity constituted through them) that reject openness in favor of preemptive closure, uncertain transformation in favor of the controlled maximization of human capital, and encounters with what is unfamiliar in favor of domesticating management. My aim in developing the understanding of vulnerability proposed throughout this chapter has been to provide a sense of vulnerability that is both more accurate and not so easily accommodated by these norms, practices, and forms of subjectivity. Implicit in the ethos of entrepreneurial subjectivity and the ideal of invulnerability is the view that vulnerability is susceptibility to harm. Their logic depends on regarding vulnerability negatively, as a condition of inadequacy, weakness, passivity, and powerlessness. To decenter these logics, we must destabilize the view of vulnerability they presuppose. We cannot so readily, so unquestioningly, pursue and admire invulnerability, impermeability, independent self-determination, and complete self-control if the complexity of vulnerability is recognized and the reductively negative view of it is dislodged from its position as a given. Thus, I aimed to show how Merleau-Pontian and Deleuzian ontologies can help us circumvent the trap of the dualisms that are presupposed by much of the history of philosophy and by the reductively negative conception of vulnerability. Furthermore, it is crucial to emphasize again that many of the very features that define vulnerability—its status as potential that occasions transformation, as fundamental and univocal, and as ambiguous—lie at the root of disavowals of vulnerability despite a lack of awareness of these features. Vulnerability becomes an appropriate object of fear and anxiety when it is viewed in a reductively negative way and defined as susceptibility to harm. With such a simplistic sense of vulnerability, we can continue to eschew it without recognizing that what we fear is not harm per se—or not harm alone—but the ambiguity and uncertainty that define vulnerability. We are, therefore, unable to recognize either the nature of vulnerability or what about vulnerability produces fear and anxiety. Thus, we can understand the failures and misrecognitions that accompany experiences of vulnerability only by articulating, comprehending, and working through what vulnerability truly means for us. The concept of vulnerability developed herein is integral to making sense of and dealing with ethical lapses concerning vulnerability, such as an unwillingness to be vulnerable that leads to the exploitation of others' vulnerability. Our aim, consequently, ought not be to dispense with the discourse of vulnerability, but rather to ensure that the language we use to speak and write about the experience of vulnerability does some justice to the variety and ambiguity of those experiences, and so does not reiterate and perpetuate the problematic dualisms (such as active/passive, capable/incapable, admirable/pitiable) that lead to oppressive, controlling, and stigmatizing consequences.

NOTES

1. For an overview of dominant accounts of Merleau-Ponty's account of flesh and, in contrast, a specifically relational account see Bannon 2011.
2. Distance is a mechanism that preserves difference and all figures of spatial distance or temporal noncoincidence are ways of signifying alterity. Further, just as distance, gaps, and divergences are the condition of perception and experience, so is alterity the condition of self-identity. On this point see Murphy 2010.
3. A relational ontology may be defined as one in which relationships are constitutive of objects, subjects, things, bodies, etc., and so take priority over what we call properties or attributes in our understanding of these things. The things of the world are not isolated individuals dispersed in space and time, given to us in this particular form, but rather are generated and distinguished from one another through continuing and intertwining processes.
4. It is also tempting to see continuity between Cixous' view of the 'feminine' economy and mode of relating, and the values advocated in feminist care ethics. There are some basic similarities—the emphasis on connectedness and relationality as typically feminine in contrast to separation and individuality as typically masculine—but, as will become clear, the most noteworthy features of Cixous' account are not necessarily echoed by care ethicists.

6 Vulnerability in Social Life
Sexuality and Pornography

One of the overarching themes of this work has been the need to examine the experience of vulnerability and the significance of images of vulnerability in their social context. This chapter considers one dimension of the social life of vulnerability—that of sexuality—with the aim of articulating more precisely how vulnerability can operate as an ethical resource. Sexuality is both a dimension of social life through which individuals commonly experience vulnerability in diverse ways, and a mode of experience that is saturated with ethical significance. Though the chapter begins by exploring sexuality broadly as a site of vulnerability, the central argument turns to the ways sexuality and vulnerability are represented in pornography and experienced in relation to that medium. As I argued in the preceding chapters, if vulnerability is the basis for ethical relation, then how we relate to vulnerability is an ethical matter of fundamental importance. Harm and wrongs occur not just through the exploitation of others' vulnerability or failure to respond well to it, but also find their precondition in disavowal of one's own vulnerability and denials of relationships. The culturally pervasive understandings of vulnerability and invulnerability, which permeate our social milieu and shape the practices in which we engage and the ends to which we aspire, impact how we relate to vulnerability—our own and that of others—and facilitate such denials and avoidance. Thus, the question of how the nexus of meanings surrounding vulnerability and invulnerability impacts how we experience and live sexuality is both a socially and an ethically significant one. Accordingly, the aim of this chapter is neither to condemn nor to condone the wide array of sexual imagery, but rather to take stock of how vulnerability is imagined in this context, what kinds of ideas and experiences of vulnerability are facilitated for viewers, and what sense of sexual subjectivity is formed in relation to them. Although I conclude that representations of and approaches to vulnerability that are reductive, and thus conducive to its exploitation or repudiation, are likely ethically problematic whereas those that express or enable experience of the full complexity of vulnerability are likely more ethically valuable, my aim is not to render judgment about the content of pornography or behavior in relation to it. Rather, by analyzing the issue of pornography from the perspective of vulnerability, I seek to furnish a perspective on the ethics and politics of pornography that moves beyond the stalemate in feminist discussion of the topic.

Pornography might appear passé as a topic of feminist discussion: the "sex wars" that dominated feminist discourse in the 80s are decades past, and the debate over pornography has been reduced to irreconcilable anti-porn and pro-sex/sex radical standpoints. Yet, given the dramatic increase in availability and variety of pornographic material on the internet, there has been a surge of interest in pornography as a social and cultural phenomenon. Mass-market books with titles such as *Pornified* and *The Porning of America* point to the continued relevance of the topic and heightened concern about the role pornography plays in American culture in particular. For instance, Ariel Levy's recent book *Female Chauvinist Pigs: Women and the Rise of Raunch Culture* charts the relationship between feminism and contemporary sexual culture in the U.S., wondering why women have acceded to a model of sexuality and sexiness dictated by the pornographic imagery of what she calls raunch culture. Although we might attribute this fascination with pornography to a prudish American culture enthralled with what it deems perverse, the predominance, normalcy, and increasing social acceptance of pornography indicate that it has become a common feature of everyday experiences of sexuality. Increasingly, pornography is a medium through which people express, engage with, and understand their own sexuality. Although it is not unlike other media and forms of entertainment, in certain ways it is not quite like them either since the express purpose of pornography is to arouse, to produce a specific bodily response in the viewer, to engage the viewer as a sexual being. Pornography is an influential representation and expression of sexuality, and it is fair to say that individuals now develop their sense of themselves as sexual beings in a context in which pornographic imagery is the dominant representation of sexuality. A social world in which pornography is mainstream, along with the attendant revival of interest in the subject, calls for renewed discussion of what might seem an old topic.

SEXUALITY, EMBODIMENT, AND AMBIGUITY

Before turning to the more specific topic of pornography, it is necessary to explore the salience of sexuality as a mode of experience through which vulnerability and invulnerability are felt and understood. Why consider sexuality as a unique instance of vulnerability? Throughout this section I will offer four intertwined reasons in order to contextualize the focus on sexuality and, thus, on the topic of pornography and the feminist debates surrounding it. I consider, first, the way sexuality is integral to embodiment and embodied self-identity; second, the centrality of sexuality to feminist understandings of the self, ethics, and politics; third, the way sexuality exemplifies the ambivalence and ambiguity that defines vulnerability; and fourth, the intensity with which sexuality has been subject to normalization and the correspondingly intense critique of such norms.

The body's sexual capacities, its ability to experience sensations as sexual and its openness to sexual meaning, point us to the unavoidably embodied nature of our existence. As sexual, we are embodied beings; as embodied beings, we are sexual. Sexuality is often aligned with our more 'animal' nature and considered a facet of human experience that is instinctual. As such, sexuality easily fits into dualist paradigms—associated with the body, emotions, animality, nature, and characterized as unruly, uncontrollable, and disruptive—and thus experienced as an aspect of life that is threatening. To the extent that it threatens order—social, political, or intrasubjective—sexuality calls for regulation and the exercise of control. The image of sexuality as an unruly and rebellious force can be, and often is, idealized, with sexuality's 'naturalness' invoked as an antidote to the repressive forces of culture. Regardless of the validity of this conception of sexuality, it possesses a certain potency. As Foucault's work amply demonstrates, however, branding sexuality as 'natural' obscures the sociocultural work done to construct sexuality as we experience it—all the specific ways of thinking and speaking about bodies and desires, and specific ways of doing things with and to those bodies—and so obscures the way sexuality is a fundamentally intersubjective and collaborative domain. Additionally, the construction of sexuality as 'natural,' 'animal,' and so on, fabricates sexuality as a force (albeit one within us, such as desire) to which we (being more appropriately identified with our minds than our bodies, of course) are vulnerable and in relation to which we should attempt to make ourselves invulnerable in various ways: that is, by exercising control over our sexuality whether it be by abstaining from sex until marriage, on the one extreme, or, on the other, by mastering sexual techniques and accumulating sexual partners in order to be the best entrepreneur of one's sexual self that one can be. Yet, sexuality is neither inherently threatening nor inherently revolutionary. Its salience lies in its intersubjective nature, and thus the way sexuality renders us vulnerable is far more ambiguous and far more nuanced.

Recent accounts of embodied subjectivity such as those of John Russon and Debra Bergoffen are helpful resources for understanding the centrality of sexuality to intersubjective self-identity, particularly because both highlight the way sexuality is a locus of vulnerability. On Russon's account, as sexual beings "we experience the nonisolability of our bodily identity from the significance others place upon it" (2003, 106). That is, as Butler also often notes, experiences of sexuality reveal how we are inevitably linked to others and to the social contexts of significance we inhabit along with them. Sexual meaning—attraction, desire, arousal, objectification, titillation, and so on—emerges in relation to others; it comes from them and is directed toward them. We never engage in sexuality alone, even when we are alone. Sexuality thus initiates us into a particular web of social significances in virtue of which we are especially open and vulnerable to others. Because sexuality is always enacted in a given social milieu, being an embodied, social being means being a sexual being. The specific vulnerability of sexual experience derives from how sexual experiences depend upon another person regarding and responding to one's bodily self in a particular way: as an object of desire, worthy of idealization, lust-inducing, eliciting touch, and so on. Sexuality is thus definitively embodied and receptive; to engage as a sexual being is to be receptive to the ways others apprehend one's bodily being. Sexual self-identity is exemplarily intersubjective. Indeed, Russon defines sex as "the experience of one's embodiment as a locus of intersubjectivity" (2003, 108). This experience points to the corporeal reality of sexuality: my body elicits erotic response from the other's body and vice versa. The experience is one of the mutual intertwining of self and other, and the reciprocal self-definition that can take place through that intertwining.

Bergoffen's account highlights the intertwining of sexual and other forms of meaning. She articulates three facets of embodied subjectivity that are central to human integrity and dignity: the instrumental, the sensuous, and the sensual forms of engagement define human meaning-making capacities (2009). In all three cases, meaning is created through *embodied* interaction; in working, sensing, and desiring, one creates meaning and value via one's body. Thus, integrity and dignity are, on Bergoffen's account, made material rather than abstract concepts; they are rooted in concrete bodily capacities that generate socially, culturally, and personally significant value. Yet, as on Russon's account, the intrinsically embodied and social nature of human subjectivity renders us vulnerable as well. Of particular significance for this discussion is Bergoffen's emphasis on the ambiguity of these three distinctive modes of engagement. Each is rooted in our bodily being but gives rise to a meaning that transcends that bodily being. Our vulnerability lies in the ambiguous quality—immanent and transcendent, material and symbolic, personal and social—of our meaning-making capacities: "Since the values I bring to the world are always articulated through my embodiment; and since they always exist in the materialities of the world, that is, since they are specific expressions of my ambiguity, it is as the embodiment of certain values that I am targeted for bodily abuse" (2009, 312). To exploit another's vulnerability is thus not just to abuse her or him as a physical being, but is also to target and exploit the expressive nature of bodies and bodily capacities, what the body means and what it is capable of conveying. This intuition has been crucial to many feminist critiques of sexual violence, and Bergoffen extends this key point through a sustained analysis of the way rape has been used a weapon of war.[1] The use of rape as an instrument for waging war is premised upon the basic human need and desire for intimacy, the meaning-making powers of the sensual body, and the way social-cultural contexts bestows gendered symbolic meaning upon bodies (2009, 317). When used as a weapon of war, rape alters the meaning of women's femininity; where women's bodies might traditionally have been "coded as passive and useful for two purposes: giving pleasure and birthing babies[,]" when a woman is raped by enemies she "is humiliated because by giving pleasure to enemy men and giving birth to 'his' children, she becomes a whore" (2009, 315). The kind of meaning that can be made is constrained by gender norms that identify masculinity with power, strength, invulnerability, and the role of protector, and femininity with weakness, vulnerability, and the need for protection. A woman's body is used to express what those who rape her want to express; her embodied capacities for meaning-making are appropriated, and used against her and her community. Bergoffen states, "Her raped body carries, and is intended to carry, a message to the men of her community: You are not men; like your women who are now ours, you too are subject to our power" (2011, 43). This kind of violation is one that exploits the ambiguity of human vulnerability, using the way a person's body speaks against that person and her community.

Although we will explore this point—the way the body's meaning-making powers are utilized—further, the key point here is that sexuality is a core dimension of embodied subjectivity. Qua sexual, the body has particular and significant meanings, especially gendered ones, to oneself, to those with whom one is sexually intimate, and to those who are part of one's broader sociocultural world. As Bergoffen's analysis underscores, the import of the sensual body extends far beyond what we might normally consider the domain of the sexual: thoroughly intertwined with gender roles and gendered norms for behavior, perceived as both threatening and exhilarating, censured and obsessed over, sex lies at the heart of culture. Thus, as Sallie Tisdale observes, "[w]ithout crossing through the country of sex, there's a lot of other territory we can't begin to traverse" (1994, 7).

Sexuality is also a core feminist concern. As a site of regulation and control, it has historically been the bodies, desires, and behaviors of women and sexual minorities that have been subject to scrutiny, management, and subjugation. As a site of vulnerability, it has historically been the bodies of women and sexual minorities that have been subject to systemic violation, exploitation, objectification, and commodification. The gendering of the reductively negative understanding of vulnerability also ties it to sexuality. If women are typically considered more vulnerable than men, it is because of their bodies, which are deemed both weaker and more sexually stimulating. Both of these traits—inferior strength and sexualization—comprise the specificity of feminine vulnerability and constitute it as a dualist, reductively negative form of vulnerability: one is vulnerable because one's body is the kind of object upon which others, active male subjects, seek to act and because one cannot prevent them from doing so. To be a woman is to inhabit the kind of body that is perceived as inciting lust and thus as inviting sexual attention, whether desired or not. Conceived in this reductive way, feminine vulnerability is not just susceptible to any kind of harm but rather is thought of as a particularly sexual vulnerability. For instance, in her recent book *The Female Thing: Dirt, Sex, Envy, Vulnerability* (2006), cultural critic Laura Kipnis devotes the entire chapter on "vulnerability" to a discussion of the gender politics of rape and fear of rape, thus equating women's vulnerability with susceptibility to sexual violence. Kipnis scrutinizes the cultural preoccupation with women's sexual susceptibility, but also reflects and affirms it by failing to consider what vulnerability might mean or be like outside of this narrow context. The view that women's bodies are inherently susceptible to sexual harm is especially problematic for various reasons. It naturalizes weakness, passivity, receptivity, and object-status as properties of a female body, and strength, activity, and subject-status as properties of a male body. Myriad feminist thinkers have criticized and questioned these assumptions and associations from various angles, and problematized their role in women's oppression. Coding sexual vulnerability as feminine is also problematic for male victims of sexual violence because it precludes them and others from understanding themselves as victims, and prevents many of them from reporting their assaults and seeking and receiving help. If being vulnerable (and victimized) is associated with femininity, then male victims of sexual violence may experience a heightened sense of shame and inadequacy related to their gender identity. If to be violated is to be feminized, then "men also face a challenge to their sense of masculinity. Many feel they should have done more to fight off their attackers. Since they may believe that men are never raped, they may feel isolated and reluctant to confide in anyone" (Rabin 2012).

Given the intimate connection between sexuality, gender norms and identity, and vulnerability, for an ethic of vulnerability to be a feminist ethic, it must concern itself with sexuality. Yet, a consideration of vulnerability in the context of sexuality must also move beyond the reductively negative view of vulnerability because of this view's complicity in gender inequality and oppression. When understanding vulnerability reductively, we understand it dualistically and so perpetuate the series of binaries that are integral to oppressive ideologies and practices. Identifying women's bodies as inherently susceptible naturalizes violence (as an inevitable outcome of male aggression and female violability), prevents apprehension of male vulnerability, and obscures the fundamentally ambiguous character of sexual vulnerability. A feminist ethic of vulnerability, however, enables us to take stock of the ambiguity of sexual vulnerability and its centrality to self-identity, while also questioning the perceived relationship between gender and vulnerability. If, as Ann Murphy notes, the theme of vulnerability is "deeply vexed in the context of feminist theory" especially regarding "the issue of sexual violence," then a critical perspective on the relationship between vulnerability, sexuality, and gender is crucial (2012, 70).

The obfuscation of the ambiguous character of sexual vulnerability is especially problematic. In effacing the ambiguity of vulnerability, we divorce negative instances from positive ones, regarding the bodily availability that defines erotic love and that which enables sexual assault as radically different rather than as possibilities that arise from the same basic corporeal openness. In so doing, clear boundaries are created where they do not exist and the myriad forms of sexual experience that fit neatly into neither category are rendered unintelligible. Given the prevalence of acquaintance rape and coercive and/or alcohol-fueled sex, on the one hand, and the continued dominance of the idea that what counts as rape is only violent, forcible, resulting in noticeable physical harm, on the other hand, many people are unable to make sense of their sexual experiences. If it is not rape, per this conception, but neither is it mutually respectful erotic engagement, then what is it? And who am I in the context of this interaction? Failing to recognize the ambiguity and complexity of sexual experiences means that there are only dichotomous alternatives for making sense of them: positive or negative, harmful or beneficial, overtly consensual or overtly nonconsensual, mutual or forced. Both the ambivalence and ambiguity of vulnerability are amply present in sexual vulnerability in particular, and call for deeper exploration in order to do justice to the full range of experiences of sexual vulnerability. Sexuality is thus exemplary of these dimensions of vulnerability and consideration of it will facilitate understanding of the nature of vulnerability in general.

The extant discourse on sexuality supplies another reason for finding sexuality to be a valuable sphere for expanding our analysis of vulnerability. Sexuality has been widely analyzed from a perspective that is critical of social norms. In particular, Foucaultian-influenced critique of disciplinary power, gender norms, and discourses surrounding sex has become an indispensable part of understanding sexuality.[2] As articulated in previous chapters, this mode of critique—Nietzschean, Foucaultian, Butlerian—is integral to this project. An ethic of vulnerability must be one that adopts a deliberately critical perspective, recognizes the continuity between ethical and social norms, and considers critique itself to be a crucial ethical activity. Given the plethora of feminist and other critical treatments of sex and gender, the issue of sexuality allows us to bring a critical lens to bear on *vulnerability* in specific as it pertains to sex and gender.

VULNERABILITY, INVULNERABILITY, AND PORNOGRAPHY

The discourse on pornography, especially the feminist discourse, is one in which the language of vulnerability appears clearly but also quite problematically. Vulnerability is also central to the experience of pornography in all its permutations from participating in its making to viewing it most simply because these are sexual experiences, ones that affect us as embodied selves. In virtue of how pornography visually depicts vulnerability and how critical work about it interprets this depiction, pornography and the discourses surrounding it are of special interest to an ethic of vulnerability. Pornography, as well as writing about pornography, is a site where the meaning of vulnerability is constructed, and where the construction of vulnerability strongly intersects with the construction of gender. Both rely and play upon the viewer and reader's vulnerability—our openness to being affected—and, at the same time, shape how we regard vulnerability. As I seek to show, the reductively negative image of vulnerability appears often in both pornography and arguments against pornography. Indeed, the complexity and ambiguity of sexual experience in relation to pornography is not often captured by the discourses surrounding it, and the way the language of vulnerability is used does a particular disservice to these experiences.

Debate over pornography in feminism for the most part has taken place in quite oppositional terms and primarily focused on two core issues, harm and freedom, which are concerns for those on both sides of the issue. Whereas radical antiporn feminists focus on the harm done to women by pornographic imagery that portrays them as objects for sexual use, feminist sex radicals focus on the harm done to women's capacity for sexual self-determination by censorship. Feminist sex radicals are concerned with maintaining freedom of speech and sexual expression, which they regard porn as facilitating, and radical antiporn feminists are concerned with maintaining freedom from sexist subordination, which they regard porn as perpetuating. As Lynn Chancer recounts, in the 1980s and 90s, feminism fragmented over the answer to the question "should sexual oppression or sexual repression be given more attention?" (2000, 78). Thus, little common ground has been reached between these two camps and an impasse characterizes many discussions of pornography. We might attribute this impasse to a tendency to simplify and underestimate the complexity and ambivalence of pornography in particular and sexual culture in general. The terms upon which discussions of pornography are conducted seem to be persistently narrow ones; they are the terms of a debate, a pro/con dispute, in which participants argue already established views rather than seek to find common ground or question their core assumptions (see Chancer 2000). In this respect, I follow Amy Allen who asserts that the "debate remains unresolved precisely because it is irresolvable in the terms in which it has been posed" (2001, 512). Allen seeks to shift the terms of the debate by analyzing and critiquing the competing and antithetical conceptions of power presumed by feminist sex radicals and antiporn feminists, contending that neither is sufficient; a richer, less reductive, Foucaultian-inspired conception of power is needed (522–523). In a similar spirit of reframing and reconciliation, my aim is to shift the focus of feminist thinking on pornography by engaging in a similar critique of the way vulnerability is framed by both pornography and discourse about it. By situating pornography in the context of vulnerability, I develop an alternative ethical framework for understanding pornography from a feminist perspective. The main focus throughout is twofold: to interrogate how vulnerability and invulnerability are portrayed in pornography and debates over it, and to explore how vulnerability and invulnerability are experienced in relation to pornography. I make no causal claims about pornography—e.g., that it causes either the objectification of women or the liberation of repressed sexual desires—but rather seek to articulate how pornography as one particular influential genre of visual media can dictate and reinforce norms about the meaning and value attached to vulnerability, about who ought to be vulnerable and who ought to eschew vulnerability how, when, and where. Pornography is part of a broader social, cultural context, explored in Chapters Three and Four, that validates and encourages the pursuit of invulnerability. The main question for the remainder of this chapter is how this context and the pornographic imagery that pervades it shape sexual experience, and how we might begin to assess its ethical implications.

Images of Vulnerability in Pornography

In the most simple sense, pornography is an instantiation of human vulnerability because it depicts bodies engaged in sexual activity, laying bare for viewers forms of interaction that are typically private and hidden from view. The exposure involved in sexual desire and activity alone renders us vulnerable, open to others, but in pornography, vulnerability is heightened. Bodies are portrayed that are vulnerable in virtue of their simple nudity and the effect they have on one another, but also in virtue of their public availability. Just as the vulnerability entailed by sexuality in general is not solely corporeal but also social, so is the vulnerability expressed in pornography. Whereas in private sexual acts one is most directly vulnerable in relation to one's partner(s), pornography implicates the vulnerabilities of myriad others, including those who are present during its creation—camera operators, directors, other actors and actresses, etc.—and those who view the final product as consumers. Yet, as a publicly and freely distributed product, through which images of and ideas about sex circulate widely, pornography also puts into play the vulnerability of even those who do not view it.

Antipornography feminists have been particularly attuned to how pornography might make women vulnerable, and their critique relies upon an idea of vulnerability in two ways. First, the harm of porn lies in the way it exploits women's vulnerability. Second, it exploits women's vulnerability by portraying them as especially vulnerable and susceptible to harm. The depiction of women in pornography affirms the sense of feminine vulnerability discussed above and sanctions the sexual exploitation of women on its basis. Pornography exploits women's preexistent disproportionate bodily vulnerability, rendering them more vulnerable to sexual violence, for instance. It does so by advancing images of vulnerability and invulnerability in which women's bodily vulnerability and men's bodily invulnerability are naturalized and sexualized. In this way, on the antipornography account, porn constructs both a conception and a distribution of vulnerability along gender lines that enables the continued exploitation of the vulnerability of both women and men; it institutes gender-based sexual precarity.

How, in particular, is vulnerability imagined in porn? According to well-known feminist critics of pornography Andrea Dworkin and Catharine

MacKinnon, pornography makes vulnerability a property of women and defines being a woman as being sexually vulnerable.[3] Female vulnerability is manifest in the way women are portrayed as submissive, powerless objects that are acted upon and often harmed by men. Typical scenes involve women serving men by giving them pleasure (paradigmatically through oral sex), being dominated by, obeying, and submitting to men (e.g., taking orders from them, being told what they want and responding affirmatively), and being displayed or displaying themselves as objects for men, as when the camera focuses on eroticized parts of the body such as breasts, genitals, buttocks, mouth, which are sexualized in virtue of how they can be used by a male sexual partner.[4] Porn titles and dialogue commonly reinforce these visual elements, sometimes emphasizing what is perceived to be the extreme nature of the sexual acts performed, their aggressive quality, and the impact they might have on the woman (for instance, calling attention to the size of the man's penis, the effect it will have on the woman's body during oral, vaginal, or anal sex, the number of men with whom a woman will have sex either simultaneously or in succession, and so on). As Ann Garry explains in her account of the antiporn view, a common theme in mainstream heterosexual pornography is the polarization of gender roles: women are positioned as submissive, passive, powerless, acted upon harmed objects, and men are positioned as dominant, active, powerful, acting, harming subjects (Garry 2002, 350).

One of the central claims of antipornography feminism is that pornography sexualizes this hierarchy of submission/dominance, receptivity/aggressivity, and vulnerability/invulnerability. Not only does it sexualize women's bodies, but it also sexualizes women's submission and thus gender inequality. This account depends on the view that pornography determines sexuality and consequently determines how men treat women: MacKinnon states, "Gender is sexual. Pornography constitutes the meaning of that sexuality. Men treat women as who they see women as being. Pornography constructs who that is. Men's power over women means that the way men see women defines who women can be. Pornography is that way" (1984, 326). MacKinnon and Dworkin's view is thus constructivist through and through; sex and gender—what it means to be female or male, feminine or masculine—are constructed by power relations, and since gender is sexual, sexuality is constructed in terms of gender inequality. Pornography manifests that inequality, reinforces it, and thus "is a central practice in the subordination of women" and the maintenance of male dominance (Dworkin 2000, 30). Dworkin parses four aspects of subordination—hierarchy, objectification, submission, and violence—each of which appears in an eroticized fashion in mainstream pornography (Dworkin 2000, 30–31). Hierarchy may be evident in the way women cater to men's desires, for instance; submission is manifest in the fact that it is often men who command and women who obey; violence is eroticized most obviously in scenes of rape, but also through the persistent reliance on tropes of violation; objectification is evident in the close-ups of sexualized parts of women's bodies that have the effect of reducing women to those parts of their bodies and reducing those parts to tools for another's sexual pleasure.[5] Overall, the conclusion is that when pornography constructs sexuality, arousal is contingent upon inequality. Female vulnerability and powerlessness in conjunction with male invulnerability and power are eroticized.

Accordingly, antipornography feminists like MacKinnon and Dworkin emphasize that pornography is not *representation* but reality; it does not *depict* sexuality but "is sexual reality" (MacKinnon 1984, 326). MacKinnon summarizes this idea by noting the impact pornography has on experiences of sexuality:

> Pornography does not simply express or interpret experience; it substitutes for it. . . . As society becomes saturated with pornography, what makes for sexual arousal, and the nature of sex itself . . . change. What was words and pictures becomes, through masturbation, sex itself. As the industry expands, this becomes more and more the generic experience of sex, the woman in pornography becoming more and more the lived archetype for women's sexuality in men's, hence women's, experience. (MacKinnon 1993, 25–26)

Pornography is viewed as shaping how men view women—what they want and expect them to be—and thus shaping how women view themselves (through the eyes of men, which view them through the lens of pornography). Pornography can shape sexual reality because of the kind of response it provokes: a masturbatory one. Recounting the antipornography argument, Joshua Cohen summarizes the two mechanisms by which pornography is believed to reproduce gender inequality, making it the reality of sex itself. The cognitive mechanism describes how concepts of subordination and force are linked to sex and pleasure; given that sexual desires are "concept dependent," that is, are experienced socially and in terms of dominant concepts and patterns of interpretation, they end up reflecting "the pornographic conception of sexuality" (2006, 266).[6] The behavioral mechanism refers to the way in which masturbation to pornography "reinforces an association between sexual excitement and subordination" (ibid). Thus, on the antipornography view, not only does pornography delimit oppositional and hierarchical gender and sexual roles, it also elicits one type of fixed response: to do harm via sex, to exploit female vulnerability. MacKinnon claims, "the physical response to pornography is nearly a universal conditioned male reaction, whether they like or agree with what the materials say or not" (1993, 37). As eroticized in pornography, a limited image of feminine vulnerability provokes a limited response: arousal at the potential for violation.

The view that pornography shapes sexual reality is meant to refer not only to those who consume pornography but further to the sexual experiences of women and men in general. It licenses and enacts the abuse and sexual exploitation of women in general, but how? On MacKinnon's view, pornography and the law surrounding it silences women. Considered a 1st Amendment issue, the protection of pornographic speech enhances the power of pornographers. Free speech law, however, is plagued by an abstractness and formalism that prevents it from recognizing the practical ways speech is used in real life and the effects it has; it cannot take into account the context of inequality—gender hierarchy—in which speech takes place, and thus it is complicit in helping the powerful retain their power and silencing the powerless. Thus, MacKinnon's refrain is that pornography is not a moral issue but a political one. What is at stake is power: the power of men to dominate women and the powerlessness of women that "provides the appearance of consent and makes protest inaudible as well as rare" (1984, 336–337). As the speech of the powerful, what is said and portrayed in pornography—the view of women and men, of sex and harm—is far from unconventional. Indeed, "[i]t is the ruling ideology" (ibid, 337). By portraying the aforementioned dominance/submission dynamics as prevalent, desirable, and as the predominant model for heterosexual sex, porn makes oppositional, hierarchical sexual relations seem inevitable and natural. Men just are dominant, women just are submissive; women want to be desired, men have and act on desires; men command, women obey.[7] Given the ubiquity of these images, male power and dominance, and female powerlessness and submission are conceived as normal and, as such, unproblematic: "the harm cannot be discerned from the objective standpoint because it is so much of 'what is.' . . . To the extent pornography succeeds in constructing social reality, it becomes invisible as harm" (MacKinnon 1984, 335).

The implication of their view is that porn sexualizes dualism by sexualizing gender inequality via an enactment of static, oppositional sexualized gender roles. Of interest for this discussion is the predominance of the power/powerlessness dualism, which is the lens through which vulnerability is conceived: "The vulnerability of women's projected sexual availability—that acting we are allowed: asking to be acted upon—is victimization" (MacKinnon 1984, 327). Thus, the image of vulnerability at play in both mainstream porn and feminist criticism of it is the reductively negative one, vulnerability as susceptibility to harm and injury. Just as porn polarizes gender roles such that women are figured as passive, harmed objects and men as active, harming subjects, so it aligns vulnerability along these two poles, attributing it to women and not to men. The problem with this division is not simply that it is dualist but that it fragments human vulnerability, dividing the world cleanly into victims and perpetrators, sufferers and darers, or protectors and those in need of protection. As Bergoffen notes, this division "creates a world where women are required to carry the vulnerability of the human condition as a burden so that men can imagine that they can escape the vulnerabilities of being human" (2011, 318). From the antipornography perspective, the world is already arranged thus; porn portrays women as sexually vulnerable—open to exploitation—because women in general already are vulnerable. It makes women more vulnerable—susceptible to sexual harm—because it exacerbates a political situation in which women are powerless and men are powerful. Thus, women's (paradigmatically sexual) vulnerability is construed as pervasive powerlessness.

In response to this perspective, feminist critics contend that antipornography feminists subscribe too fully to the view of sexuality, gender, and power that they find in pornography. Following Wendy Brown, Amy Allen claims, "they are too willing to *mirror* the view of women that they see in pornography in their own theories" (Allen 2001, 516; see also Brown 2000 and Tisdale 1992). MacKinnon and Dworkin, among others, believe strongly in the power of pornography to construct the reality of sex and our sexual experience. Because they view pornography as so pervasive, defining, and dominating, as well as one-dimensionally misogynistic, the notions of power and vulnerability they invoke are ones generated in and by a pornographic culture and, thus, also appear to be misogynistic and one-sided. By maintaining that pornography *is* sexual reality, they deny women's agency. Thus, Sallie Tisdale's protest conflates moralist conservative and radical feminist critiques of pornography:

> Always, the censors are concerned with how men act and how women are portrayed. Women cannot make free sexual choices in that world; they are too oppressed to know that only oppression could lead them to sell sex. . . . What a misogynistic worldview this is, this claim that women who make such choices [e.g., to watch pornography] cannot be making free choices at all—are not free to make a choice. Feminists against pornography have done a sad and awful thing: They have made women into objects. (1992)

Although Tisdale's objection is at most hyperbolic and, at the very least, unfair, she expresses a vital worry: that the antipornography perspective confirms the worldview it aims to critique. It proposes that gender inequality and sexual subordination are constructed rather than natural, but, as many critics have noted, fails to give much of an account of how this all-encompassing construction functions (op. cit). The reality that is constructed is one in which men jettison vulnerability while it is reduced to a reified 'natural' property of women, a property that indicates their fitness and desire for sexual use.

Besides articulating the flaws of the antipornography view, feminist sex radicals have sought to offer a different perspective on sexuality, gender, and power, and thus on vulnerability (see Snitow, Stansell, and Thompson 1983; Vance 1984, Duggan 1995; Segal and McIntosh 1993; F.A.C.T. 1992). This set of positions can be summarized as having at least three main concerns: to articulate the positive importance of liberty and sexual expression, to voice concern about the effects of censorship, especially on non-normative sexualities, and to contest the description of pornographic imagery given in antipornography feminism, emphasizing instead (1) the diversity of material available, (2) the complexity of meaning in this material, and (3) the variety and ambivalence of responses to sexual material.

Concerning the first point, the creation and availability of sexual materials is regarded as crucial for feminism and women's sexual liberation. Pornographic depictions of sexuality in particular are lauded because they portray sex divorced from marriage and reproduction, embrace promiscuity and sexual pleasure for its own sake, and challenge other entrenched, often patriarchal, sexual mores; "the subversive quality of 'pornography' challenges the entire status quo, including social structures that inhibit women's freedom" (Strossen 1993, 1133). The upheaval of the sexual status quo is particularly important for women and for combating sexual repression given the long history of sexual double standards. If women have been considered sexually vulnerable—passive or receptive rather than active—then sexual representations that afford women opportunities to experience and understand their own desires, and also authorize them to act on them, will be crucial to their sexual empowerment. As Chancer concludes, "[a]ccording to this argument, some pornographic images are experienced as liberating in their effects, especially when expression of any sexual feelings has often been historically tabooed based on gender" (2000, 81). Wendy McElroy's account summarizes some additional benefits pornography has for women: it provides sexual information in the form of knowledge about the diversity of sexual possibilities available, offers this information in the form of experience rather than didactically, "provides women with a *safe* environment in which they can satisfy a healthy sexual curiosity[,]" and so enables women to gain this information and explore their desires in a setting that is less emotionally fraught because it is in the context of fantasy (1995, 130). Cohen likewise argues for the importance of expressive liberty on the basis of three core interests—informational, deliberative, and expressive—we have in such liberty. He postulates that it is crucial to deal openly with sexual subject matter, especially ones that deal with domination, submission, and violence. Since sexuality is intimately intertwined with power, regardless of what we make of this intertwining, surrendering free expression about it avoids the reality of sexual experience and obstructs attempts to make sense of it. Moreover, if the aim is to alter a misogynistic and moralistic status quo, then refraining from giving expression to the intertwining of sex and subordination, power and pleasure, submission and dominance, and violence and vulnerability seems akin to burying one's head in the sand to avoid the sun's glare. Instead, "it may be in part by working with that fusion and acknowledging its force, rather than by simply depicting a world of erotic possibilities beyond power, that we establish the basis for transforming existing forms of sexuality" (Cohen 2006, 288).[8]

Feminist sex radicals devote much effort to remedying some of the obvious oversimplifications in the picture of pornographic material drawn by antipornography feminists. As Cohen summarizes, "sexually explicit expression" has three features that call into question the value of censorship and contribute to the importance of expressive liberty: "its diversity, its interpretability, and uncertain connections with sexual practice" (2006, 286). First, not all pornographic material fits the description MacKinnon and Dworkin offer, which most accurately describes mainstream heterosexual porn and low-budget, hardcore 'gonzo' productions, in particular. For instance, BDSM scenes in which women dominate submissive men are quite common, queer pornography (versus 'lesbian' scenes designed for heterosexual men), in which dynamics of heterosexual domination are absent, is growing, and feminist pornography awards have been created to publicize non-mainstream pornography.[9] Second, many thinkers contest the idea that the meaning of sexually explicit material is univocal and clear and that the responses of viewers is correspondingly one-dimensional and fixed, oriented toward the sexual subordination of women. Rather, pornography contains contradiction, ambivalence, and polysemicity; it presents "intricate identity and gender crossings, the validity of female desire, and myriad forms of inversion and contradiction" (McClintock 1993, 115; see also Soble 2002). The complexity of significance is directly related to the potential for complex and ambiguous responses. As Strossen indicates, "no text or image has any 'objective,' fixed meaning, but rather has a different meaning for each member of its audience[,]" and, indeed, has this different meaning because of the particularity of the audience members (Strossen 1993, 1128). Kobena Mercer advances this claim as well in his consideration of Robert Mapplethorpe's *Black Book,* a 1988 volume of images of Black men, many nude and explicitly erotic. Mercer contrasts his initial impression that the effect of the images is to "stabilize the invisible and all-seeing white subject at the centre of the gaze, and thereby 'fix' the black subject in its place" with his realization that the allusion to sexualized racist stereotypes (that of black male hypersexuality, for instance) both reveals and problematizes these stereotypes as well as the general invisibility of black men in this artistic genre (the aesthetic nude) (1993, 99). He thus highlights the variation in and ambivalence of viewers' response to sexually explicit images and the need to understand the shifts and complexities in viewers' identifications, such as his own shift from identifying with the Black men who were portrayed to realizing how as a gay man he also identified as the purportedly masterful spectator (104).[10] The "social identity" of viewers, their particular desires, personal history, and social context shape how images are interpreted. Recognizing "the ambivalence of the text" as well as "the emotional ambivalence experienced by different audiences[,]" "foreground[s] the uncertainty of any one, singular meaning" (104, 102, 105). As a consequence of the ambivalence of both the pornographic 'text' and viewers' responses, the connection between sexually explicit material and sexual practices is unclear; pornography cannot be said to be unequivocally the central tool in the subordination of women.

It would appear that the feminist sex radical standpoint aligns better with the tenets of an ethic of vulnerability. Unlike antipornography feminism, there is no equation of vulnerability with femaleness or adherence to a reductively negative view of vulnerability. The ways sexually explicit material may affect a viewer cannot be determined in advance to be harmful and viewers are not conceived as preemptively vulnerable or invulnerable depending on their gender. Rather, the endorsement of polysemicity, complexity, and ambivalence converges with the idea that vulnerability is a form of potential defined by ambiguity and ambivalence. Although on the surface the sex radical perspective accords with the concept of vulnerability, there are two problematic inconsistencies within the position that limit the extent to which it can make sense of the experience of vulnerability in relation to sexuality and pornography. First, pornography and sexual expression in general are unproblematically conceived as liberatory forces that have been or are in danger of being repressed. Second, although they endorse the "post-structuralist" or "deconstructionist" view that pornography has no fixed or objective meaning (Strossen, 1128), in a move that is wholly inconsistent with the 'deconstructability' of the image, they also posit an autonomous, self-determining subject who interprets the pornographic text.

Amy Allen's analysis of the conceptions of power at work in antiporn and sex radical feminism illuminates both of these points. On Allen's account, both sides of the debate have overly simple understandings of power. Antiporn feminists equate power with domination, power wielded *over* others, whereas feminist sex radicals conceive of power in terms of empowerment, the power *to* act freely. Both miss the dimension of power the other side emphasizes. Whereas the antiporn view is reductive and appears to render female agency impossible, the sex radical view is too rosy and makes empowerment seem easy. In particular, they presume the existence of a repressive culture and so assume that the derepressive nature of porn is good for women. As a consequence, "consuming pornography is seen as in itself an act of resistance to patriarchy" (Allen 2001, 520). The view that sexual materials are inherently liberatory is tied both to the presumption of repression and to the intuition that there is something about sexuality—and thus about sexual expression—that is nonconformist, rebellious, and transgressive (see Kipnis 1996 and 2003). This assumption is flawed for a number of reasons. It posits sex as a 'natural' force that is inherently disruptive of the status quo and thus must continually contest its own repression. Setting aside the problematic invocation of the 'naturalness' of sex, this view lacks substantive recognition of the ways sexual acts, desires, and fantasies are always culturally mediated even as it relies on the cultural mediation of sexuality in order to conceptualize it as transgressive (i.e., the appeal of particular sexual acts, images, and ideas inheres in the perception that they have a transgressive quality, yet they are only experienced as transgressive because of how they are socially and culturally situated as violating social mores). Moreover, as Allen concludes, "The feminist sex radicals' faith in the repressive hypothesis leads them to ignore the ways in which the very agency and empowerment that they claim for women may be implicated in the relations of domination and subordination that feminists are trying to criticize" (521). That is, there is a difference between being empowered to act and acting in ways that resist domination. A woman may be empowered to pursue her own desires, but the fact that she derives pleasure from doing so does not make her actions intrinsically nonconformist or a mode of resistance. It is important to be able to take stock of the ways in which our desires may be complicit in domination and this kind of critical analysis is not tantamount to labeling women dupes of patriarchy if they enjoy pornography (as Tisdale imagines MacKinnon doing).

For pornography to possess this derepressive function, viewers are assumed to be autonomous, critical, and self-determining subjects. The emphasis sex radical feminists place on autonomy both stems from the background of liberal theory that informs the position and constitutes a rejoinder to what is perceived to be a denial of women's agency and autonomy in the antiporn view. Immediately following her reference to the "post-structuralist" or "deconstructionist" view that pornography has no fixed or objective meaning, Strossen asserts that the view that pornography "instills misogynistic attitudes, or even behavior, in viewers . . . denies individual autonomy" (1129).[11] Freedom of sexual expression, on the other hand, acknowledges and advances individual autonomy. This move comprises a mere reversal of the antiporn perspective. Rather than a wholly impressionable, fully constructed subject, implanted with sexist ideas, the subject is a self-determining agent who possesses full critical capacities and thus is impervious to the myriad messages of sexual media except those he chooses to receive. Foregrounding autonomy and individual liberty in this manner prevents recognition of how the subject herself is destabilized along with the destabilized polysemic text, and thus of how the relationship to sexual media is formative of subjectivity and desire. To return to the claims of section I, pornography is a social medium, one that mediates sexual desire and interaction. As a consequence, we may interpret the pornographic text, but we never interpret it alone or without a broader social context that may induce us to accept or reject certain messages, experience repulsion or attraction, be intrigued or bored, feel shame or titillation, become aroused or turned off. As Allen states, the paradox of subject formation is that the conditions that constitute us as subjects make possible at the same time domination and resistance:

> [A]lthough pornography can be understood as a medium for the transmission of relations of power that subordinate women to men, this mechanism of subordination is accomplished only by creating women as sexual subjects who are subjected to the relations of domination that pornography depicts; however, the fact that subjection is always

> Janus-faced means that these relations of domination themselves provide for the possibility of resistance. (526)

Accordingly, it makes as little sense to presume a fully autonomous, critical viewer as it does to presume that viewers are impressionable blank slates who merely assimilate the messages contained within pornography. Critical capacities are developed and practiced. If resistance to domination requires the capacity for critical interpretation of one's own desires as well as of sexually explicit material, then what we need is not an endorsement of pornography's role in women's empowerment but an exploration of the conditions that facilitate such critical response. A critical disposition in relationship to porn can only be achieved via education and, given the proliferation of internet pornography, is likely part of being a critical consumer of media in general.

In seeking to expand the discussion of sexuality and women's oppression beyond pornography, feminist sex radicals have called for improved sexual education, greater openness concerning sexuality, fostering women's ability to refuse coercive sex, and women to gain increased knowledge about their bodies, desires, and develop the capacity to ask for what brings them pleasure. In so doing, they recognize how sexist social contexts and expectations prevent women from readily achieving sexual liberation and pleasure. Yet, they dismiss the way pornography has a hand in these contexts when what is needed is an understanding of its role. A critical investigation of images' meanings and viewers' responses is relinquished in light of the diversity of images, meanings, and responses. Because we are unable to predict or know exactly what any particular viewer feels, thinks, or desires, the proliferation of images and desires is good enough, on the sex radical view. As a consequence, they fail to offer any way of thinking about what different types of images mean for different types of viewers, any sense of how the aforementioned prescriptions relate to pornography, or critical accounts of the relationship between pornography and sexual experience in general.[12] The implication of these points is that the feminist sex radical perspective is not entirely different from the antiporn perspective when it comes to vulnerability; that is, it is correspondingly one-sided. The viewer's openness to sexually explicit material is mitigated by her critical capacities and autonomy. Although she may encounter images and acts that repulse her or prompt ambivalent emotional responses, these are not described as having a lasting effect or generating harm because the interactions at stake are only with images rather than with others. Whereas the antiporn view solidifies pornography as sexual reality itself, the sex radical view confines it to the ostensibly safe domain of fantasy and individual exploration, forgetting the way sexuality is always an intersubjective field of experience. As a consequence, the range of the viewer's vulnerability is theoretically narrowed, that is, the impact pornography might have on sexual experience is limited to positive, derepressive effects, obscuring the nature of sexual vulnerability.

Pornography and Control

I turn now to a brief consideration of the theme of control as it appears in experiences of pornography. A gloss of how control is sought, asserted, and perhaps relinquished is central to understanding how sexually explicit material can function as an occasion for the pursuit of invulnerability, as well as to investigating to what extent the ambivalent and ambiguous character of vulnerability is preserved in common experiences of sexuality and pornography. From an antiporn perspective, pornography is the paradigmatic expression of male power, enacting and depicting male sexual power over and control of vulnerable women. Yet, use of pornography is also frequently understood as a performative manifestation of the absence of male control and power in contemporary culture; men must turn to pornography to feel secure and in control with respect to sexuality and relations with women. For this reason, pornography is a site where control over sexuality, one's own and that of others, is reasserted. Interaction with pornography may operate as an anxious shoring up of stereotypical masculinity, which is hidden behind a rhetoric that invokes the 'naturalness' of the masculine visual orientation and 'need' for sexual stimulation and relief, and simultaneously as a forum for an entrepreneurial approach to sexuality.

If, on the one hand, consumption of pornography indicates men's sense of powerlessness, it is also a manifestation of their experience of themselves as vulnerable in particular negative ways. Alan Soble's defense of male enjoyment of pornography illustrates how the medium enables consumers not to have to experience their vulnerability either in its negative aspects or as a more fundamental, ambiguous condition.[13] On Soble's account, the appeal of pornography lies in the sense of power and control that it affords men, who frequently feel powerless in relation to women (1998). Pornography is a form of compensation for men, of whose desires women have become less and less accommodating in the wake of feminism. It provides the typical fantasy in which one can pick and choose exactly the kinds of activities, situations, and 'partners' that one finds arousing. Chloë Taylor confirms and extends this point in a more critical fashion, noting that "[t]he fantasy world of much pornography produced for men is one in which women enjoy doing or having done to them what gives men pleasure. Such a fantasy is surely soothing in an era when women are demanding their own pleasure (which may not necessarily correspond with what brings men pleasure), and are judging men on their performance with the option of shopping around for better lovers should men fail to perform" (2009, 37). Contrary to claims that pornographic imagery involves a fixed, stereotypical, and repetitive sequence and conditions viewers to find inequitable, sexist, and violent depictions erotic, however, Soble contends that porn actually "allows men a great deal of autonomy in constructing sexual images" (1998, 560). It provides material with which to construct the fantasies in which one finds sexual satisfaction. This constructive dimension of pornography and the accompanying feeling of freedom makes it a fulfilling alternative to the boredom, dissatisfaction, and feelings of powerlessness that pervade men's lives, sexually and otherwise.

Soble's account accords with some of the experiences of many men who regularly view pornography. They echo the view that their consumption of pornography constitutes a realm of specifically male freedom, one that many wish to keep separate from relationships with women (Paul 2005). They regard pornography as a reprieve from the pressures of face-to-face sexual interaction, many especially enjoy viewing types of sexual activities in which they might not usually engage although others take pornography as a paradigm for sexual interaction, and consider the ability to select which women they watch—and perhaps about whom they fantasize—a key to the pleasure they take in pornography. The physical attractiveness of the women in pornography is important, but equally important is the unbridled enthusiasm the women show for sex and for men. In her study of consumers of pornography, Pamela Paul concludes that one of the main sources of pornography's appeal is the way it acts as reassurance:

> Pornography literally creates the man's world as he would ideally have it, free of exclusion, discomfort, stressful competition, and rejection.... In porn, she treats a man the way he wants to be treated, relieving him of the fears that plague everyday male-female interaction. In the porn world, men retain the power and the control. (Paul 2005, 32, 33)

In effect, the men viewing pornography regain a sense of power and control by dictating the terms of the sexual interaction, which they cannot do in the flesh with another person (hence the common reluctance to watch pornography with a partner and/or to give up watching it solo). This sense of control is admittedly one born of freedom from the hassles of intimacy and sex with other people; "pornography explicitly offers men the option of sex without risk, without vulnerability, without the potential to be hurt" (Paul 2005, 41). Thus, as compensation, it makes up not for a real absence of sexual autonomy—an inability to make substantive choices about sexual interaction or be free from coercion—but for the loss of an illusory invulnerability that many men desire to recoup, especially given the way masculinity is conceived as thoroughly intertwined with invulnerability. The loss of invulnerability is felt as a loss of masculinity and privilege in the sexual realm. Pornography acts as compensation for the erosion of (white, upper-class, heterosexual) male sexual privilege in the sense that it makes up for the inability to have one's desires fulfilled completely as one wishes them to be. It is an attempt to compensate for the way male sexual access to women is increasingly less taken for granted and gender inequality is subjected to greater scrutiny. The kind of control that is lost is the control that defined male dominance, and gender inequality and oppression. Thus, contra Soble, the autonomy that men may find in viewing pornography derives from experiencing sexual desire and pleasure without encountering the other who incites such feelings as an other who has her own experiences, subjectivity, and desires.[14] Thus, it is a privatized experience in which one has no responsibility to others because one is not interacting with another who is present and, further, is distanced from the others on the screen, conceiving what they do as the provision of entertainment rather than an intimate act. One avoids feeling vulnerable in the way Soble describes—a generalized sense of male powerlessness born of the advent of female empowerment—but one also evades experiences of vulnerability as a core part of what it is to be an embodied, social being: vulnerability as ambiguous potential.

A feeling of control is also pursued by seeking epistemic mastery through pornography, that is, through the acquisition of information about the human body, sexual acts, sexual preferences, and 'normal' or idealized modes of sexual comportment. Although feminist sex radicals defend sexually explicit materials precisely because they provide a plethora of information about human sexuality and facilitate sexual exploration, they do not account for some of the common uses of this information, which I contend foreclose experiencing vulnerability. The central questions to address are what knowledge is acquired through viewing pornography and for what purpose? Pornography is experienced as doing more than simply providing information about different sexual options.[15] Those performing in pornography are considered sexual experts of sorts (they have sex for a living after all, whereas the rest of us just have sex recreationally), and the knowledge sought and acquired is not only about the variety of sexual acts that exist, but about how to perform them and what to expect or ask others to do. As Taylor observes, "in so far as advocates say that pornography (or prostitution) is educational, they mean that it teaches sexual *skills* or *techniques*" (2009, 27). That pornography is taken as the chief source of practical knowledge about sex is evidenced by the proliferation of instructional pornography, often featuring popular porn stars who coach viewers on how to have anal sex, give good oral sex, venture into S&M, and so on. Per "exemplification theory," the sexual acts performed in pornography are seen as exemplars of what sex is like and thus as a basis for building one's sexual skill set (Paul 2005, 18). Pornography, thus, is a guidebook for acts, an avenue for increasing one's sexual repertoire; one learns a transferrable series of acts and techniques, an 'expert' mode of sexual comportment, and seeks to master one's body so it performs appropriately. What is not usually modeled in pornography, however, is how to deal with miscommunication, differing expectations, disappointment, and the all vagaries of human bodies, which cannot be willed to function as desired on command. Of particular concern for feminists, pornography does not provide guidance for dealing with coercion, discussing consent, or communicating one's desires to a partner; that is, it does not model modes of comportment that involve attunement and attentiveness to the specificity of one's partner and openness to the unexpected.

In addition to being a vehicle for the accumulation of sexual skills, pornography consumption also allows viewers to mold their sexual identities. The kind of consumption behavior that characterizes viewing pornography—behavior through which one exercises control—helps consumers to figure out who they are sexually. Feminist sex radicals also considered this form of knowledge a boon to women in particular. Yet, on Taylor's analysis, the issue is not as simple as merely acquiring a deeper understanding of preexistent sexual preferences and thus of one's identity. Consuming pornography, especially on the internet, is a process of discovery that often involves a search for the images that are most arousing. Viewers regard the preferences that are revealed as telling them who they are; their sexual identities are discovered through pornography. From a Foucaultian perspective, however, consuming pornography is not merely a process of discovery but rather creates particular kinds of sexual subjectivity. The preferences and desires realized are not inherent but produced through interaction with sexually explicit material among other things. Since viewers conceive themselves as uncovering something essential and true about themselves, however, they form a fairly rigid sexual identity:

> Pornography thus allows viewers to realize a sexuality or taxonomical sexual type, providing them with the opportunity to identify with one of many kinds of sexuality. . . . Now he knows the sites that specialize in the things he likes. Every time he types in what he wants to see in his search engine, he self-consciously reaffirms and reinscribes his sexual type. It therefore seems that pornography allows consumers to experiment with different kinds of pleasures that might not otherwise have been available to them and thus allows for a proliferation of sexualities; however, pornographic consumption also contributes to an identification with one kind of sexuality. (Taylor 2009, 41)

The control one can exercise over the kinds of acts and performers one watches consolidates that identity—one only views images that fit with one's 'type' of sexuality—and precludes exposure to images that would challenge one's sense of one's sexual type. Thus, the flexibility of sexual identification touted by Soble and feminist sex radicals is perhaps overstated or at least is absent from accounts of many men's experiences given the dominant form subjectivity takes. Rather, sexual self-identity is also predictable, knowable, and controllable and, as such, a site for entrepreneurial capacity enhancement. Thus, consuming pornography in this way embodies the values of Cixous' masculine economy; given presumptions of scarcity and fears about loss of status, sexual access, pleasure, and so on, control is exerted and alterity elided in order to regain those things in order to shore up a stable, fixed sense of self-identity. In a complementary vein, Margret Grebowicz contends, "Pornography is problematic when understood as a 'tool' . . . that requires the disappearance of the secret existence, of the possibility of real otherness . . . It is the perfect manifestation of [Baudrillard's idea of] the babbling political body, in which every subject is interchangeable for every other, exercising its rights and expressing, expressing, more and more, telling us what we already know, climaxing, always recognizable and predictable" (2011, 161–162). The expression involved in pornography is problematic on Grebowicz's view because it demands that all is seen and told, and so eliminates uncertainty, ambivalence and ambiguity, and any possibility of 'secrecy.' There is no hint, in pornography, that sexuality might involve encountering another person in her or his singularity. If everything about sex, bodies, desires, and pleasure is "always recognizable and predictable" then they pose no threat, their meaning is transparent, and one remains invulnerable even as one is physically exposed.[16] Thus, following Soble's account to its logical conclusion, consuming pornography can be a way of avoiding one's own vulnerability by supplanting feelings of powerlessness with those of control, however illusory, rather than facing that experience and responding to it.

Although not all pornography contains scenes in which men exert control over women or women relinquish control to men, and not all men view pornography in order to obtain a sense of sexual security, risk-free pleasure, and avoid emotional and physical vulnerability with a physically present sexual partner, the desire for a sense of control—over sex, their bodies, their relationships, and in some cases, the bodies and sexual experiences of women with whom they have sex—animates the impetus many feel to view pornography. The tendency in feminist critique of pornography has been to censure its content as a manifestation of men controlling women, making them into what men want them to be. Yet, when considering the experiences of consumers, it becomes clearer that the primary difficulty in the consumption of pornography is not the content per se but the sociopsychic rationales—preexisting or developing—that exist for its use: to be entertained, to attain sexual release without complication, to figure out how to define one's sexual subjectivity (including one's preferences regarding the physical attributes of partners, the kinds of acts that are arousing, and/or in which one wishes to engage), to obtain information. The first three motivations dilute the beneficial effects of the last. If one immediately closes a window when one encounters something strange or undesirable, the information one gains is only the information one was previously seeking and open to finding. The diversity, complexity, and contradiction that is said to characterize sexually explicit materials is hardly experienced when one sticks to what one knows and likes. Openness to sexual experience and vulnerability therein dissipates as one defines oneself as a sexual self who is turned on by hyper-enthusiastic slim brunettes over 5'5" with B/C cup-sized breasts, anal sex, and 'facials', for instance. In many ways, thus, the tendencies of viewers along with the commodification of sexuality (see Levy 2005) reinforce invulnerability as an ideal for sexual comportment. The sexual dimensions of the self are often governed by entrepreneurial imperatives and an ignorance of relationality that make sexual vulnerability an experience to avoid. This mode of avoidance has clear implications for comprehension of both the sexual vulnerability of others and vulnerability as a fundamental condition.

RESPONDING TO PORNOGRAPHY

From the perspective of an ethic of vulnerability, what ethical analysis can we offer of the content of sexually explicit materials and modes of interaction with them? That is, how does foregrounding the experiences of vulnerability and invulnerability alter the kinds of ethical analyses made? The main ethical criterion supplied by an ethic of vulnerability is that of responsiveness to vulnerability. The argument developed throughout previous chapters sought to expand our understanding of what constitutes responsiveness to vulnerability as well as how to understand exploitation of vulnerability, the latter of which is achieved not just by taking advantage of those who are disadvantaged and disempowered but further enabled by disavowals of vulnerability. The foregoing discussion vulnerability and invulnerability in relation to pornography should also make clear that exploitation of vulnerability takes place not only when someone in a perilous situation is abused but when the open, ambiguous, undetermined character of vulnerability is reduced, narrowed to a fixed, ostensibly pregiven, and overly determined way of being affected. To exploit vulnerability, there must be some who are exploited and others who do the exploiting (or the protecting), and vulnerability is accordingly divvied up inequitably and perceived reductively as negative, fixed, and homogenous. The exploitation of vulnerability consists of the appropriation of the capacity to affect and be affected for a particular, narrow end; it restricts a person's experience of vulnerability—what her body feels and communicates—and overrides its ambiguity and plasticity. Bergoffen's example of how the meaning-making powers of the human body can be seized and turned against the individual aptly demonstrates this point. So, exploitation of vulnerability reduces the condition and experience of vulnerability to a particularly negative one, which only facilitates the desire to disavow vulnerability and project it onto others. Hence, framing the issue of pornography in terms of vulnerability reorients the question of what is at stake in ethical and feminist discussions of it: one the one hand, preserving the ambiguity and indeterminacy of vulnerability, and, on the other hand, dealing with the exploitation of vulnerability that renders it a wholly negative condition, the experience of which is implicitly gendered (eschewed by masculinity and carried by femininity), and so results in a fixed, hierarchical distribution of the vulnerability that is a condition that pertains to all.

From this perspective, what exactly might be ethically problematic about pornography? As argued in the previous sections, the main issue we might take with consumer interaction with pornography is the way it fosters the pursuit of invulnerability and the cultivation of entrepreneurial subjectivity. Much mainstream heterosexual pornography may facilitate viewers' imperviousness to their own vulnerability, except as it manifests as susceptibility to arousal. The modes of comportment made possible by pornography tend to focus on sexual achievement and mastery rather than on an uncertain openness to unfamiliar and unpredictable kinds of experiences. Mediating one's sexuality—what one knows, how one identifies, the language one uses, what one finds arousing—through pornography can also encourage detachment and quests for control. Lastly, the imagery and language of much mainstream heterosexual pornography persists in overtly and exaggeratedly articulating gender binaries, if not gender hierarchy, and related dualisms such as passive/active, small/large, weak/strong, dominant/submissive, being served/serving, and so on. A dualist perspective on vulnerability is particularly apparent in the way that masculinity is portrayed as invulnerable and femininity as vulnerable, although this depiction is much less rampant than the antipornography perspective alleges since women in porn are often portrayed as especially enthusiastic if not nymphomaniacal. Although it is possible to play with such binaries, to tweak them to achieve subversive signification, there is not usually enough context in pornographic materials to turn the invocation of these tropes into transgressive elements rather than reinscriptions of orthodoxy. Nor is there enough critical attention on the part of viewers given their purposes in consuming pornography; the majority watch pornography for sexual stimulation and release, not to engage critically with their own desires and their social context or even to explore new dimensions of their sexuality.

What, then, is required for ethical response to vulnerability in this context? First, ethical response requires more than merely not causing harm. Constructive response begins with acknowledging vulnerability rather than eschewing it and then moves on to problematizing the social norms that attend vulnerability—in this case, those surrounding sexuality and gender—in order to move beyond the inequity of the sufferer/darer, exploiter/exploitee binaries. Thus, part of coming to terms with vulnerability entails rejecting these dualistic terms as givens and so not reifying vulnerability as a condition inherent to female sexuality. Response to our fundamental vulnerability requires recognizing it as a condition that transcends gender, which therefore entails portraying and experiencing it in this way. More generally, to respond to vulnerability demands comprehension of its character as univocal potential, ambiguous and ambivalent, and manifesting in diverse ways so that we might see how these features of vulnerability are covered over or exploited. Thinking about pornography in terms of vulnerability allows us both to comprehend the ways in which its consumption can be problematic—perpetuating inequality, reinforcing gender stereotypes, foisting unachievable expectations onto many—and to account for positive experiences with pornographic material. More importantly, however, when considering pornography in terms of how it depicts vulnerability and shapes experiences of vulnerability, we take stock of the ambivalence and ambiguity of affective and corporeal experience. Sexual experience may often be ambiguous: at once ecstatic and alienating, isolating and intimate, pleasurable and painful, producing meaning and causing anxiety, and so on. The vulnerability inherent in sexuality is likewise ambivalent; it may be the condition for intimate connection but also for violation. To present sexuality in a way that suggests none of this ambiguity and complexity is to depict an idealized fiction, a cartoonish display, or a mechanical demonstration as a reality. For instance, in pornography, on some occasions the infliction of pain is portrayed as producing pleasure. Though this kind of depiction indicates the intertwining of pain and pleasure, it eclipses the ambiguity of this intertwining by painting pleasure as unconditional and ecstatic. The nature of pornographic material is such that virtually no one stops the action of the scene, hesitates, voices qualms, expresses discomfort, or renegotiates the terms of the sexual encounter.[17] The aim of the scene is the production of pleasure or the appearance of pleasure. Pain may be a means to pleasure but it does not coexist with and complicate it in a way that might precipitate a more tenuous, changing, and mutable human interaction.

Accordingly, we can evaluate pornography and our interactions with pornography on the basis of whether it enables us to be responsive to the types of vulnerabilities it puts in play (e.g., bodily, psychological, emotional vulnerability). Images that make it possible for viewers to perceive vulnerability as a shared condition as well as to experience and reflect on their own ambiguous vulnerability are ones that allow for necessary critical reflection and ethical erotic engagement with others. Images that offer up what Drucilla Cornell describes as a frozen scene likely prevent viewers from experiencing their own vulnerability and from recognizing vulnerability as shared (2000). They may portray vulnerability as exclusively feminine, as an inevitable susceptibility to harm, as always subject to exploitation, or as a condition that merits punishment. Much mainstream heterosexual pornography likely functions to disconnect individuals from their own vulnerability, perhaps even displacing it—an undesirable weakness—onto the female figure (or women in general). These kinds of depictions of vulnerability cover over the features that make it a fundamental condition: its potentiality, its univocity, its ambiguity and ambivalence, and its diversity of manifestations. As I have suggested in the previous section, the development of fixed sexual identity—strong, specific, and unchanging sexual preferences that are taken as revelatory of the truth of one's sexual self—may be one way experiencing vulnerability is foreclosed. Other ways include (1) seeking as much knowledge as possible to eliminate uncertainty and gain epistemic control, (2) striving to develop mastery over one's body's sexual capacities, one's physical appearance in general, and consequently over the body's meaning-making capacities so that it conveys only the messages one intends for it to represent, and (3) asserting control over others by expecting them to meet certain norms for physical appearance, sexual willingness, and sexual performance.

The aim of this and the foregoing discussion has not been to establish an argument against pornography or to condemn its typical content or some of the common ways consumers interact with it, but rather to meditate on how sexually explicit media are often received and perceived in U.S. culture and, in particular, how they figure into the formation of a sense of sexual subjectivity. I have sought to raise some issues with respect to how vulnerability is represented and experienced in relation to pornography, and thus to interrogate pornography as a site where entrepreneurial subjectivity is cultivated with respect to sexuality. The persistence of sexual violence, the centrality of embodiment to self-identity, and the hyper-focus on bodily appearance in contemporary culture make sexuality an important axis for understanding experiences of vulnerability and invulnerability. As embodied and as sexual beings we experience a keen sense of ourselves as vulnerable: physically open, emotionally susceptible, and caught in a complex web of social significance, norms, and values. When it comes to sexuality, vulnerability is eschewed in part because sex is paradigmatically embodied, making the desires, fears, and responses it brings on physically, often visibly, manifest. We cannot hide vulnerability as easily when it is written on the body, thus the body is the locus of a heightened imperative for control. Moreover, given our contemporary commonplace notion that our sexuality defines our self-identity, these responses hit close to home; we take them to be central to our sense of ourselves, revelatory of our self-identity. What one's body looks like, what it does, how others respond to it or do to it make one feel especially vulnerable in a culture that is especially concerned with bodily appearance and the place of sexuality in self-identity. Thus, sexuality may readily be experienced as a facet of life where invulnerability is needed and so comprises a prime site for cultivating an invulnerable entrepreneurial self, one over which one has control and through which one presents a masterful image to the world. None of which is to say that pornography operates unequivocally to produce entrepreneurial dispositions and so serves to maintain ignorance of vulnerability. Rather, it is to express a need for images and language that point to the complexity of experiences of sexuality as a locus of human vulnerability. Pornography can, and indeed much nonmainstream material does, work to undermine and contest firmly entrenched ideas about sex, gender, and vulnerability. Yet, as Angela Carter writes, pornography is subversive only when "it begins to comment on real relations in the real world" (2000, 539). These "real relations" are ones in which we are all vulnerable in some way, thus the only way for porn to be subversive is for it to attempt to show this vulnerability.

NOTES

1. For further discussion of the use of rape as a weapon of war and genocidal rape, see Card 1996 and Miller 2009 for example.

2. For a selection, see Allen 2008, Bartky 1990, Bordo 2003, Butler 1999 and 2004b, Heyes 2007, Huffer 2010, McLaren 2002, Sawicki 1991, Taylor and Vintges 2004, Warner 1999.
3. Here I take MacKinnon and Dworkin's work to be exemplary of feminist critique of pornography, but other representative work includes Longino 1980, Kittay 1984, Whisnant and Stark 2004, Langton 2009, and Dines 2010.
4. MacKinnon and Dworkin's definition of pornography is as follows: "Pornography is the graphic sexually explicit subordination of women, whether in pictures or in words, that also includes one or more of the following: (i) women are presented dehumanized as sexual objects, things or commodities; or (ii) women are presented as sexual objects who enjoy pain or humiliation; or (iii) women are presented as sexual objects who experience sexual pleasure in being raped; or (iv) women are presented as sexual objects tied up or cut up or mutilated or bruised or physically hurt; or (v) women are presented in postures of sexual submission, servility or display; or (vi) women's body parts—including but not limited to vaginas, breasts, and buttocks—are exhibited, such that women are reduced to those parts; or (vii) women are presented as whores by nature; or (viii) women are presented being penetrated by objects or animals; or (ix) women are presented in scenarios of degradation, injury, torture, shown as filthy or inferior, bleeding, bruised, or hurt in a context that makes these conditions sexual" (MacKinnon 1984, 321). As Garry (2002) notes, this statement builds harm, and thus moral wrong, into the definition itself. A more neutral definition is "explicit sexual materials intended to arouse the reader, listener, or viewer sexually" (Garry 2002, 346).
5. Martha Nussbaum has astutely argued that objectification has at least seven distinct senses: denial of subjectivity, denial of autonomy, instrumentality, fungibility, inertness, violability, and ownership or commodification (1999). All seven are likely present in different examples of pornography, including what are, on Nussbaum's account, some of the more pernicious forms such as denial of autonomy and denial of subjectivity.
6. See Garry 2002 for an analysis of the cultural conceptual link made between sex and harm, and its implications for respect for women.
7. On the tendency to postulate opposing, complementary male and female sexual tendencies as 'natural' see Bordo 1999b.
8. Cohen's argument dovetails with one aspect of that offered by Nadine Strossen: that censorship would have detrimental consequences for work that is of particular interest for feminists and sexual minorities. The use of censorship laws in Canada to target queer bookstores and, reputedly, to confiscate feminist work, including Andrea Dworkin's, has also been cause for concern (see Strossen 1993, 1143–1146). Since legislation like that which MacKinnon and Dworkin sought to pass vests additional power in the State and the law, representative of the status quo, "such censorship poses a special threat to any sexual expression that society views as unconventional" (Strossen 1993, 1145). The contention is that such legislation makes gay, lesbian, queer, and feminist work more susceptible to censorship.
9. See https://www.facebook.com/FeministPrnAwards and http://www.goodforher.com/fpa_2013
10. On viewers' shifting and unconventional identifications in relation to pornography see Williams 1989 and Kipnis 1996.
11. I note the proximity of these two points only to highlight the inconsistency in endorsing them both. It is tantamount to saying that we can call into question the fixity of the text without calling into question the fixity of the subject who interprets it. Part of the 'post-structuralist' and 'deconstructive' move is also to deconstruct the subject. If the text's meaning is destabilized,

rendered deconstructible and reconstructible, so are readers, who are themselves subjects constituted through complex social relations. What they view affects them in the sense that it shapes their subjectivity; they do not interpret it from some pure and established position of autonomy.
12. See Cindy Gallop's Make Love Not Porn TED Talk (http://blog.ted.com/2009/12/02/cindy_gallop_ma/) and website (makelovenotporn.com) for an example of critical interaction with pornographic imagery and the effect it has on sexual experience.
13. Since the demographic on which Soble's argument, and most other considerations of the topic, centers is heterosexual men, the following discussion narrows its focus to heterosexual men as well.
14. The point here is not that the many men who regularly use pornography for sexual satisfaction eschew intimate relationships with women in favor of pornography (although there is some evidence that sexual interaction between partners declines with regular use of pornography), but rather that consumption of pornography treats what is a fundamentally intersubjective domain—sexuality—as a solipsistic one since the 'partner' is the image of a pornographic actress on a screen with whom there is no spontaneous, unpredictable, and uncontrolled interaction.
15. According to a 2002 poll by the Kinsey Institute, the most common sentiment expressed about pornography is that "it can educate people"; 86% of respondents expressed this sentiment. See http://www.pbs.org/wgbh/pages/frontline/shows/porn/etc/surveyres.html
16. For an explanation of how sexual 'normalcy' reveals underlying neurosis, which involves a need to manifest control and invulnerability in contexts of sexual vulnerability, see Russon 2003, 107–110.
17. There are obviously some exceptions to this claim. For instance, the premise of Tristan Taormino's *Rough Sex* is that the actresses script and act in their own fantasies, dictating their partners and the terms of the sexual encounter. Each scene is preceded by an interview with the performers. The scene between well-known pornographic actress Sasha Grey and actor Danny Wylde includes a fair amount of verbal communication, expression of limits, and renegotiation of the terms of the sexual encounter.

7 Conclusion

This work has sought to develop a few interwoven lines of reasoning. By charting the ways a concept of vulnerability has been articulated and utilized in the context of ethics, I have sought to demonstrate its salience for normative endeavors while raising some questions about these accounts, beginning with a critique of what I have throughout called a reductively negative understanding of vulnerability. To be clear, not all 'negative' uses of the term vulnerability entail such an understanding; vulnerability is a condition of potential and as such can precipitate harm along with myriad other consequences. My aim has not been to reject this use of the term but to question its predominance and the way it is taken as the essence of what it is to be vulnerable. Rather, a reductively negative view of vulnerability is one that has the non-logical implication of avoidance and disavowal of vulnerability. This non-logical implication occurs when vulnerability is defined either expressly or implicitly as a negative, homogenous, and static state, the attribution of which is necessarily asymmetrical. Given this implicit understanding, many failures attend vulnerability, ranging from denials of one's own vulnerability to the inability to perceive and respond to the vulnerability of others to the adoption of a posture of persecution intended to legitimate defensive actions. All of these failures presuppose a reductively negative understanding of vulnerability, reduce what is a shared condition to a negative property, and fragment a common vulnerability by divvying it up along lines of gender, race, socioeconomic class, ability, nationality, and other salient social differences. The reductive understanding of vulnerability is thus complicit in oppression and facilitates the persistence of inequality. These failures call for a critique of the norms and ideals that comprise their conditions of possibility: the pursuit of invulnerability, profound ignorance of vulnerability, and entrepreneurial subjectivity, all of which are mundane features of everyday life in the post-industrial, capitalist West and all of which perpetuate arrogance, oppression, and denials of responsibility.

An ethics of vulnerability thus requires both such a critique and a more expansive understanding of what vulnerability is, which I have sought to offer throughout and, in particular, in the fifth chapter. Overall, we might summarize an ethics of vulnerability as one defined by responsiveness and a critical disposition. Such an ethic calls us to be responsive to our own vulnerability and to the vulnerability of others, but also to be critical of the norms that orient those responses. In this context, critique in the name of ethics entails questioning how we think of vulnerability, the way vulnerability in general is framed, the ways different vulnerabilities are framed differently, the connection between our ideas about and our experiences of vulnerability, whether and how we perceive vulnerability, and whether and how we are able to respond to it. A critical disposition is a crucial aspect of an ethics of vulnerability precisely because of the failures that attend vulnerability. Yet, critical attention needs to be directed not only at the ways we may fail to take responsibility but also at our own activities in the service of ethics. That is, the very personal virtues that would comprise an ethic of vulnerability—those of openness and receptivity, for instance—have the potential to be co-opted by entrepreneurial subjectivity. Cultivating openness, receptivity, or what Brené Brown calls "wholeheartedness" (2010) can become just another way to develop status and social capital, especially when these virtues are regarded as having instrumental value (e.g., creating a more efficient work environment).[1] Social critique is necessary to prevent the virtues of vulnerability from being co-opted in this way since what distinguishes them, as dimensions of an ethic, from just socially esteemed character traits is the way they require rejection of privatizing, individualizing tendencies. Openness, receptivity, avowal of vulnerability must be ways of opening the self to others who compose the self's community and thus ways of contesting rather than persisting in denied dependency. They are, as MacIntyre names them, virtues of acknowledged dependence rather than character traits that merely make one a better person as an individual.

Thus, one implication of an ethics of vulnerability is the imperative to shift the sense of self with which we function both theoretically and in terms of everyday practice. As feminist thinkers from diverse schools of thought have amply demonstrated, there are many problems with traditional and socially dominant conceptions of subjectivity. The individualism and solipsism of the sense of selfhood that imagines persons to be bounded, coherent, unified, rational individuals, ones who ought to be self-sufficient, independent, and masterful, coincides with and presupposes the ideal of invulnerability. An ethics of vulnerability necessitates an idea of the self as reciprocally constituted by others, always fundamentally interconnected and interwoven with the selves of others, permeable, and both mutable and in the process of altering. The displacement of invulnerability as a norm dislodges ideals of self-sufficiency, masterful control, and certainty and allows space for more sustaining ideals of interdependence, affirmation of uncertainty, and working through ambiguity with hesitation, questioning, and critical reflection. Only given this shift in the sense of the self can responsibility be undertaken more adequately, and expanded from the usual realm of concern—responsibility to one's self and for one's own individual actions—to that of the living in shared vulnerability.

This conclusion brings us to another implication of an ethics of vulnerability, which is the idea that experiencing vulnerability is itself central to ethical response to vulnerability. This notion is key for Butler, for instance, who contends that recognition is not "the best way to register precariousness" (2009, 13). Comprehension of precariousness and vulnerability is not achieved through a cognitive acknowledgement, but rather is a matter of experience: of undergoing, seeing, feeling, and sensing. Moreover, recognizing vulnerability in a merely cognitive way does it a disservice by failing to capture what is significant about it. We may look to the objective features of a situation in order to determine the nature of the vulnerability without comprehending their significance and impact on those who inhabit that situation. To understand how others experience their vulnerabilities, though, requires embodied, imaginative capacities. Thus, for vulnerability to have the kind of normative significance that we aspire for it to have—for it to motivate and sustain responsibility—it must be experienced. That is, it must constitute a basis for an expansive practice of empathy like that described at the outset of this work. It is not the case that such experience of vulnerability is unequivocally ethical or necessarily prompts ethical response, but rather it is a requisite starting point for such response that one actually feel vulnerable rather than shut down such feelings as soon as one finds oneself in a condition of vulnerability. This implication entails that we begin to live our vulnerabilities differently and make of everyday life a practice in experiencing vulnerability otherwise. As should be clear, the idea is not to avow potentially harmful forms of vulnerability and seek them out, but to alter how we perceive vulnerability's ambiguity, regarding it not as threat but as an unavoidable, pervasive condition. In particular, altering our prereflective relationship to vulnerability involves developing greater awareness of positive forms of vulnerability so that we might both feel this dimension of vulnerability in a wider array of circumstances, and conceptualize and apply the idea of vulnerability in ways that emphasize the '-ability' facet of the concept. If to be vulnerable is defined simply as being capable of or open to being wounded, then, as Nancy Annaromao notes, such capability is equally that of being "open as Webster defines open, namely, 'being in a position or adjustment to permit passage'" (1996, 6). The ability or capacity of vulnerability is, as Cixous describes, that openness that allows us to move forward, to change, to experience something new, to pass from what we take ourselves to be to what we are becoming, and so perhaps learn.

All philosophical argumentation effectively functions as narrative, advancing stories from particular perspectives and inventing or endorsing particular ways of framing issues. To the extent that it contains assumption, every narrative also contains omissions, some more dire and consequential than others, of course, and this one is no exception. I think it is fitting, thus, to conclude from a place of epistemic vulnerability. As Kimberly Hutchings suggests in her analysis of invulnerable judgment, recognizing the vulnerability of judgment entails "an extension and intensification of the responsibilities of the scholar" (2013, 38). I am uncertain if I have undertaken such responsibility, as a scholar and as a person, as well as I could have. There are many gaps in this narrative, not all of which I am yet aware. I wish, for instance, to have had more space to give voice to peoples' own accounts of their experiences of vulnerability and invulnerability as well as to have been able to indicate more directly how vulnerability and the ethics it sustains necessarily extends beyond the human domain, entailing different modes of relating to animals and the natural world. There is likewise much more that needs to be said about vulnerability in relation to race, gender, and sex, issues upon which I have only touched. These areas are avenues for future inquiry and contemplation for both myself and others. Though all perspectives are only partial, glimpses of a sliver of what is the case for us, my aspiration has been to articulate a perspective that casts a different light on what we mean when we speak, think, and theorize about vulnerability and what we experience when we find ourselves exposed, open, and uncertain. I only hope a fragment of the thoughts contained herein do so and thus gesture to some form of experience that called for response.

NOTE

1. This concern is what I take Critchley and Webster to be expressing in their piece concerning authenticity in *The Stone* (2013).

Bibliography

Adorno, Theodor and Max Horkheimer. 1972. *The Dialectic of Enlightenment.* New York: Continuum.
Alcoff, Linda. 2007. "Epistemologies of Ignorance: three types." In *Race and Epistemologies of Ignorance,* edited by Shannon Sullivan and Nancy Tuana, 39–57. Albany, NY: SUNY Press.
Allen, Amy. 2001. "Pornography and Power." *Journal of Social Philosophy* 32 (4): 512–531.
———. 2008. *The Politics of Ourselves.* New York: Columbia University Press.
Annaromao, Nancy. 1996. "A Feminist Interpretation of Vulnerability." *Philosophy in the Contemporary World* 3 (1): 1–7.
Baker, Tom and Jonathan Simons. 2002. "Embracing Risk." In *Embracing Risk: the Changing Culture of Insurance and Responsibility,* edited by Tom Baker and Jonathan Simons, 1–26. Chicago: University of Chicago Press.
Bankoff, Gregory. 2001. "Rendering the World Unsafe: 'Vulnerability' as Western Discourse." *Disasters* 25 (1): 19–35.
Bannon, Bryan E. 2011. "Flesh and Nature: Understanding Merleau-Ponty's Relational Ontology." *Research in Phenomenology* 41: 327–357.
Bartky, Sandra. 1990. *Femininity and Domination.* New York: Routledge.
Bayoumi, Moustafa. 2008. *How Does it Feel To Be a Problem?* New York: Penguin.
Beattie, Amanda and Kate Schick. 2013. *The Vulnerable Subject.* New York: Palgrave Macmillan.
Beck, Ulrich, 2006. "Living in a World Risk Society." *Economy and Society* 35 (3): 329–345.
Benhabib, Seyla. 1987. "The Generalized and the Concrete Other." In *Women and Moral Theory,* edited by Eva Feder Kittay and Diana T. Meyers, 154–177. New York: Rowman and Littlefield.
Bergoffen, Debra. 2003. "February 22, 2001: Toward a Politics of the Vulnerable Body." *Hypatia* 18 (1): 116–134.
———. 2009. "Exploiting the Dignity of the Vulnerable Body: Rape as a Weapon of War." *Philosophical Papers* 38 (3): 307–325.
———. 2011. *Contesting the Politics of Genocidal Rape.* New York: Routledge.
Bordo, Susan. 1999a. *Twilight Zones: The Hidden Life of Cultural Images from Plato to O.J.* Berkeley, CA: University of California Press.
———. 1999b. "Gentleman or Beast?: The Double-Bind of Masculinity." In *The Male Body,* 229–264. New York: Farrar, Strauss, Giroux.
———. 2003. *Unbearable Weight: Feminism, Western Culture, and the Body.* Berkeley, CA: University of California Press.
Brown, Brené. 2010. *The Gifts of Imperfection.* Center City, MN: Hazelden.

Brown, Kate. 2011. "'Vulnerability': Handle with Care." *Ethics and Social Welfare* 5 (3): 313–321.
Brown, Wendy. 2000. "The Mirror of Pornography." In *Feminism and Pornography*, edited by Drucilla Cornell, 198–217. New York: Oxford University Press.
Butler, Judith. 1999. *Gender Trouble*. New York: Routledge.
———. 2004a. *Precarious Life: The Powers of Mourning and Violence*. New York: Verso.
———. 2004b. *Undoing Gender*. New York: Routledge.
———. 2004c. "What is Critique? An Essay on Foucault's Virtue." In *The Judith Butler Reader*, edited by Sarah Salih, 302–322. New York: Wiley-Blackwell.
———. 2005. *Giving an Account of Oneself*. New York: Fordham.
———. 2007. "Reply from Judith Butler to Mills and Jenkins." *differences* 18 (2): 180–195.
———. 2009. *Frames of War: When is life grievable?*. New York: Verso.
Calhoun, Cheshire. 1988. "Justice, Care, and Gender Bias." *Journal of Philosophy* 85 (9): 451–463.
Card, Claudia. 1996. "Rape as a Weapon of War." *Hypatia* 11 (4): 5–18.
Carter, Angela. 2000. "Polemical Preface: Pornography in the Service of Women." In *Feminism and Pornography*, edited by Drucilla Cornell, 527–539. New York: Oxford University Press.
Cavarero, Adriana. 2009. *Horrorism*. Translated by William McCuaig. New York: Columbia University Press.
Chancer, Lynn. 2000. "From Pornography to Sadomasochism: Reconciling Feminist Differences." *Annals of the American Academy of Political and Social Science* 571: 77–88.
Cixous, Hélène and Catherine Clément. 1986. *The Newly Born Woman*. Translated by Betsy Wing. Minneapolis: University of Minnesota Press.
Code, Lorraine. 2006. *Ecological Thinking*. New York: Oxford University Press.
Cohen, Joshua. 2006. "Freedom, Equality, and Pornography." In *Prostitution and Pornography: Philosophical Debate about the Sex Industry*, edited by Jessica Spector, 258–295. Stanford, CA: Stanford University Press.
Collins, Patricia Hill. 2000. "The Social Construction of Black Feminist Thought." In *Black Feminist Thought* 2nd ed. New York: Routledge.
Cornell, Drucilla. 2000. "Pornography's Temptation." In *Feminism and Pornography*, edited by Drucilla Cornell, 551–568. New York: Oxford University Press.
Counihan, Carole. 1999. *The Anthropology of Food and the Body*. New York: Routledge.
Critchley, Simon and Jamieson Webster. 2013. "The Gospel According to 'Me.'" *New York Times*, June 29. Accessed July 5, 2013. http://opinionator.blogs.nytimes.com/2013/06/29/the-gospel-according-to-me/
Dean, Jodi. 2008. "Change of Address: Butler's ethics at sovereignty's deadlock." In *Judith Butler's Precarious Politics*, edited by Terrell Carver and Samuel A. Chambers, 109–126. New York: Routledge.
De Beauvoir, Simone. 1976. *The Ethics of Ambiguity*. New York: Citadel Press.
———. 2011. *The Second Sex*. Translated by Constance Borde and Sheile Malovany Chevallier. New York: Vintage.
Deleuze, Gilles. 1994. *Difference and Repetition*. Translated by Paul Patton. New York: Columbia University Press.
———. 1985. *Différence et répétition*. Paris: Presses Universitaries de France.
Dines, Gail, 2010. *Pornland*. Boston: Beacon Press.
Diprose, Rosalyn. 2002. *Corporeal Generosity*. Albany, NY: SUNY Press.
Duggan, Lisa, ed. 1995. *Sex Wars: Sexual Dissent and Political Culture*. London: Routledge.

Dunkel, Tom. 2010. "Vigor Quest." *New York Times Magazine*, January 15. Accessed January 19, 2010. http://www.NYtimes.com/2010/01/17/magazine/17antiaging-t.html?pagewanted=1&hpw
Dworkin, Andrea. 2000. "Against the Male Flood: Censorship, Pornography, and Equality." In *Feminism and Pornography*, edited by Drucilla Cornell, 19–38. New York: Oxford University Press.
Estabrook, Barry. 2011. *Tomatoland*. Kansas City, MO: Andrews McMeel Publishing.
Ewald, François. 2002. "The Return of Descartes's Malicious Demon: An Outline of a Philosophy of Precaution." In *Embracing Risk*, edited by Tom Baker and Jonathan Simon, 273–300. Chicago: University of Chicago Press.
F.A.C.T. Book Committee. 1992. *Caught Looking: Feminism, Pornography, and Censorship*. East Haven, CT: LongRiver Books.
Fineman, Martha. 2008. "The Vulnerable Subject: Anchoring equality in the human condition." *Yale Journal of Law and Feminism* 20 (1): 1–23.
Foucault, Michel. 1990. *The History of Sexuality, Volume I*. Translated by Robert Hurley. New York: Vintage.
———. 1995. *Discipline and Punish*. Translated by Alan Sheridan. New York: Vintage.
———. 1997. "What is Enlightenment?" In *Ethics: Subjectivity and Truth*, edited by Paul Rabinow, 303–319. New York: The New Press.
———. 2008. *The Birth of Biopolitics*. Trans. Graham Burchell. New York: Palgrave Macmillan.
Frye, Marilyn. 1983. *The Politics of Reality: Essays in Feminist Theory*. Freedom, CA: The Crossing Press.
Garry, Ann. 2002. "Sex, Lies, and Pornography." In *Ethics in Practice*, edited by Hugh LaFollette, 344–355. Malden, MA: Blackwell.
Gilson, Erinn. 2011. "Responsive Becoming: Ethics between Deleuze and Feminism." In *Deleuze and Ethics*, edited by Nathan Jun and Daniel W. Smith, 63–88. Edinburgh: Edinburgh University Press.
———. 2013. "Review Essay: Ann Murphy, *Violence and the Philosophical Imaginary*." *Journal of French and Francophone Philosophy* 21 (1): 173–182.
Goodin, Robert E. 1985a. *Protecting the Vulnerable: A Reanalysis of Our Social Responsibilities*. Chicago: University of Chicago Press.
———. 1985b. "Vulnerabilities and Responsibilities: An Ethical Defense of the Welfare State." *The American Political Science Review* 79 (3): 775–787.
Gottlieb, Robert and Anupama Joshi. 2010. *Food Justice*. Cambridge, MA: MIT Press.
Grebowicz, Margret. 2011. "Democracy and Pornography: On Speech, Rights, Privacies, and Pleasures in Conflict." *Hypatia* 26 (1): 150–165.
Guenther, Lisa. 2006. *The Gift of the Other*. Albany, NY: SUNY Press.
Held, Virginia. 1998. "Feminist Reconceptualizations in Ethics." In *Philosophy in a Feminist Voice*, edited by Janet A. Kournay, 92–115. Princeton, NJ: Princeton University Press.
Heyes, Cressida. 2007. *Self-Transformations: Foucault, Ethics, and Normalized Bodies*. New York: Oxford University Press.
Hoagland, Sarah Lucia. 2007. "Denying Relationality: epistemology and ethics and ignorance." In *Race and Epistemologies of Ignorance*, edited by Shannon Sullivan and Nancy Tuana, 95–118. Albany, NY: SUNY Press.
Honneth, Axel. 2008. *Reification*. New York: Oxford University Press.
hooks, bell. 2000. *Feminist Theory From Margin to Center*. Cambridge, MA: South End Press.
Huffer, Lynne. 2010. *Mad for Foucault: Rethinking the Foundations of Queer Theory*. New York: Columbia University Press.

Hutchings, Kimberly. 2013. "A Place of Greater Safety? Securing Judgement in International Ethics." In *The Vulnerable Subject,* edited by Amanda Beattie and Kate Schick, 25–42. New York: Palgrave Macmillan.
Jen, Gish. 2010. *World and Town.* New York: Vintage.
Jenkins, Fiona. 2007. "Toward a Non-Violent Ethics: A Response to Catherine Mills." *differences* 18 (2): 156–179.
Kessler, David. 2010. *The End of Overeating.* New York: Rodale.
Kingsolver, Barbara. 2007. *Animal, Vegetable, Miracle.* New York: Harper Collins.
Kipnis, Laura. 1996. *Bound and Gagged.* New York: Grove Press.
———. 2003. *Against Love.* New York: Vintage.
———. 2006. *The Female Thing.* New York: Vintage.
Kittay, Eva Feder. 1984. "Pornography and the Erotics of Domination." In *Beyond Domination: New Perspectives on Women and Philosophy,* edited by Carol Gould, 145–74. Totowa, NJ: Rowman.
———. 1999. *Love's Labor.* New York: Routledge.
———. 2011. "Ethics of Care, Dependence, and Disability." *Ratio Juris* 24 (1): 49–58.
Kittay, Eva Feder and Ellen K. Feder. 2002. *The Subject of Care: Feminist Perspectives on Dependency.* New York: Rowman and Littlefield.
Langton, Rae. 2009. *Sexual Solipsism.* New York: Oxford University Press.
Lazzarato, Maurizio. 2009. "Neoliberalism in Action: Inequality, Insecurity, and the Reconstitution of the Social." *Theory, Culture, and Society* 26 (6): 109–133.
Levy, Ariel. 2005. *Female Chauvinist Pigs.* New York: Free Press.
Lloyd, Moya. 2008. "Towards a Cultural Politics of Vulnerability." In *Judith Butler's Precarious Politics,* edited by Terrell Carver and Samuel A. Chambers, 92–105. New York: Routledge.
Longino, Helen. 1980. "Pornography, Oppression, and Freedom." In *Take Back the Night,* edited by Laura Lederer, 40–54. New York: William Morrow.
Lorde, Audre. 1984. *Sister Outsider.* Freedom, CA: The Crossing Press.
Luna, Florencia. 2009. "Elucidating the Concept of Vulnerability: Layers Not Labels." *The International Journal of Feminist Approaches to Bioethics* 2 (1): 121–139.
Lupton, Deborah. 1999. "Introduction: risk and sociocultural theory." In *Risk and Sociocultural Theory: New Directions and Perspectives,* edited by Deborah Lupton, 1–11. New York: Cambridge University Press.
MacIntyre, Alasdair. 1999. *Dependent Rational Animals: Why Human Beings Need the Virtues.* Chicago: Open Court Press.
Mackenzie, Catriona and Natalie Stoljar, ed. 2000. *Relational Autonomy.* New York: Oxford University Press.
MacKinnon, Catharine. 1984. "Not a Moral Issue." *Yale Law and Policy Review* 2 (2): 321–345.
———. 1993. *Only Words.* Cambridge, MA: Harvard University Press.
Mader, Mary Beth. 2007. "Foucault and Social Measure." *Journal of French Philosophy* 17 (1): 1–25.
Marsden, Jill. 2004. "Deleuzian Bodies, Feminist Tactics." *Women: A Cultural Review* 15 (3): 308–319.
McClintock, Anne. 1993. "Gonad the Barbarian and the Venus Flytrap: Portraying the Male and Female Orgasm." In *Sex Exposed: Sexuality and the Pornography Debate,* edited by Lynne Segal and Mary McIntosh, 111–131. New Brunswick, NJ: Rutgers University Press.
McCluskey, Martha T. 2002a. "Subsidized Lives and the Ideology of Efficiency." In *The Subject of Care,* edited by Eva Feder Kittay and Ellen K. Feder, 115–137. Lanham, MD: Rowman and Littlefield.

——. 2002b. "Rhetoric of Risk and the Redistribution of Social Insurance." In *Embracing Risk: the Changing Culture of Insurance and Responsibility*, edited by Tom Baker and Jonathan Simons, 146–166. Chicago: University of Chicago Press.
McElroy, Wendy. 1995. *XXX: A Woman's Right to Pornography*. New York: St. Martin's Press.
McHugh, Nancy. 2007. "It's in the Meat: Science, Fiction, and the Politics of Ignorance." In *SciFi in the Mind's Eye: Reading Science through Science Fiction*, edited by Margret Grebowicz, 39–56. Chicago: Open Court Press.
McLaren, Margaret. 2002. *Feminism, Foucault, and Embodied Subjectivity*. Albany, NY: SUNY Press.
McMillan, Tracie. 2012. *The American Way of Eating*. New York: Scribner.
McNay, Lois. 2009. "Self as Enterprise: Dilemmas of Control and Resistance in Foucault's *The Birth of Biopolitics*." *Theory, Culture, and Society* 26 (6): 55–77.
Mercer, Kobena. 1993. "Just Looking for Trouble: Robert Mapplethorpe and Fantasies of Race." In *Sex Exposed: Sexuality and the Pornography Debate*, edited by Lynne Segal and Mary McIntosh, 92–110. New Brunswick, NJ: Rutgers University Press.
Merleau-Ponty, Maurice. 1968. *The Visible and the Invisible*. Translated by Alphonso Lingis. Evanston, IL: Northwestern University Press.
Meunnig, Peter, Haomiao Jia, Rufina Lee, Erica Lubetkin. 2008. "I Think Therefore I Am: Perceived Ideal Weight as Determinant of Health." *American Journal of Public Health* 98 (3): 501–506.
Mies, Maria and Vandana Shiva. 1993. *Ecofeminism*. New York: Zed Books.
Miller, Sarah Clark. 2009. "Moral Injury and Relational Harm: Analyzing Rape in Darfur." *Journal of Social Philosophy* 40 (4): 504–523.
Mills, Catherine. 2007. "Normative Violence, Vulnerability, and Responsibility." *differences* 18 (2): 133–156.
Mills, Charles. 1997. *The Racial Contract*. Ithaca, NY: Cornell University Press.
——. 2007. "White Ignorance." In *Race and Epistemologies of Ignorance*, edited by Shannon Sullivan and Nancy Tuana, 13–38. Albany, NY: SUNY Press.
Mohanty, Chandra. 2003. *Feminism without Borders*. Durham, NC: Duke University Press.
Moss, Michael. 2009. "Food Companies Are Placing the Onus for Safety on Consumers." *New York Times*, May 14. Accessed July 18, 2013. http://www.NYtimes.com/2010/01/17/magazine/17antiaging-t.html?pagewanted=1&hpw
Murphy, Ann V. 2010. "'All Things Considered': Sensibility and Ethics in the Later Merleau-Ponty and Derrida." *Continental Philosophy Review* 42 (4): 435–447.
——. 2012. *Violence and the Philosophical Imaginary*. Albany, NY: SUNY Press.
Nussbaum, Martha. 1999. *Sex and Social Justice*. New York: Oxford.
Oliver, Kelly. 2001. *Witnessing: Beyond Recognition*. Minneapolis: University of Minnesota Press.
——. 2004. "Ecological Subjectivity: Merleau-Ponty and a Vision of Ethics." *Studies in Practical Philosophy* 4 (1): 102–125.
——. 2008. *Women as Weapons of War*. New York: Columbia University Press.
O'Neill, John. 2005. "Need, Humiliation and Independence." In *The Philosophy of Need*, edited by Soran Reader, 73–97. New York: Cambridge University Press.
Ortega, Mariana. 2006. "Being Lovingly, Knowingly Ignorant: White Feminism and Women of Color." *Hypatia* 21 (3): 56–74.
Patel, Raj. 2007. *Stuffed and Starved*. New York: Melville House.
Paul, Pamela. 2005. *Pornified*. New York: Times Books.
Pollan, Michael. 2008. *In Defense of Food*. New York: Penguin.
Plumwood, Val. 1993. *Feminism and the Mastery of Nature*. New York: Routledge.

Rabin, Roni Caryn. 2012. "Men Struggle for Rape Awareness." *New York Times*, January 23. Accessed June 7, 2013. http://www.nytimes.com/2012/01/24/health/as-victims-men-struggle-for-rape-awareness.html?emc=eta1&_r=0

Roff, Robin Jane. 2007. "Shopping for Change? Neoliberalizing Activism and the Limits to Eating Non-GMO." *Agriculture and Human Values* 24: 511–522.

Rogers, Wendy, Catriona Mackenzie, and Susan Dodds. 2012. "Why Bioethics Needs a Concept of Vulnerability." *International Journal of Feminist Approaches to Bioethics* 5 (2): 11–38.

Rough Sex. Directed by Tristan Taormino. 2008. Los Angeles: Vivid, 2008. DVD.

Royalle, Candida. 2000. "Porn in the U.S.A." In *Feminism and Pornography*, edited by Drucilla Cornell, 540–550. New York: Oxford University Press.

Russon, John. 2003. *Human Experience*. Albany, NY: SUNY Press.

———. 2009. *Bearing Witness to Epiphany*. Albany, NY: SUNY Press.

Sartre, Jean Paul. 2001. "The Humanism of Existentialism." In *Existentialism: Basic Writings*, edited by Charles Guignon and Derk Pereboom, 290–308. Indianapolis, IN: Hackett.

Satz, Ani. 2009. "Animals as Vulnerable Subjects." *Animal Law* 16 (2): 1–50.

Sawicki, Jana. 1991. *Disciplining Foucault*. New York: Routledge.

Schor, Juliet. 1998. *The Overspent American*. New York: Harper Perennial.

Segal, Lynne. 1993. "Sweet Sorrows, Painful Pleasures: Pornography and the Perils of Heterosexual Desire." In *Sex Exposed: Sexuality and the Pornography Debate*, edited by Lynne Segal and Mary McIntosh, 65–91. New Brunswick, NJ: Rutgers University Press.

Segal, Lynne and Mary McIntosh, eds. 1993. *Sex Exposed: Sexuality and the Pornography Debate*. New Brunswick, NJ: Rutgers University Press.

Shildrick, Margrit. 2002. *Embodying the Monster: Encounters with the Vulnerable Self*. London: Sage.

Shilliam, Robbie. 2013. "Who Will Provide the West with Therapy?" In *The Vulnerable Subject*, edited by Amanda Beattie and Kate Schick, 133–148. New York: Palgrave Macmillan.

Snitow, Ann, Christine Stansell, and Sharon Thompson. 1983. *Powers of Desire*. New York: Monthly Review Press.

Soble, Alan. 1998. "Why Do Men Enjoy Pornography?" In *Philosophy and Sex*, edited by Robert Baker, Kathleen Wininger, and Frederick Elliston, 556–566. Amherst, NY: Prometheus Books.

———. 2002. *Pornography, Sex, and Feminism*. Amherst, NY: Prometheus Books.

Solnit, Rebecca. 2013. "The Separating Sickness." *Harper's Magazine*, June.

Spelman, Elizabeth. 2007. "Managing Ignorance." In *Race and Epistemologies of Ignorance*, edited by Shannon Sullivan and Nancy Tuana, 119–131. Albany, NY: SUNY Press.

Stark, Christine and Rebecca Whisnant. 2004. *Not for Sale*. North Melbourne, Australia: Spinifex Press.

Strossen, Nadine. 1993. "A Feminist Critique of 'the' Feminist Critique of Pornography." *Virginia Law Review* 79 (5): 1099–1190.

Taylor, Chloë. 2009. "Pornographic Confessions?" *Foucault Studies* (7): 18–44.

Taylor, Dianna. 2009. "Normativity and Normalization." *Foucault Studies* (7): 45–63.

Taylor, Dianna and Karen Vintges, eds. 2004. *Feminism and the Final Foucault*. Champaign, IL: University of Illinois Press.

Tisdale, Sallie. 1992. "Talk Dirty to Me." *Harper's Magazine*, February.

Tronto, Joan. 1995. "Care as a Basis for Radical Political Judgments." *Hypatia* 10 (2): 141–149.

Tuana, Nancy. 2004. "Coming to Understand: Orgasm and the Epistemology of Ignorance." *Hypatia* 19 (1): 194–232.

———. 2006. "The Speculum of Ignorance: The Women's Health Movement and Epistemologies of Ignorance." *Hypatia* 21 (3): 1–19.
Turner, Bryan. 2006. *Vulnerability and Human Rights*. University Park, PA: Pennsylvania University Press.
Vance, Carole, ed. 1984. *Pleasure and Danger: Exploring Female Sexuality*. London: Routledge.
Walker, Margaret Urban. 2007. *Moral Understandings* 2nd ed. New York: Oxford University Press.
Warner, Michael. 1999. *The Trouble with Normal*. Cambridge, MA: Harvard University Press.
Wendell, Susan. 2008. "Toward a Feminist Theory of Disability." In *The Feminist Philosophy Reader*, edited by Alison Bailey and Chris Cuomo, 826–841. New York: McGraw Hill.
Williams, Linda. 1989. *Hard Core*. Berkeley, CA: University of California Press.
Williams, Patricia J. 1991. *The Alchemy of Race and Rights*. Cambridge, MA: Harvard University Press.
Winterson, Jeanette. 2000. "A Green Square." In *The World and Other Places*, 189–203. New York: Vintage.
Young, Iris Marion. 1990. *Justice and the Politics of Difference*. Princeton, NJ: Princeton University Press.
———. 2002. "Autonomy, Welfare Reform, and Meaningful Work." In *The Subject of Care: Feminist Perspectives on Dependency*, edited by Eva Feder Kittay and Ellen K. Feder, 40–60. New York: Rowman and Littlefield.
———. 2004. "Responsibility and Global Labor Justice." *Journal of Political Philosophy* 12 (4): 365–388.
———. 2011. *Responsibility for Justice*. New York: Oxford University Press.

Index

activity 32, 90, 129–30, 133, 139, 142–5, 153
Alcoff, Linda 76
ambiguity 8, 66, 78–9, 83, 95, 121–2, 129, 134, 138, 140–1, 143–4, 146–7, 149–55, 166, 170–3, 178–9
ambivalence 8, 45, 129, 134, 138, 140–1, 144, 154–5, 161–3, 165–6, 170, 172–3
animals 4, 18–19, 27, 38n1, 90, 119, 121, 175n4, 180
autonomy 7, 9, 18, 32, 39n5, 69n13, 135–6, 164–7
avoidance 3, 7, 73, 78, 89–90, 93, 96, 99, 109–10, 112, 115, 129, 148, 171, 177

Bergoffen, Debra 150–2, 159, 171
bodily vulnerability *see* vulnerability, corporeal
Bordo, Susan 79–80, 83, 85, 92, 118
Butler, Judith 6, 12n6, 40–70, 73, 77, 87, 122, 128, 134, 141, 150, 179

Calhoun, Cheshire 5, 9
care 3, 16–17, 19–20, 29, 32
Cixous, Hélène 7, 10, 129, 140–5, 169, 179
community 2, 5, 8, 20–1, 25, 43, 55–6, 66, 94, 152, 178
control 3, 7, 50, 68n6, 74, 76, 79–80, 83–5, 95–6, 98–101, 103–7, 109–10, 116, 118–23, 127, 146, 172, 174; absence of 43, 48, 83, 89–90, 134; and sexuality 150, 152, 166–70, 173; social 33–5, 99, 107

de Beauvoir, Simone 10–11, 78, 138, 145
Deleuze, Gilles 7, 10, 129, 134–40, 143
denial 16, 18, 31–2, 37, 59, 73–6, 78, 86, 88–93, 148; *see also* disavowal
dependence 5–6, 9, 16–26, 28–30, 32, 39n5, 68n1, 87–9, 111, 121–2, 132–3, 138, 178
disability 10, 17–18, 20–5, 36–7, 89–90, 97n6
disavowal 3, 43, 61, 67, 71, 73, 75, 77, 80, 87, 92–3, 99, 116, 128, 146, 148, 171, 177; *see also* denial
dispossession 56, 69n17, 127, 143–4
dualism 8–9, 32, 35, 66, 96, 120, 128–30, 133–4, 145–7, 150, 152–3, 159, 172; mind/body, 18, 83–4, 95, 150

embodiment 43, 82, 90, 142, 149, 151, 174
entrepreneurial subjectivity 7, 98–9, 104, 107–23, 127, 139, 142, 146, 150, 166, 169, 171–2, 174, 177–8
environment 15, 27, 75, 120
epistemic vulnerability 74, 93–7, 122, 139–40, 145, 179
ethical responsiveness 5–6, 8, 31, 41, 51, 61–2, 128, 171, 173, 177
ethic of vulnerability 6, 11, 31, 37, 51, 58, 73–4, 86–7, 127–9, 145, 153–4, 171, 177–9
exploitation 27–8, 32, 45, 86, 91–3, 145–6, 148, 156, 159–60, 171
exposure 3–4, 8, 127, 138, 144, 156, 169

190 Index

failure 10, 12, 32, 59–60, 65–6, 73–4, 80, 92–3, 118, 144, 146, 148, 177–8
fear 2–3, 7, 24, 32–3, 56, 60, 64–5, 83, 90, 94, 106, 115, 121, 127, 142, 146, 169, 174
feminism 8–11, 92, 94, 96, 129, 141, 149, 155–71, 178; feminist ethics 9, 12n5, 17, 68n1, 73, 147n4
fixity 7, 34–5, 129, 134, 137, 140
food 116–22
Foucault, Michel 7, 10, 44, 52, 69n10, 92, 96, 98–108, 113, 115, 150, 154–5, 169
freedom 11, 78, 105–7, 113, 146, 155, 161, 164, 167

gender 10, 17, 32, 36–7, 66, 79, 90, 116, 142, 151–63, 167, 171–2, 174, 177, 180
Goodin, Robert 6, 12n5, 25–31, 41, 47, 51, 55, 58, 73, 86, 128

habit 7, 54, 74, 79–81, 84, 92, 95–6
Heidegger, Martin 39n6
Held, Virginia 9
hierarchy 7, 35, 129, 134, 136–7, 157–9, 171–2
Hoagland, Sarah Lucia 88, 90, 93, 145
homogeneity 7, 124n5, 129, 131, 134–5, 138, 140
humanity 4, 43, 82, 85; human condition 5, 8, 9, 11, 15–18, 21, 37, 58, 83, 128, 138, 145

ignorance 7, 20–1, 74–9, 109, 120, 171, 174, 177; epistemology of 73–5; willful 76–9, 81, 85–96
independence 7, 9, 19, 22, 24, 28, 134
individualism 110, 123, 178
injustice 2–4, 10, 15, 27, 41, 56–7, 59, 145–6
interdependence 9, 17, 22, 28, 43, 48, 50, 55–6, 63, 88, 109–10, 121, 132, 134, 178
invulnerability 2, 6, 28, 34–5, 57, 67, 74–7, 79–96, 98, 100, 110–12, 122–3, 137, 140, 144–6, 148–9, 150, 152, 155–8, 163, 167, 170–4, 178–80; as ideal 7, 91–2, 96, 98, 127, 146, 178; as ignorance 74, 76, 86; invulnerable self 7, 77, 87, 89, 92, 98, 120; pursuit of 7–8, 74–6, 80–6, 91–3, 96, 98, 156, 166, 172, 177

Jenkins, Fiona 49

Kant, Immanuel 15
Kittay, Eva Feder 9

learning 2, 38, 93–4, 145
Levinas, Emmanuel 12n6
life 4, 11, 24, 35, 37, 43–8, 55–7, 98, 100–2, 116, 121, 128, 134, 137, 145
Lloyd, Moya 62–3, 69n8
loss 11, 22–3, 43, 46, 56–7, 64–5, 142, 144–5, 167
love 32, 38, 39n3, 56, 64–5, 127, 153

management 7, 80, 83, 98–108, 113, 120–1, 146, 152; of the self 105, 107, 115, 118, 123
MacIntyre, Alasdair 6, 17–25, 30–2, 39n5, 46, 51, 55, 73, 83, 86, 90, 127–8, 178
Merleau-Ponty, Maurice 7, 10, 129–34, 136
Mills, Catherine 49, 61
Mills, Charles W. 77, 87
Murphy, Ann V. 130, 153

Nietzsche, Friedrich 10–11, 51, 154
non-logical implication 5, 9, 128, 177
normative 5–6, 9–11, 15–16, 29, 43, 46–7, 51–5, 58, 60–4, 67, 92, 139, 146, 177; judgment 10, 54; prescription 10–11, 29, 31, 36, 53–4; significance 6, 15, 51, 55–6, 63, 67, 98, 112, 179; theory 9, 52, 54–5, 58, 60; violence 49, 68n4, 68n6
norms 6, 21, 29, 42, 46–52, 54, 59–61, 63, 66–8, 80, 87, 90–2, 100–1, 115, 123, 139, 144–6, 150, 156, 177–8; as "doubled" 6, 41, 48, 52; ethical 6, 41–2, 48, 51–2, 67, 154; gender 66, 90, 152–4; social 6, 10, 21, 24, 30, 31, 36, 41, 49–52, 90, 98, 118, 141–2, 154, 172–3

openness 2–3, 10, 25, 37, 46–7, 58, 64–5, 67, 76, 84, 86–7, 91, 93–4, 96, 121, 127, 129–46, 153, 155, 168, 170, 172, 178–9
oppression 10, 74, 77–8, 85–95, 141, 145–6, 153, 165, 167, 177

passivity 9, 25, 37, 66, 87, 90, 113, 127–34, 139, 142–3, 145–6, 153
persecution 56–7, 61, 63, 68, 73–4, 87, 89, 177
Plumwood, Val 8–9, 85–6, 120
pornography 8, 148–9, 154–76
potential: condition of 8, 23, 135–8, 140, 177; for violence 50, 58, 62, 93; vulnerability as 122, 127, 129, 134–8, 141, 146, 163, 168, 172–3
power 32, 34–6, 38, 152, 158–61, 163, 166–7; dynamics and relations of 10, 41, 76–7, 157; Foucaultian view of 52, 92, 99–108, 154–5
powerlessness 1, 3, 5, 32, 35, 37–8, 63–4, 79, 92, 136, 146, 157–60, 166–8, 170
practice 2–4, 6–7, 12, 28–9, 37–8, 45, 52, 60–3, 67, 75–6, 79–83, 92, 95, 100–1, 146, 148, 153, 162, 178–9
precariousness 6, 42–9, 51, 55–60, 63, 67–9, 73, 134, 179
precarity 42–7, 51, 67, 68n1, 115, 156
privatization 99, 104, 110–23
protecting the vulnerable 15, 26–31, 68, 86, 112, 171

race 10, 17, 37, 66, 78, 80, 82, 87, 88, 177, 180
recognition 47, 73, 179; of others 43–4, 65–8; of vulnerability 6, 24, 30, 35, 37, 63, 65, 67, 93, 98, 115, 128, 146, 172–3, 179
reductionism 80–5, 93, 97
responsibility 6–7, 25–32, 34–8, 41, 47, 51, 55–6, 59–61, 64, 69n15, 73, 92, 98–100, 108–23, 128–9, 168, 177–80
risk 7, 22, 33–4, 40, 46, 96, 98–124, 127
Russon, John 84, 150–1, 176n16

Sartre, Jean Paul 10–11, 78
Scalia, Antonin 66, 80
Security 2, 3, 16, 54, 103, 105–7, 109, 115, 123, 170
September 11th 1, 3, 49, 61
sex 38, 108, 134, 136, 150–70, 173–6

sexuality 8, 148–74
sovereignty 7, 57–9, 61, 63, 68, 73–5, 87, 122
suffering 6, 16, 20, 22–3, 38, 40, 42–3, 56–8, 63, 65, 127
susceptibility to harm 5–6, 22–5, 30, 32, 37, 42, 64, 68, 121, 127–8, 138, 140, 146, 159, 173

terrorism 1, 4, 92, 98
Tronto, Joan 9
Tuana, Nancy 76–7, 94

univocity 129, 134, 136, 140, 173

violence 4, 6, 11, 42, 47–69, 73–5, 78, 90, 92–3, 97n2, 128, 130, 153, 157, 161
virtues of acknowledged dependence 20, 32, 178
vulnerability: as capacity 3, 24, 34, 123, 131–3, 138–9, 171, 179; corporeal 37, 42, 95, 151, 153, 156, 173; criticism of 32–5; as exceptional state 16–18, 129; experience of 3, 10, 36–8, 55, 64–5, 67, 73, 76, 79, 86, 88, 91, 115, 118, 122, 127–9, 134–41, 144–9, 151, 154–5, 163, 166–8, 171–4, 178–80; as fundamental condition 8, 10–11, 15–16, 23, 36–8, 57–9, 75, 90, 138, 140–1, 145, 173, 177; the meaning of 4–5, 32, 64–7, 140, 154; ontological 37–8, 75, 90, 129, 134, 137, 140–1, 145; reductively negative understanding of 5–6, 9, 31–5, 40, 58–60, 63, 66, 75, 98, 115, 121, 127–9, 146, 152–3, 159, 163, 177; sexual 152–4, 160, 165, 171; situational 37–8, 129; *see also* openness
"vulnerability model" 25–30

Walker, Margaret Urban 11, 28–31
war 4, 48, 56, 66, 92, 151
welfare 27–8, 30, 111, 113, 115
Wendell, Susan 89–90

Young, Iris Marion 10, 39n5, 76, 92

An environmentally friendly book printed and bound in England by www.printondemand-worldwide.com

This book is made entirely of sustainable materials; FSC paper for the cover and PEFC paper for the text pages.

#0013 - 040615 - C0 - 229/152/11 [13] - CB - 9780415656139